READINGS IN RESTORATIVE JUSTICE

READINGS IN RESTORATIVE JUSTICE

Editors

SHEILA M. MURPHY

MICHAEL P. SENG

ALLISON R. TRENDLE

Readings in Restorative Justice

Editors
Sheila M. Murphy
Michael P. Seng
Allison R. Trendle

Published by:

Vandeplas Publishing, LLC – July 2021

801 International Parkway, 5th Floor
Lake Mary, FL. 32746
USA

www.vandeplaspublishing.com

978-1-60042-538-7

TABLE OF CONTENTS

Restorative justice is coming into its own. Since the publication of our first book, RESTORATIVE JUSTICE IN PRACTICE: A HOLISTIC APPROACH, in 2015, many courts and school have embraced restorative justice practices. The City of Chicago has established its first restorative justice community courts. The Illinois legislature has passed a bill to provide a privilege when restorative justice practices are used and to encourage the use of restorative justice practices in the settlement of all disputes. There is growing recognition that the old ways of solving crime and settling disputes are not working. From a simple cost/benefit analysis, punitive justice is not effective. New and creative approaches are under consideration.

This book brings together some of the most creative thinkers in the United States on restorative justice practices. They write from different perspectives and illustrate the breath of restorative justice innovation. They demonstrate that many sectors of society beyond the criminal justice system can benefit from restorative justice practices. Several of the authors are students or former students who are perhaps the most enthusiastic proponents of restorative justice. The book does not provide a definitive blueprint for the practice of restorative justice, rather it consists of a series of essays intended to provoke thoughtful analysis.

The primary audience is college and universities students in such fields as sociology, political science, public health, psychology, or criminal justice. The book is also for law students, who hold the future of justice in their hands. Community and study groups can use the chapters as starting points for discussing local problems. The purpose of the book is not to provide definitive solutions. It is to promote new ways of thinking and to encourage communities to seek broader solutions when confronting local problems, whether they be public safety, public health, civil rights, or environmental concerns.

The authors of the chapters have seen the successes produced by restorative justice practices in their schools and communities. Restorative justice is not just a process for resolving disputes. It is a philosophy. Its premise is the idea that justice must arise from the ground up and that justice is the work of not just legislators, attorneys, police officers, or judges. Justice is the work of each of us. We will only have truly just communities when every voice is raised and when everyone acknowledges their role in producing the injustices and inequalities that exist in our society. We cannot sit idly by and expect others to solve our society's many problems. We all play a role in creating the problems and we all must play a role in providing a solution.

By reading these essays and considering the discussion questions, either by individual reflection or ideally through discussions in community-wide circles, we hope to foster thinking and practices that reflect the principles espoused by the authors.

May 2021

PART I
RESTORATIVE JUSTICE AS AN Effective TOOL
FOR EDUCATORS

"They are stealing our future."

SHEILA M. MURPHY AND MICHAEL P. SENG

"They are stealing our future." This is the conclusion that many of our law students came to during the last 11 years since we started teaching Restorative Justice at what is now the UIC John Marshall Law School. The students, who attend a class each week where they learn about restorative justice and restorative techniques, bring what they learn in the classroom to grade and high school students in the City of Chicago. The law students begin to see clearly that when a child is denied a good education, all of us are harmed.

Our law students counseled a high school student whom the school had labeled a disciplinary problem because she was habitually tardy. Our students learned that the reason the high school student was late was that both of her parents worked and she had to accompany her younger sister who was in kindergarten by bus to school and then take a different bus to the school she attended. Her parents feared for the younger girl's safety because of the violence prone neighborhoods she had to pass through on her way to school. No one in the school asked the student why she was tardy or proposed any solution to her problem. Instead, school officials methodically recorded the instances of tardiness on her record, compiling a record that would accompany her throughout her career and prevent her from advancing to a better school.

In a similar incident at another school, a young girl in elementary school consistently was absent and was marked down for her bad behavior. Our law students talked to the girl and discovered that she was living alone with her mother, who was undocumented and spoke no English. The girl and her mother had no relatives in the area. The mother had been diagnosed with cancer and given a short time to live. She needed her daughter to take her for medical treatment because she could not communicate with the medical personnel. No one at the school had inquired why the girl was missing her classes or had any sympathy for her plight.

These young women were stigmatized for doing what they and their parents considered good behavior. As a result, they had school records that would undoubtedly stand in the way of their ever becoming doctors, lawyers, or teachers where they could have a real impact in the future. They were punished because they were compassionate daughters and big sisters. No one at school saw the effect of what the school was doing. Neither school had a counselor to talk to the girls and assist them. Both girls were taught at home to be submissive to authority and, therefore, did not question the demerits the school gave them.

We became involved in the Chicago schools fortuitously. A brilliant teacher and retired engineer, Katherine Doolin, was teaching science to a class where one girl began making noise in the classroom and the teacher threatened to send her to the Principal. The girl had a brush in her hand and she threw it at the teacher. The girl missed, but the teacher, in a rage, called the police. A black Chicago policeman came to the classroom. He was upset. "Do you know that you have just given this child a record that will follow her beyond the doors of this high school for the rest of her life? You need to learn about restorative justice." The teacher telephoned The John Marshall Law School. She had heard that we were starting a class for law students in restorative justice and asked the Principal to allow the law students to instruct the teachers and students about restorative justice.

This high school was in an area of the city divided by gangs. The school was periodically placed on lockdown because of shootings in the neighborhood. Both teachers and students were traumatized. There were no sports for the girls, no art, no music, no orchestra or band, no real library at this high school. Chicago police officers paroled both outside and inside the school. Their presence only aggregated police/community tensions.

Into this atmosphere, our brave law students entered. They were not the same thereafter. The law students learned to listen actively. If they came led by their egos, they lost their egos. If they were trained in an atmosphere of indifference and bias, they became compassionate and understanding. They began to think like the men and women they were when they decided to go to law school. Their idealism returned. They now saw why they were in law school – not to make a pile of money and hold a position of respect, but to help those in need, and the need was everywhere. They lost the bad habits they acquired in their first year of law school. Law was no longer simply remembering legal formulas to be repeated on an examination. Law was not one-upping a classmate or gaining an advantage over an opponent. Law was service to the community. Law involved transforming the society wherever the student eventually landed.

The law students began to ask and seek answers to the underlying questions: Why do some schools lack the most basic resources that are routine in other schools? Shouldn't education be a fundamental right? Isn't denying a child a good education effectively putting that child in the pipeline to prison? Why don't we devote the same amount or more money on education as we do on prisons? Why am I commuting from a well-kept neighborhood in the suburbs to a decaying neighborhood that lacks the most basic services? How did these neighborhoods become segregated? Why can't children use the playground or walk down certain blocks without putting their lives at risk? What is accomplished by our present punitive system of justice? Isn't freedom from fear a basic human right? Why is it that some students have never traveled but a few blocks outside of their neighborhoods? Just by raising these questions, the law students will never think about law the same again.

Nor were the grade and high school students that our law students counseled the same thereafter. Sometimes, for the first time in their lives, they met someone who looked like them who had gone to college and was pursuing an advanced professional degree. These children now had someone with whom they could discuss their problems without worrying about how the information might be used against them. Rarely in school are the students allowed to discuss the problems that really concern them. For, instance, it was the policy in many of the schools to ignore the environment where the school was located. Shootings occurred, persons were killed, but school went on without any acknowledgement of the trauma experienced by the students (or the teachers).

The children suffered trauma in silence until they gathered in a peace circle and shared their fears and hopes with each other and with the law students. On several occasions the law students were concerned about how they could not get the students to open up, but after a few meetings it all came gushing out. In one circle that met every week the students were unusually quiet until one of the students was absent. Then the students, without saying why, suddenly opened up about the pressures they were under to join a gang. Girls who were in constant fights sat down and discussed their problems and became friends. In one case, girls were making fun of a classmate because she smelled. It was discovered in the circle that the girl lived in an apartment with no running water. A plan was quickly devised to help the unfortunate girl without embarrassing her.

Our law students learned to read the newspapers in anticipation of their visits to the schools. On one occasion, a shooting occurred at a funeral home, and several of the elementary students lived within blocks of the home. They knew the people who were present and some of the people who had been shot. They came to school traumatized. Talking about the incident in a circle helped alleviate their anxieties.

The biggest beneficiaries of the restorative justice experience is the law students. They learn what it really means to interview and counsel a client. They learn that confrontation and abrasiveness does not really work, that law is something more than doing battle with one's adversaries. Law is most effective when it brings people and communities together. The experience has made them better human beings and, therefore, better lawyers. By causing them to recognize that law can be restorative, many law students reassess their career goals and consider choices they had never before considered within the legal profession.

Our law students see the value of circles in not only assisting school children but also in helping themselves. Since the pandemic of 2020, our law students have been meeting online to engage in the circle process at regular times outside of class and without the presence of faculty. They discuss problems that they are having in school and in their personal lives. Many of them state that this is enabling them to cope with the isolation of the pandemic and the many hassles they experience as law students. Some state that they doubt that they would have continued in the legal profession if it had not been for the fellowship created through the restorative justice process.

Nonetheless, the continuing effect of what the law students accomplish in the grade and high schools is outside their control. Control lay with the teachers and the administrators. Although restorative justice is the official policy of the Chicago schools, it is left to the individual schools how to implement it. The cooperation of the teachers is essential. It does little good to provide restorative practices in a school where retribution is the rule in the classroom. Also, restorative justice will not be effective if the teachers see it only as a form of punishment: "If you are unruly, I will send you to a restorative justice session." Yet the teachers themselves are overloaded and treated with a lack of respect by the school and the community. Under these circumstances, we can hardly expect teachers to be effective practitioners of restorative justice in the classroom.

The tone in the school is set by the principal. In those schools where we are welcomed by the principal and where the principle encourages the faculty to use restorative techniques in the classroom, restorative justice flourishes. When the principal does not believe in restorative justice, there is little that can be done. Over and over again our students introduced successful restorative justice programs in a school. Truancy and delinquency incidents decreased and things began to proceed harmoniously. The law students left in the spring anticipating even more success the following fall and the children were anxiously awaiting their return. Then during the summer, the principal was transferred and a new principal appointed. If this principal was hostile or indifferent to restorative justice, the process fell apart. In many instances, the principal was sent into the school to increase the student's test scores and saw time spent on restorative justice as wasted time. Restorative justice needs its own physical space in the school. It needs time to be allocated so that the students can meet with their counselors regularly. If the Principal will not facilitate these conditions, the process is doomed.

What is needed is restorative justice for teachers and school administrators. The kids understand the value of restorative justice. Teachers eventually accept restorative justice if they know they are supported from the top down. They see the benefits in the classroom when restorative justice practices are introduced. But restorative justice cannot be forced. It must be freely embraced. School administrators have to be persuaded. We need to persuade them to sit in a circle where they can explore their fears about restorative justice and how restorative justice can be an effective tool for educating children to succeed in life.

In the past several years, our law students have been working with the Union League Club's Boys and Girls Clubs in Chicago. The Clubs work in some of the schools in the late afternoon after classes and are also situated in two additional independent sites. Personnel in the Clubs have embraced restorative justice techniques. During the pandemic, the law students continued with the children online. While perhaps not as effective as in-person encounters, the online experience has worked and brings new, alternative opportunities to do restorative justice.

The restorative justice movement is growing. IT MAKES SENSE. By training a new generation of lawyers in restorative justice (and why not education, psychology, public health, and sociology majors as well), we are making a difference. The hard questions can and should be asked, and maybe, just maybe, solutions will be found through the circle process.

What makes restorative techniques, particularly the circle process, so effective?

How do we persuade restorative justice skeptics to embrace the movement?

How can universities implement restorative justice programs?

Give some examples where adults have learned from children?

PART II
THE TOOLS OF RESTORATIVE JUSTICE:
EMPOWERMENT, LOVE, TRUTH, KINDNESS, AND
MERCY

"Justice is what love looks like in public, just like tenderness is what love feels like in private."[1]

This Chapter is dedicated to Brigid Tonia Wolff, our daughter who was my first teacher of Restorative Justice. I was arguing with her and raising my voice. At the time she was a freshman at Saint Ignatius College Prep High School. She stopped me and said, "Wait," and drew a circle on the rug around us both. Then Brigid said, "We love each other. Love is the only thing allowed in the circle." She now teaches at Marist High School in Chicago. I am told that her circles include all humanity, nearly always a smile and laughter.

Special thanks to Maeve Ann Wolff, who graduated from Saint Ignatius College Prep High School and is a rising Junior at St. Louis University. Maeve's amazing technological help makes everything possible. Additionally, I am grateful for the research and assistance of Alison Chan, former Restorative Justice law student and currently an Assistant State's Attorney of Cook County.

Sheila M. Murphy

---

1   Cornel West, Address at Howard University (April 2011).

EMPOWERMENT OF COMMUNITY IS RESTORATIVE JUSTICE

SHEILA M. MURPHY AND JOY LINDBERG LEE

PREFACE

When you read this Chapter, please rethink the whole Court system. What is its intended purpose? What purpose does it actually serve? Is it a system of case management? Every week, thousands of people are loaded onto buses with bars on the windows on their way to state and federal prisons. Children who live in segregated areas and have brown or black colored skin are more often pushed through the school to prison pipeline and then blamed for their deficiencies instead of getting the medical attention they need to improve. It is high time that we listen to teachers. They know the children who have been traumatized as they are the ones who act out in class. Before I went to law school, I was a primary teacher. In Washington D.C., where I taught at Charles Quincy Adams School, one fifth grader tried to jump out of a window and also tried to hurt other children. I wrote letters to the Principal, the Superintendent, and to St. Elizabeth Hospital to try and get help for him. No one helped. We need to start helping these traumatized children in preschool and kindergarten. It is the right thing to do and much cheaper than locking them up when they grow up. Remember that hurt children hurt others unless they are treated with kindness and compassion.

When the judicial system was developing, scientists had not yet discovered the impact of trauma on the brain. We knew nothing about the neurobiology of the brain. It has since been discovered that change is indeed possible when medical needs are met. Across our land, judges sentence people without knowing their neurobiological background. They are sent to prisons where they are not provided the tools they need to succeed. When they are released from prison, they have the same medical needs as when they arrived, but their symptoms are exacerbated and now they are sicker. Hurt people, hurt people.

If we have a friend or family member who has a mental health issue or is addicted to alcohol and narcotics, we know how to help them. They may be detoxed at first, then sent to treatment. If the first treatment does not work, then there are other options. After treatment, halfway houses assist with reentry into society. Slowly, new neurological paths to the brain are developed after engaging in a 12-step peer meeting program.

Abraham Lincoln said, "Those who have suffered by intemperance personally, and have reformed, are the most powerful and efficient instruments to push the reformation to ultimate success."[2] He did not say to lock them in prisons with others who have unmet medical needs or in solitary confinement. The current system makes people worse. In order to have a chance of healing and making reparations, people need to fit perfectly into a small box. If they have any history of violence or crime, they are not eligible for Specialty Courts. If they are in a district or before a judge that does not implement the values of Restorative Justice, they will be sent away to prison for many years as well. There is an infinitesimally small number of people who are given the tools and resources they need to recover and move forward. The ones who do not fit into that tiny box are locked away for years.

After serving their time these prisoners are released. However, they do not return to the community of the judge and prosecutor who sent them away. They go back to their original community forever changed by their time in prison. They are unemployable for the most part because they are forced to disclose their criminal record to any potential employer. Additionally, their mental illness has worsened, trauma on trauma. If they pick up the first drink of beer, their probation officer will be there to send them back to prison.

This is what "case management" looks like in the Courts. This is what taxpayers pay for. With that in mind, please read the summary below of how one Court empowered the community. The community became a partner with the Court. As wonderful as this story may be, it is not enough. Every Court should be able to provide for people with medical needs by partnering with medical professionals. Every Criminal Court should have probation officers, lawyers and police who can recognize what they do not know and what they need to know. As you read, imagine that every Court could be even better than the Markham Court described below. If individual police, lawyers, judges, and probation officers had

---

2   Abraham Lincoln, Temperance Address in Springfield, IL (February 22, 1842).

full partnerships with communities, we would be better. We would come into this century and leave our medieval ways behind.

One of the pillars of Restorative Justice is empowerment of the community.[3] Even though the judicial system is hierarchical, change comes when the Court becomes a partner of the community. This is not only possible, but necessary. After serving as a Cook County Public Defender for seven years and a Federal Defender for eleven years, I had ideas on how restorative practices need to be brought into the Court. Unfortunately, I was not in a position to implement them because I was not a member of the judiciary. Suddenly, I was appointed as an Associate Judge of Cook County and three years later was elected a Circuit Court Judge. I received over one million votes because the voters loved that I was fighting to bring Children's Rooms to courthouses that put signs on the Courtroom doors saying, "No smoking and no children allowed." It was time for humanizing the Courts.

The Chief Judge, Harry Comerford, started the first children's room in a courthouse when he was assigned to Adoption Court. He sent me 20.1 miles away to the Markham Courthouse, where I was appointed the Presiding Judge, with 23 judges and 37 towns in my jurisdiction. I was overwhelmed, but I recognized the Markham Court because it was the site of my first Death Penalty case. Out of the entire jury, there was only one older man, and he was also the only Black person. He held out for a not guilty verdict through the night, resulting in a hung jury. At the end, the State's Attorney offered my client a plea bargain where he would plead guilty and the State would not ask for the death penalty. I later learned that as a child, the juror had witnessed a lynching and that was why he refused "to cooperate in the killing of a person." Markham was a tough Court with the biggest call of criminal cases in Cook County besides the Criminal Court in Chicago. I knew I needed additional help when I was appointed presiding judge.

As a defense lawyer, most of the people I represented in the Markham Court had co-occurring conditions: mental health issues and addiction. There had been one judge in the courthouse who was in recovery himself, and he was the best judge of all. He addressed those who came before him with the voice of a Father, a kind Father. He would say, "WE cannot use drugs or alcohol." The clients listened for the first time. It was the voice of love that this judge had for each

---

3   Kelly Richards, *Restorative Justice and "Empowerment": Producing and Governing Active Subjects through "Empowering" Practices*, 19 Critical Criminology 91 (2011). https://doi.org/10.1007/s10612-010-9106-8.

person that called them to their better selves. He told them, "Down deep you have a light on at all times. I am here to help you. If you fail your drug test, we will increase your treatment. You will become your best self." This judge died before I was appointed, but another judge, who was also in recovery, took his place. To help the people of the Markham Court community, the Court needed a professional who was experienced in helping people recover. Her name is Joy Lindberg Lee.

Joy Lindberg Lee was a very successful businesswoman before becoming the Court Administrator. She was a realtor and the owner of three animal hospitals. She was also a certified counselor for alcohol and drug treatment. In her treatment capacity, she was aware that judges were enablers. When defendants appeared before the Court at bond hearings, no medical conditions of bond were set because the judges did not know their medical histories. No one told them the medical history of the person before them when they first appeared unless it was in a record. Sheriff's buses came from Chicago daily, loaded with prisoners. If the individuals were found guilty, probation officers gave a background report that may have included addiction and mental health issues. Social workers also interviewed many people. But unless there is trust, the truth is often hidden. Alcoholism, drug addiction, mental health, and trauma need to be addressed and taken into account at every stage of the criminal justice process. Many defendants ended up in prison where there was little hope of treatment but great possibilities of increasing trauma. The families in the community are hurt deeply. Community members sat in the Courtrooms and watched as their sons and daughters were sent to prison. The children lost the most. Most prosecutors recommended prison whenever possible. These men and women may have been traumatized before they went to prison, but afterwards, the trauma was increased. If they went to prison without reading at a third grade level, they came out the same way. The school to prison pipeline got them to prison in the first place, and it would get them back to prison. Communities suffered the most. Their citizens were tired. Tired of seeing their sons and daughters in buses bound for prison. Tired of not feeling safe in their homes.

Joy and I discussed the possibility for a Drug Treatment Court with all 23 Judges. They approved the idea for the Markham Court. I presented the idea to the Chief Judge and he was excited about the idea of a Court dedicated to helping people with addictions and mental health, but the county did not take federal funds. He had tried to convince the Court to accept federal funds for years before when he was assigned to Boys Court. Despite the lack of federal funding, the Chief Judge assured me that it could begin with the education for judges in Restorative Justice practices. Chief Judge Harry Commerford grew up above a tavern. He understood how good people could become alcoholics, and he knew of many who recovered with the help of Alcoholics Anonymous.

So, we began by having speakers talk to the judges. One of the Markham judges knew a great deal about mental health issues. Some of the judges were more excited about it than others. We were able to get many of the judges trained in restorative practices. We? learned that speaking like a Father or Mother, with kindness, could work. Kindness helped defendants stop hurting themselves. Some judges had seen it work with their own families and friends.

At a conference, one of the speakers was Dr. Michael O. Smith, M.D. He was a psychiatrist who spoke on trauma — how the brain is affected by trauma as a child or emerging adult. Trauma causes Association Disorder. They look upon authority with fear and in their mind go somewhere else, even though they look at the judge, and nod their head in agreement. There is no agreement. They are not there. Dr. Smith's Protocol for Drug Treatment Court was designed to help the judge and the person before the Judge get peace of mind and the ability to listen.

We still had hopes that we could have federal funds for the Drug Treatment Court. This was made possible by Black Ministers who met monthly in the community. They said that their children were not the only children in the land who had addiction problems. In White neighborhoods, those who were addicted were not always sent to prison like their children. They told the same story to members of the Cook County Board who then authorized the federal funds. The community demanded a Drug Treatment Court, a Restorative Justice Court. It opened because the community empowered the Chief Judge to do the right thing. Other communities in the State of Illinois followed this model pioneered by the Markham Court community.

Restorative Justice is not a new concept in North America. Centuries ago, tribes practiced it before the White settlers arrived.[4] Tribes met in circles, where they passed a talking piece, sometimes an eagle wing. The peace pipe was really used, but in many homes, there was no peace in the community. Children called the police at all hours begging them to come and save their Mother. There were three Domestic Violence courts in the City of Chicago and none in the suburbs.

---

4   Mark Umbreit, *Talking Circles*, Center for Restorative Justice & Peace (2003), http://rjp.dl.umn.edu/sites/rjp.dl.umn.edu/files/talking_circles.pdf.

There were six courthouses in Cook County and not one of them had a stand-alone Domestic Violence Court. It was sorely needed. The community called for it. Teachers were aware of it as the children were traumatized by what was happening at home. The 37 police departments met at the courthouse. Ministers, priests and rabbis demanded protection of the innocent. The first Domestic Violence Court was opened. It was the result of attending community meetings, listening, and then acting. We believed that the community could do anything. It seemed that there was a door opening somewhere, somehow as soon as the community undertook the needs of people The first Domestic Violence Court outside of Cook County was opened because of the community.

The community was filled with wonderful people who lived there, such as the Gavin Family. Judge Marvin Gavin was a humble judge who served in Traffic Court where he was close to the people and could help them. He was a graduate of Harvard Law School. His sister, Dr. Katherine Gavin, reported that schools had a zero tolerance policy. Due to this policy, young people were expelled from many schools. Young people were arrested for various things, and if they did not follow the rules of probation, they would be sent to prison. Dr. Gavin proposed to the community that a condition of bond be set that these young people attend school. Not the neighborhood schools but a school that she wanted to set up in the basement of the courthouse. Judge Murphy and Dr. Gavin conceived a plan where schooling and tutoring would become available for these offenders/ students. This was seen as a shining example of purpose becoming accomplishment. The community received a grant from the U.S. Department of Education.

There is little doubt that the community, as well as the lives of many young students, were well served by this "School in the Courthouse." Offense became an opportunity. And young people were schooled, and in most cases avoided punishment and possible incarceration but rather became schooled citizens better able to serve the community, their families and themselves.

Drug testing was established and made available in the courthouse. Test results were sent to the Drug Treatment Court Judge. The mandated accused, usually a member of an underserved minority community was able to receive mandated services at the convenient courthouse location. Also instituted were acupuncture services from licensed acupuncturist, Arthur Pinckney. The NADA Protocol of auricle acupuncture was developed by Dr. Michael Smith and was a supportive therapy to those fighting addiction. This service was also available in the courthouse.

Michael O. Smith, MD, DAC, founder and founding chairman of NADA, visited the courthouse often from his New York base. He trained, encouraged and inspired the judges, staff and visiting professionals. As a prominent advisor of the development of Drug Courts throughout the United States, Dr. Smith also shared his expertise and experience. He was extremely helpful in helping the women in Drug Treatment Court. He explained to the judges that women suffered greatly from sexual abuse, sometimes from childhood. The stress of authority and fear causes them not to listen. He recommended that we offer the opportunity of ear acupuncture. Dr. Smith said that this would give them peace long enough to listen closely and follow Court orders. The community helped bring funds from the Violence Against Women Federal Fund. The numbers of women in treatment soared. We learned from them that women were not getting treatment. Many had children and their lives were hurt already by their mother's untreated trauma and addiction.

One of the Markham judges saw how well the acupuncture worked in the courthouse. He asked, "Why not the judges? We have tension too. We need it." On Wednesday after the Court call, judges paid for acupuncture and liked it very much. The judges at Markham were quite remarkable. They suggested partnerships with Governor's State University. The President, Paula Wolff, brought in speakers that were extraordinary and shared them with judges and staff. At our meetings we spoke to each other over delicious lunch every month. If we did not agree on an issue, we did not vote. We simply thought about it for a month and acted only when we were all in agreement.

Bar Associations for generations have hosted yearly nights to honor judges. Our judges decided to invite the Southwest Bar Association to the courthouse. Members of the community did the decorations and cooking. The keynote speaker was a Black woman who had been arrested 35 times. Judge Reginald Baker never gave up on her and helped her find treatment for the trauma in her life. She no longer used drugs and told the audience that "I am clean and sober and now have found my best self." The audience clapped for five minutes.

Judges were helped by having Joy Lee in the Court every day. She welcomed employees who were recovering and opened 12 step programs in the courthouse. The judge who heard Bond Court cases was in recovery himself. He talked to the defendants like a Dad or big brother. They would get sober and come back to this wonderful judge so that he could witness their wedding. He would do so in his chambers. Then you would hear the music from his Chambers playing, "To dream, the impossible dream…"

The Executive Committee of Judges met once a month. We learned that the women in the jail had no treatment program. It was a fake on paper. A group of us visited the jail at the time the treatment was allegedly taking place. The women sat in an old gym with rain coming down into buckets. We also visited pregnant women who complained of the constant cigarette smoke. We assisted the Sheriff in getting federal grants for effective treatment for women in recovery in the jail so they could leave clean and sober.

Joy decided that the community needed some music, like outside the City Courthouse in Chicago. The Navy Jazz Band came one afternoon. Seeing people sing and dance in the courthouse was one of our best memories of these years.

JOY

Judge Sheila Murphy as Presiding Judge attracted many good people to the office of Presiding Judge's courthouse team. Here is a sampling:

Court Administrator, Joy Lee was creative and smart. She allowed no one to answer the phone unless kindness was used entirely. She ran the Court just like she did her Animal Hospitals. It was a business for sure. She was in the business of saving people.

Linda Johnson was the Executive Assistant. She is Black and beautiful and brilliant. She is still helping people. Linda is now a registered nurse.

Claudia Conlon served as Court Administrator when Sheila Murphy was first assigned her position as Presiding Judge. A skilled lawyer, Claudia served until being elected to the bench in Cook County and becoming Judge Conlon. I (Joy) was proud to follow her in this position with a totally different skill set. (The Children's room in the Markham Courthouse is the K.C. Conlon room, named for the darling son of Claudia and Kevin Conlon who died in childhood.)

Sherewood Williams was in charge of the Sheriff's Office. My first week as Presiding Judge, I parked under the building by the prison bus. I heard that this was available for Presiding Judges. Now I could stay warm. A few minutes after Court started, Sheriff Williams quietly asked for my car keys. I told them that it was wonderful that I could park under the building and stay warm. Sheriff Willliams said, "Judge Murphy I have no duty to keep you warm. My duty is to save your life." How grateful I am to him and to all the Staff that worked so hard.

Barbara Blaine was an activist social worker and one time Director of the Catholic Worker House. The highly educated Barbara saw an opportunity to better serve the community if she returned to school and became a lawyer. Barbara had already founded SNAP, Survivors network of those Abused by Priests. Barbara served as law clerk of the Sixth District and brought with her dedication, personal experience and intellect. She went on to practice Restorative Justice by going to the U.N., where she succeeded in having sexual abuse of children named "torture." She helped hundreds of people who were sexually abused by Catholic Priests in North America, Central America, South America and Europe before her untimely death in 2017.

Joyce Murphy Gorman served as a law clerk at the Markham Courthouse and contributed multiple talents including activism, passion for the community, persuasive and skilled ability as a writer. Judge Joyce Murphy Gorman is retired. Her last assignment was on the bench at the Markham Courthouse.

Kathleen Bankhead[5] was an Assistant State's Attorney at Markham. She is now the Ombudsman for Children in Detention in Illinois. She is a powerful speaker, and her theme is that there can be no Restorative Justice if there is bias and prejudice. Our law students love her speech, "No Restorative Justice without casting prejudice away for good."

Charles Burns was the supervisor of the Markham State's Attorney's office. Judge Burns is now assigned to the Leighton Court and uses restorative practices to help prostitutes recover and find new lives.

Joy Lee is retired and lives in Tucson, Arizona. She continues to help women in recovery. She is studying Zen Buddha meditation "as, Buddha was one of the first Restorative Justice advocates."

Several foreign law students served as clerks in the Markham Court including Marc Lofthus from Ballina, in the Republic of Ireland and David Hasson from Derry in Northern Ireland. These law students brought the Restorative Justice ideas to us all. Northern Ireland by statute has laws of Restorative Justice. In later days at John Marshall Law School, we have had many students from the Czech Republic and Slovakia in our Restorative Justice classes. They have returned to their countries and one is now a judge, another is a judicial clerk in

---

5   Kathleen Bankhead authored *Law and Order?*, a chapter in this textbook.

the Constitutional Court of the Czech Republic.[6] Foreign law students trained at the courthouse and brought with them international exchange benefits from their home countries, while training and utilizing American methods and law.

Upon the Opening of the K.C. Conlon Children's Room, Mary O'Donohue Haugh was the Supervising Director of the children's room. It was a place for the most vulnerable members of the community, the children, whose families had business in the Court. It was a place where children were nurtured with fun, food and kind attention. It was a safe place. A community partnership with St. Xavier University School of Education brought Professor Meg Kelly who taught the staff monthly. Rose Filter, who formerly owned a Maria Montessori School, came weekly to the Children's Room, A gentle soul, she showed the parents how to talk with their children. In the basement on Thursday afternoon, Patrick Filter, Rose's husband, volunteered at the Legal Aid Clinic. He was an outstanding lawyer.

The office of the Presiding Judge established strong ties within the internal community of the courthouse for all Court services present at the Markham Courthouse.

One of the most memorable manifestations of community was the first celebration of Black History held in February which had been designated as Black History Month. It was decided that the Court community would invite the entire community to celebrate the heritage of the Black History. A stage was made by the janitors and we all heard the many accomplishments of the Black Community. Present were community dignitaries and clergy, elected officials, residents and even members of decorated Tuskegee Airmen, several of whom lived in the district. It was a wonderful celebration featuring displays and presentations and closing with a program of speeches, talks and rousing music. It was a day we were empowered as one community.

The outcome of the celebration was an invitation to the Cook County Bar Association. The Cook County Bar Association is the oldest Black Bar association in the country. Several members spoke at the Black History Month celebration. We asked their members who were experienced lawyers to come to the Markham Courthouse and represent individuals who were able to pay lawyers, usually 10% of the bond. White lawyers from another Bar Association had a monopoly from the time the courthouse was built. It helped me when I first

---

6   Lenka Křičková co-authored *Restorative Justice Abroad: A Case of the Czech Republic* in this textbook with Terezie Buková.

became a lawyer to see another woman in the Court practicing law. It would help the community to see lawyers that lived there. It was an example of prejudice that these lawyers were not invited when the Court opened. It took time for the clerks and deputies to recognize them for who they were.

This is the end of the tale of the Markham Court from 1992-1999. The community brought the Court forward for the new century. Now we know the value of community and unity. We learned together not to beat children, but to show them love; that if a child is acting out, listen to the teacher and get medical help for the child. In this new century we learn about neurobiology. The brain is not fully grown until we are 28. Patience, help, and above all love opens new paths in our brains. We are learning in this new age to flip it. Here is an example. Judge Alexander Calabrese presides in the Red Hook Court in Brooklyn, New York. He was asked by a law student, "How many hot drops does a defendant have in your Court before you send him to prison.?" The judge answered, "It is my fault if he continues to use drugs. He needs better and more intensive treatment. I will help him get it. It may take a long time, but he will get well."

In other words, love is the secret ingredient. We are all one. We are all together.

Love grows mercy and other good things. We can only find the good things if we love.

2021

Chief Judge Timothy Evans is a believer in Restorative Justice. Three Community Courts have opened in areas of Cook County that requested them. Judges, lawyers and Court personnel from the community are trained in restorative practices including circles. Judge Evans asks the community members to design the courts to their needs. He is there for them at all times.

Professor Michael P. Seng and I are Co-Directors of the Restorative Justice Project. We have had the joy of teaching law students Recently we did training for the Community Court Judges. Communities are lining up to receive their own courts.

The U.S. District for the Northern District of Illinois has developed multiple Courts where restorative practices are used. There are several Courts for reentry of former prisoners and a Diversionary Court as well. Our law students observe these Courts and are lectured each semester by the Federal Defender,

John Murphy. Mr. Murphy tells the students that the Federal Defender's job is not only to represent clients in Court, but to help them become their best selves.

Our law students bring restorative practices to grade school and high school children. Currently, we partner with the Union League Boys and Girls Club. The law students develop active listening skills and compassion. We learn from our students more than we teach at UIC John Marshall Law School. We are grateful to all whose grants have made our work possible. We wish our readers to join in restoring each other. One person at a time. It has been a privilege for each of us who wrote Chapters or who helped the writers. We wish our readers the height of luck in life and in Restorative Justice practices.

What is the role of courts in our society and how can courts be effective practitioners of restorative justice? What can judges do to bring restorative justice into their courtrooms?

How can the community influence what occurs in the courts?

Should courts have a psychologist, sociologist, social worker, or other trained mental health worker in residence?

What types of evidence should be admitted into trials to make them more restorative?

Are courts themselves so inherently hierarchical that any attempts to make them more restorative will fail? Therefore, should controversies be diverted away from the courts when a restorative solution is possible?

TRUTH, UNTRUTH, AND FREEDOM OF SPEECH – THE PATH TO RESTORATIVE JUSTICE

MICHAEL P. SENG

I. INTRODUCTION

Truth is essential to do justice, whether it be retributive justice, transformative justice, restorative justice, or any other kind of justice. The entire point of a criminal or civil trial is to ascertain the truth. Truth is also essential to the functioning of the democratic process. Citizens cannot fulfill their responsibilities without truthful information about what the government is doing. Legislators, judges, and executive officials cannot perform their functions without truthful information.

The First Amendment of the United States Constitution protects the dissemination of information. Yet there is a tension in American law between truth and freedom of speech under the First Amendment. This tension between freedom of speech and truthfulness is a problem in every government and in every society. It may seem expedient in the short run for the government or government officials to disseminate untruths that are to the government's advantage; however, the long-term effect will be devastating.

The dissemination of untruth inevitably destroys the credibility of the government. During the first year of the Trump presidency, the Washington Post documented that he lied an average of 5.9 times a day.[1] Unfortunately, the false information continued throughout his presidency even to his false assertions that he won the 2020 election. Trump countered that he was combating the "Fake News" that appears in the media. The result was that half the population refused to trust the traditional news media; and the other half of the population lost trust in the government. More and more persons turned to private websites

---

1   MICHIKO KAKUTANI, THE DEATH OF TRUTH 13 (2018).

that disseminated conspiracies and other nonfactual and fanciful information, resulting in a further polarization of society. This because especially apparent in the mixed reactions to the COVID-19 virus and may well have been responsible for the severity of the pandemic in the United States and many unnecessary deaths.

The First Amendment protects "freedom of speech, or of the press, or the right of the people peaceably to assemble, and to petition the Government for redress of grievances." The First Amendment protects private speech from Government interference. However, the Supreme Court has recently broadly held that the First Amendment does not apply to government speech.[2] Nonetheless, government speech has an impact on the First Amendment rights of private persons. In this essay, we will first discuss the First Amendment protection of private speech and then take up government speech.

This discussion uses the word "untruth," not "lie." This is intentional. A "lie" is a deliberate fabrication. It intends to deceive. An "untruth" is simply false. It implies an objective standard and may be intentional or unintentional. Many examples of scientific laws that we once thought to be true turned out to be false. A fixed earth at the center of the universe turned out to be untrue, but that does not mean that for millennia persons lied.

In law, we seek "truth" no matter how elusive it may be.

II. WHY IS TRUTH IMPORTANT?

When one talks of "truth," Christians automatically think of the story of Jesus before Pilot.[3] Jesus said that the reason he came into the world was "to testify to the truth." "Truth," Pilot said, "What does that mean?" We will attempt to answer that question.

One of the best books on the Trump presidency is Michiko Kakutani, THE DEATH OF TRUTH. Kakutani describes the nihilism that pervades Washington today.[4] She quotes Hannah Arendt, THE ORIGINS OF TOTALITARIANISM (1951), where Arendt states that "the ideal subject of totalitarianism is the person for whom the distinction between fact and fiction (i.e.. the reality of experi-

---

2   *E.g.*, Pleasant Grove City v. Summum, 555 U.S. 460 (2009).

3   John, 18: 37-38.

4   KAKUTANI 155,

ence) and the distinction between true and false (i.e., the standards of thought) no longer exist."[5] She quotes President Obama, who said that the biggest challenge we have today is that we no longer share a common baseline of facts.[6] She quotes Pope Francis, who warned that trusting in falsehoods has dire consequences.[7] Similarly, she challenges news reporters with a quote from CNN reporter Christiane Amanpour: "I believe in being truthful, not neutral."[8]

President Vaclav Havel of Czechoslovakia, and later the Czech Republic, saw what happens when governments ignore truth, or, worse yet, manipulate it:

> "A world where 'truth' flourishes not in a dialectic climate of genuine
> knowledge, but in a climate of power motives, is a world of mental sterility,
> petrified dogmas, rigid and unchangeable creeds leading inevitably to creedless
> despotism."[9]

As Havel states in "The Power of the Powerless," the post-totalitarian regime in Czechoslovakia required persons "to live within a lie."[10] He counters: "If the main pillar of the system is living a lie, then it is not surprising that the fundamental threat to it is living the truth."[11]

Archbishop Desmond Tutu describes the marked "therapeutic" effects of the public hearings conducted by the Truth and Reconciliation Commission that disclosed the crimes of apartheid in South Africa and their impact on both victims and perpetrators. South Africa preferred confronting truth over the "amnesia" that would have been the result of a blanket amnesty.[12] Tutu recognizes that "real reconciliation can happen only on the basis of the truth."[13] Tutu also acknowledges the relationship of truth to democracy:

---

5   *Id.* 11.

6   *Id.* 14.

7   *Id.* 14.

8   *Id.* 76.

9   Vaclav Havel, "Letter to Gustav Husak," (1975), published in VACLAV HAVEL, LIVING IN TRUTH 16 (1980).

10   Vaclav Havel, "The Power of the Powerless," (1978), published in VACLAV HAVEL, LIVING IN TRUTH 45 (1980).

11   *Id.* 57.

12   DESPOND TUTU, NO FUTURE WITHOUT FORGIVENESS 24-28 (1999).

13   Desmond Tutu, "What about Justice?" published in DESMOND TUTU, GOD IS NOT A CHRISTIAN

"What is important is to stress that a vibrant democracy is one where vigorous debate, dissent, disagreement and discussion are welcomed. No one has a monopoly on wisdom and ability. We must avoid kowtowing sycophancy like the plague. If policies are good, they can withstand scrutiny and dissent. No one is infallible. We must encourage those who ask awkward questions, for our rulers are our rulers because we chose them, and they are accountable to us. . . . Those whom we elected and whom we support should have the self-assurance of being open to scrutiny and debate and especially be able to admit they are wrong when they are."[14]

III. THE RELEVANCE OF TRUTH UNDER THE FIRST AMENDMENT.

The First Amendment itself states nothing about truthfulness or untruthfulness. Indeed, judicial opinions express skepticism about truth and impose restraints on individual speech only in the most compelling circumstances.

American jurisprudence recognizes two separate justifications for the First Amendment.

First Amendment freedoms are basic individual or human rights. They relate to the intrinsic dignity of each individual and are necessary for individual self-fulfillment. They are among the unalienable rights necessary for the enjoyment of Life, Liberty, and the Pursuit of Happiness in the American Declaration of Independence. They are enshrined in all basic international human rights documents.

Additionally, First Amendment freedoms are necessary for the functioning of democracy – in Lincoln's words, "A Government Of the People, By the People, and For the People." Thus, the free flow of information and the freedom to express one's opinions is essential to the political marketplace where democracy thrives.

---

47 (2011).

14 Desmond Tutu, "Naught for Your Comfort," published in DESMOND TUTU, GOD IS NOT A CHRISTIAN 182-3 (2011).

IV. GOVERNMENT REGULATION OF THE TRUTHFULNESS OF PRIVATE SPEECH UNDER THE FIRST AMENDMENT

The First Amendment does not guarantee that private speech will be truthful, but it does offer a path to truth. For the most part, the First Amendment does not concern itself with truth. Rather the First Amendment builds upon the premise that in the free exchange of ideas, truth will come out and prevail. One can debate whether this approach is overly optimistic. But except in very limited spheres, the truth or falsity of a statement does not determine whether it can be published.

American courts generally classify speech under the First Amendment according to its subject matter, for instance, speech on political, private, commercial, cultural, or artistic matters. Truth or falsity is irrelevant in most, but not all, instances.

A. Speech that incites to imminent unlawful action.

The first modern First Amendment cases grew out of challenges to the Espionage Act of 1917, which Congress passed during World War I to prevent conspiracies to interfere with the draft and the war effort. In *Schenck v. United States*,[15] the United States Supreme Court upheld the application of the Act. Justice O.W. Holmes held that Congress could prescribe statements that created "a clear and present danger that they will bring about the substantive evils that Congress has a right to prevent." Holmes illustrated this with his famous analogy that "free speech would not protect a man in **falsely** shouting fire in a theatre and causing a panic." (Emphasis added) However, despite the analogy, the opinion left no doubt that what Holmes was proscribing was truthful as well as untruthful speech. Speech regardless of its content can be illegal because of the circumstances. Holmes said it was all a matter of "proximity and degree."

In a companion case under the Espionage Act, *Frowerk v. United States*,[16] Justice Holmes left little doubt that legality did not depend upon veracity: the conspiracy "could be accomplished or aided by persuasion as well as by **false** statements, and there was no need to allege that **false** reports were intended to be made or made." (Emphasis added)

---

15   249 U.S. 47 (1919).

16   249 U.S. 204 (1919).

In none of the Espionage Act cases did the government prove that the statements were false, nor did the defendants allege that they were true. Truth or falsity was not an issue under the wording of the statue. Whatever brings about the end is illegal. Holmes confirms this reading in *Debs v. United States*,[17] where he stated that a jury could find the defendants guilty if "words used has as their natural tendency and reasonable probable effect to obstruct the recruiting service."

In his famous dissent in *Abrams v. United States*,[18] Holmes stated his skepticism about basing the suppression of speech on the truth or falsity of the utterance. Holmes articulated his now famous justification for freedom of speech based on the market place of ideas:

> "[T]he ultimate good desired is better reached by free trade in ideas— ... the best test of truth is the power of the thought to get itself accepted in the competition of the market."

Justice Louis Brandeis relied on the market place of ideas analogy in his concurring opinion in *Whitney v. California*.[19] Whitney was a prominent member of the Socialist Party in California. Although she did not personally advocate violence, she remained a member of the party after it adopted a platform urging the violent overthrow of the government. She was prosecuted under the California Criminal Syndicalism Statute that made it illegal knowingly to become a member of a group that advocates overthrowing the government by violence. Justice Brandeis declared:

> "Those who won our independence by revolution were not cowards. They
> did not fear political change. They did not exalt order at the cost of liberty. To
> courageous, self-reliant men, with confidence in the power of free and fearless
> reasoning applied through the processes of popular government, no danger
> flowing from speech can be deemed clear and present unless the incidence of
> the evil apprehended is so imminent that it may befall before there is opportu-
> nity for full discussion. **If there be time to expose through discussion the
> falsehood and fallacies, to avert the evil by the processes of education,**

---

17 249 U.S. 211 (1918).

18 250 U.S. 616 (1919).

19 274 U.S. 357 (1927).

the remedy to be applied is more speech, not enforced silence. . . ."
(Emphasis added)

Modern "incitement" cases ignore the question of truth or falsity.[20] Determinations of veracity appear to play no role in modern national security cases that involve freedom of speech.[21]

B. Prior Restraints on Speech

The Espionage Act cases and their successors involved criminal sanctions for previously made statements. Prior restraints are censorship prior to the publication of speech. Prior restraints on speech come to the courts with the highest presumption of unconstitutionality. Prior restraints involve situations that require government approval before one can speak or publish. They can take various forms, but the truth or falsity of the speech rarely plays a role in the discussion over whether a prior restraint is justified.

In *Near v. Minnesota*,[22] a state court had enjoined a newspaper from future publication. The newspaper was found guilty of publishing libel on numerous occasions. On appeal to the United States Supreme Court, Chief Justice Charles Evans Hughes ruled the injunction to be a prior restraint and held it unconstitutional, stating that the government has a heavy burden to justify a prior restraint. Truth or falsity was not a consideration in the Court's opinion. Although the libel published by the newspaper was false, the examples given by the Court that would justify a prior restraint involved seemingly truthful statements: "the actual obstruction to [the government's] recruiting service or the publication of the sailing dates or transports or the number and location of troops."

Similarly, truth or falsity did not enter into the Court's most famous prior restraint decision. *New York Times v. United States (the Pentagon Papers Case)*.[23] The government sought an injunction to prevent the New York Times from publishing a classified report prepared by the pentagon describing how the United States became involved in Viet Nam. The report was prepared by the government and presumably, from the government's standpoint, true. Indeed, it was

---

20   Brandenburg v. Ohio, 395 U.S. 444 (1969).

21   Holder v. Humanitarian Law Project, 561 U.S. 1 (2010).

22   284 U.S. 697 (1931).

23   402 U.S. 713 (1971).

this truth that concerned the government. The Court held that an injunction restraining publication would be an unconstitutional prior restraint. Truth or falsity did not enter into any of the multiple opinions of the Justices. Like the incitement cases, truth or falsity is irrelevant if the object of the restraint is to prevent an imminent danger that the government can avert.

C. Defamation

Perhaps the most famous case decided by the United States Supreme Court involving truth or falsity is *New York Times v. Sullivan*.[24] The Justice William Brennan held that a public official could not sue a newspaper for libel for publishing untruthful statements about him without proof of "actual malice." Recognizing that "Debate on public issues should be uninhibited, robust, and wide-open and. . . may well include vehement, caustic and sometimes unpleasantly sharp attacks on government and public officials," Justice Brennan held that requiring a newspaper to prove the truth of published statements may deter the publishing of information. "Actual malice" means that the speaker made the statement "with knowledge that it was false or with reckless disregard of whether it was false or not."

The Supreme Court has modified this standard when the speech does not involve a public official or a matter of public interest. In *Dun & Bradstreet v. Greenmoss Builders*,[25] the Court upheld an award of presumptive and punitive damages, absent a showing of "actual malice." Dun & Bradstreet had published a false financial report that injured a private contractor.

D. Right to Reply

Freedom of the press is sacrosanct under the First Amendment. In *Miami Herald v. Tornillo*,[26] the Supreme Court held that a state could not require a newspaper to publish a reply from a candidate for public office. Florida law required the right of reply when a political candidate "is assailed regarding his personal character or official record by any newspaper." Chief Justice Warren Burger held that the government cannot interfere with the editorial discretion of a newspaper by

---

24   376 U.S. 254 (1964).

25   472 U.S. 749 (1985).

26   418 U.S. 241 (1974).

telling it what it can and cannot print. In a separate concurring opinion, Justice Brennan (joined by Justice Rehnquist) stated that he understood the opinion did not decide "the constitutionality of 'retraction' statutes affording plaintiffs able to prove defamatory falsehoods a statutory action to require publication of a retraction." The Court still has not addressed this issue.

E. Fighting Words

Although often debated, the First Amendment probably does not protect fighting words, words intended to provoke a violent reaction in the hearer. Fighting words may or may not be true. In *Chaplinsky v. New Hampshire*,[27] the Supreme Court affirmed the conviction of a Jehovah's Witness who was involved in an altercation with a police officer after he called the officer "a God damned racketeer" and "a damned fascist."[28] Later in *Cantwell v. Connecticut*,[29] the Supreme Court reversed the conviction of a Jehovah's Witness who played an anti-Catholic phonograph record on the street. The speech involved "no assault or threat of bodily harm, no truculent bearing, no intentional discourtesy and no personal abuse."

The Supreme Court narrowly defines fighting words. Fighting words are addressed to the person of the hearer and not to the public at large. In *Cohen v. California*,[30] the Supreme Court reversed the conviction of an anti-war demonstrator who wore a jacket with an offensive word describing the draft during the Viet Nam War. The vulgar expression did not constitute a fighting word because no particular person was addressed.

F. Hate Speech

Unlike most of Europe and the world, the United States Constitution protects hate speech – speech that stigmatizes a person because of the person's race,

---

27 315 U.S. 568 (1942).

28 In Lewis v. New Orleans, 415 U.S. 130 (1974), the Supreme Court invalidated an ordinance that made it illegal to curse or revile a police officer in the performance of his duties. In a concurring opinion, Justice Lewis Powell stated that "a properly trained police officer may reasonably be expected to 'exercise a higher degree of restraint' than the average citizen, and thus be less likely to respond belligerently to 'fighting words.'" And see City of Houston v. Hill, 482 U.S. 451 (1987).

29 310 U.S. 296 (1946).

30 403 U.S. (1971).

ethnicity, sex, sexual orientation, religion, or disability. Almost by definition, hate speech will contain untruths that are offensive and often dangerous to the hearer and to the general public. Nonetheless, the Supreme Court has protected hate speech on the ground that the government should not regulate speech based on its content or viewpoint. Hate speech, like other distasteful speech, should be discredited in the marketplace.[31]

In *Snyder v. Phelps*,[32] the Supreme Court reversed a judgment in a common law tort action for emotional distress filed by the father of a soldier killed in war. The defendants had mounted a demonstration outside the church during the funeral. The demonstrators did not violate any time, place, or manner restrictions or engage in violence conduct. They picketed the church with anti-gay and anti-military signs expressing opposition to the military's policy allowing gays. Although certainly offensive to the father and most bystanders, Chief Justice John Roberts held that the demonstrators were speaking out on a matter of public interest and cannot be punished for the content of their speech.

Similarly, in *Virginia v. Black*,[33] the Supreme Court held a Virginia cross-burning statute unconstitutionally overbroad. Cross-burning sends a message that is intimidating to African-Americans and historically has been used to threaten them and others with violence and death. Justice Sandra Day O'Connor held that the statute unconstitutionally prohibited not only true threats of violence, which are not protected by the Constitution, but also burning a cross to express opposition to governmental policies, particularly on race and civil rights, speech that is protected by the Constitution.

In *Matal v. Tam*,[34] the Supreme Court held unconstitutional a section of the Trademark Act that prohibited the government from registering trademarks that "disparage . . . or bring . . . into contempt or disrepute" any "persons, living or dead." The Trademark Office had refused to register the name "The Slants" for a rock group on the ground that the phrase disparaged Asian-Americans."

---

31   R.A.V. v. St. Paul, 505 U.S. 377 (1992).

32   562 U.S. 443 (2011).

33   538 U.S. 343 (2003).

34   157 S.Ct. 1744 (2017).

G. Commercial Speech

Truth or falsity is relevant to commercial speech – advertising or speech that proposes a commercial transaction. The courts had formerly considered commercial speech to be outside First Amendment protection. Like any other commercial transaction, it was subject to reasonable government regulation.

In *Virginia State Board of Pharmacy v. Virginia Citizens Consumer Council*,[35] the Supreme Court held that the First Amendment protected the right of consumers to receive information. The right to speech is meaningless if it does not similarly protect the public's right to receive information. However, the Court held that the government had the right to protect consumers from false and misleading information or advertising.

Justice Harry Blackmun stated:

"Untruthful speech, commercial or otherwise, has never been protected for
its own sake. . . . Obviously, much commercial speech is not provably false, or
even wholly false, but only deceptive or misleading. We foresee no obstacle
to a State's dealing effectively with the problem. The First Amendment, as we
construe it today does not prohibit the State from insuring that the stream of
commercial information flows cleanly as well as freely."

H. Falsehoods That Cause No Injury

All lies are not outside of the protections of the First Amendment. In *United States v. Alvarez*,[36] the Court in a plurality opinion written by Justice Anthony Kennedy held unconstitutional the Stolen Valor Act, which made it illegal to represent falsely that one has been awarded any decoration or medal authorized by Congress for the Armed Forces. The law provided for an enhanced penalty if the award was the Congressional Medal of Honor.

Alvarez was indicted under the statute for lying about his having received the Medal of Honor. Justice Kennedy relied on Holmes' reasoning that "the remedy for speech that is false is speech that is true." Justice Kennedy recognized three instances where false speech could be punished, but it found none of them to be applicable here:

---

35   425 U.S. 748 (1976).

36   567 U.S. 709 (2012).

1. The criminal prohibition of a false statement made to a Government official;

2. Laws punishing perjury; and

3. Prohibitions on the false representation that one is speaking as a Government official or on behalf of the Government.

Justice Kennedy also cited *Virginia Pharmacy*'s rule that the Government can restrict speech "where false claims are made to effect a fraud or secure moneys or other valuable considerations, say offers of employment."

I. Speech of Public Employees

Government employees enjoy First Amendment protection when they speak out about matters of public interest in virtue of government employment.[37] However, the Court has more recently upheld the disciplining of public employees who speak out on purely internal personnel matters.[38] The government may also discipline employees who speak out about matters relating to the employee's official or professional duties.[39] Truth or falsity of the statement appears to be irrelevant in these cases.

In *Snepp v. United States*,[40] the Supreme Court upheld an agreement between the CIA and its employees that required employees to obtain prior clearance before publishing anything related to their government employment. More recently, the government has insisted that public employees sign these types of "Snepp" agreements outside the national security agencies. The government takes the position that these agreements apply to all matters even those that do not pose a threat to national security and regardless of the truth or falsity of the matters revealed. The agreements clearly restrict truthful information to the public through a prior restraint and they lead us directly to the problem of government speech.

---

37   Pickering v. Board of Education, 391 U.S. 563 (1968).

38   Comnick v. Myers, 461 U.S. 138 (1983).

39   Garcetti v. Ceballos, 547 U.S. 410 (2006).

40   444 U.S. 507 (1980).

Unfortunately, there is a history of Government untruth. Many American wars have started because of false information, some of it deliberately created by the government. Fabrications surrounding the Gulf of Tonkin incident led to the Viet Nam War and false reports of weapons of mass destruction led to the Iraq War. Watergate and the Iran-Contra Controversy involved lies and cover-ups of those lies. Both the Clinton and Trump impeachments involved allegations of lying. Today, we have frivolous lawsuits filed contesting so-called election fraud in the 2020 presidential election.

Each one of these events undermines trust in government, and cumulatively they run the risk of destroying democracy.

The Supreme Court has stated that First Amendment principles do not apply to government speech. In *Pleasant Grove City v. Summum*,[41] Justice Samuel Alito, not known for being a nuanced thinker, declared that:

> "The Free Speech Clause restricts government regulation of private speech; it does not regulate government speech. . . . A government entity has the right to 'speak for itself.' . . . [I[t is entitled to say what it wishes,'. . . and to select the views that it wants to express. . . ."

Justice Alito acknowledges that: "the involvement of public officials in advocacy may be limited by law, regulation, or practice. And of course, a government entity is ultimately accountable to the electorate and the political process for its advocacy."

The ability of citizens to police the government in a democracy depends upon their access to information. The United States Supreme Court has acknowledged that "informed public opinion is the most potent of all restraints upon misgovernment."[42] The Court also emphasized in *New York Times v. Sullivan*[43] that debate on public issues should be uninhibited, robust, and wide-open. Debate is meaningless if the parties lack facts to inform their discussion. Nonetheless, the Supreme Court has held that the right to government information is not

---

41   555 U.S. 460 (2009).

42   Grosjean v. American Press, 297 U.S. 233 (1936).

43   376 U.S. 254 (1964).

implicit in Frist Amendment guarantees.[44] The common law recognizes a right of access to government information, but the common law protects only the right to public information and does not apply to information that the government choses to classify as not accessible to the public.[45]

Acquiring information about the government is thus a matter left to legislative discretion at both the federal and state levels of government. The federal government as well as most state and local governments have enacted some form of freedom of information acts. The federal Freedom of Information Act is broad, but contains nine exceptions.[46] It has had a mixed history in the courts. The federal Whistleblowers Protection Act[47] and the Intelligence Community Whistleblowers Protection Act[48] provide some protection for federal employees who disclose information, but the courts have not broadly construed them. The Court's First Amendment jurisprudence places employees in jeopardy for losing their employment and for being stigmatized a traitor.[49]

Actions against both the federal and state governments directly for failing to disclose information or for disseminating false or malicious information are barred generally by the defense of Sovereign Immunity.[50] Government officials from the president on down are protected by an array of privileges and immunities that make it very difficult to maintain an action based on the truth or falsity of their official statements.[51]

---

44   Houchins v. KQED, 438 U.S. 1 (1978) (plurality opinion).

45   Schwartz v. Department of Justice, 435 F. Supp. 1203, aff'd, 595 F.2d 888 (D.C. Cir. 1979): Nixon v. Warner Communications, 435 U.S. 589 (1978).

46   5 U.S.C. § 552.

47   5 U.S.C. § 2302 (b)(8) and (9).

48   5 U.S.C. App. §8h

49   Connick v. Myers, 461 U.S. 138 (1983); Garcetti v. Ceballos, 547 U.S. 410 (2006).

50   Congress has the power to waive federal sovereign immunity. Library of Congress v. Shaw, 478 U.S. 310 (1986). Congress may also have power to waive state sovereign immunity under Section 5 of the Fourteenth Amendment in order to protect the fundamental right to freedom of speech. Fitzpatrick v. Bitzer, 427 U.S. 445 (1976) (Congress can waive state sovereign immunity to protect against sex discrimination in employment. Tennessee v. Lane, 124 S.Ct. 1978 (2004). (Congress can waive state sovereign immunity to protect the fundamental right of access to the courts.)

51   Official immunities for both federal and state public officials in damage actions are grounded in the common law and thus in theory Congress can abolish them. Nixon v. Fitzgerald, 457 U.S. 731 (1932) (President enjoys absolute immunity for damages through the common law); Butz v. Economou, 438 U.S. 478 (1978) (lower federal officials have common law immunity depending upon their function); Harlow v. Fitzgerald, 457 U.S. 800 (1982) (same). The Speech and Debate Clause in Article I, Section 6 provides Constitutional protection for members of Congress.

The Frist Amendment thus offers powerful protection against the government from interfering with private speech, whether true or false. As currently interpreted, the First Amendment provides no protection when the government lies to its citizens. Government speech is important to individuals and to society. Alito provides a simplistic answer when he states that the remedy against the government's misuse of speech is political. If the government misleads the public or if the public does not have access to government information, government untruths can inform government policies and actions. When the truth does come out, as it inevitably does, the harm may be irreversible. Cynicism provoked by government lies will ultimately undermine the democratic process

Individual exercise of First Amendment freedoms is dependent upon access to truthful government information. Truthful government information affects the ability of individuals to exercise their political and civil rights under the Constitution. If the government is giving out false information or is giving out no information at all, neither the press nor citizens can effectively perform their role in a democracy. As Archbishop Oscar Romero stated in his homily on November 25, 1979:

"If we don't tell the truth, we are committing the worse sin. We are betraying truth and betraying the people."[52]

Rarely have the similarities and differences and the relationship between private and governmental speech been analyzed. Should government speech be constrained and, if so, what would the constraints look like? How do we ensure that those who elect public officials have the facts necessary to exercise such an important right? How do we ensure that the persons we elect have access to the information they need? What role should truth play in this discussion? Should there be penalties against persons who misuse the public trust by spreading lies and untruths? Impeachment has been shown to be a cumbersome remedy and is available only in the most egregious situations. As so often happens, would new laws and penalties simply create new avenues of evasion?

Because the government cannot claim protection under the First Amendment and because citizens need truthful government information to insure robust debate, *New York Times v. Sullivan*'s concerns about inhibiting free expression

---

52 Oscar Romero, Homily, November 25, 1979, excerpts found in THROUGH THE YEAR WITH OSCAR ROMERO – DAILY MEDITATIONS (2015).

are not applicable to government speech. Nothing in the Constitution prevents Congress or a state legislature from demanding that the government and government officials be truthful and provide sanctions if they are not. As Justice Alito recognized, laws already make it criminal for public officials to make false statements to Government officials, prohibit perjury, or in making false representation that one is speaking as a Government official or on behalf of the Government. Now is a good time to debate whether existing laws provide sufficient protection for democracy and whether legislatures should supplement freedom of information laws with laws protecting the right to truthful information.

The problems of democracy are never ending. Each generation faces new challenges and must exercise vigilance in the protection of individual rights and liberties and the democratic process.

VI. CONCLUSION

We will end with the recent words of Pope Francis in his encyclical published in 2020. The Pope asks how we can reach truth in a pluralistic society. He answers, "through dialogue."[53]

"Such dialogue ought to be enriched and illuminated by clear thinking, rational arguments, a variety of perspectives, and the contributions of different fields of knowledge and points of view. Nor can it exclude the conviction that it is possible to arrive at certain fundamental truths always to be upheld."[54]

He then raises the question: how do we reach a consensus?

He gives a very simple answer, "through kindness."[55]

"Kindness opens new paths where hostility and conflict would burn all bridges."[56]

This is the prescription for restorative justice.[57] Restorative justice brings harmony out of discord. It rights wrongs that have been committed. It reforms those who have done harm. It requires offenders to acknowledge the harm that

---

53   *Fratelli Tutti* ¶ 211 (2020).

54   *Ibid.*

55   *Fratelli Tutti* ¶ 224 (2020).

56   *Ibid.*

57   See generally Murphy & Seng, editors, RESTORATIVE JUSTICE IN PRACTICE (2015).

they have caused and to make amends. Similarly, restorative justice attempts to restore the injured. Restoration comes with an assurance that the anti-social conduct has ceased. Most importantly restorative justice cannot be done without community involvement. The community must acknowledge its role in producing the wrong and create structures to prevent similar harms from recurring. Anti-social conduct does not occur in a vacuum. Restorative justice ensures that the community becomes a nurturing environment.

Restorative justice requires truth. In a pluralistic society, there is often no consensus about what is true. Truth does not occur when everyone walks lockstep with the government. Yet the architects of the American Constitution recognized that out of pluralism comes unity – *E Pluribus Unum*. The restorative process seeks truth in a way that is consistent with the democratic values found in the First Amendment of the United States Constitution.

The circle is perhaps the most iconic restorative justice practice that allows everyone to participate in the search for truth. It grew out of indigenous forms of dispute resolution. Participants agree in advance on the rules of the circle. Generally, it is agreed that matters said in the circle will remain confidential, that circle participants will listen to each other with respect, that participants will not interrupt anyone who holds the talking piece, and that participants will talk only when they are in possession of the talking piece. The talking peace is an object of symbolic value to the group and is passed from speaker to speaker in rotation. Each participant has an opportunity to make a statement, although participants have the option of passing. A circle has a dynamic of its own. It is a living process. By allowing each person to speak in turn, it diffuses anger. A well run circle has the potential for reaching consensus.

The South African Truth and Reconciliation Commission exemplifies another restorative practice. Persons from both sides who committed crimes during apartheid confessed their offenses in public and, if they were determined to be truthful, received amnesty.

The object of any restorative practice is for offenders to accept responsibility. Restorative justice practices create dialogue. The circle process treats all participants with equal respect and kindness and allows each participant to speak from the heart. Out of respect and kindness, truth emerges. Truth opens the path to reconciliation and ultimately, if we are lucky, to forgiveness. Restorative justice practices exemplify the democratic ideals inherent in the First Amendment and offer a peaceful path to "finding truth in the marketplace of ideas."

Why is truth essential for the functioning of justice?

How can we ensure that in a democracy, truthful information informs all decision?

Is the United States Supreme Court's jurisprudence correct in not considering truth as a factor when evaluating the value of most private speech?

Given the abuses that occurred under the Nazi regime in Germany, the apartheid regime in South Africa, and the Tutsi/Hutu conflict in Rwanda, as well as others, can the United States position on hate speech be justified?

Is an objective standard for truth necessary if both sides agree on a common set of facts, which may or may not be true? For instance, what are the pros and cons to parties stipulating to a statement of the facts in order to resolve a dispute when either side or both question the validity of the stipulation?

How does one come together to talk truth to a demagogue or to someone whose interest is disruption?

2 WOMEN PROVING THAT FEMININE GENIUS IS ON THE RISE IN LAW + JUSTICE

GINA MAROTTA & STEPHANIE GLASSBERG

If you feel concerned that you may not be a fit to work inside the legal and justice systems, this article will show you why and help you create your place. We begin by sharing our stories.

GINA'S DISHEARTENING LEGAL CAREER AND FINDING HER RIGHT PLACE

In my law school application, I wrote about my desire to be in a profession that required heart. To me, this meant a continuation of my work as a paralegal where I built relationships and poured my creative talents into every case. As a law student and young lawyer, I chose to focus on criminal defense work, where I believed it was my job to uphold the Constitution and protect clients as best as I could to not be squashed by what had become an increasingly heavy-handed, punishment-focused American justice system. I learned early on: being successful meant being aggressive. Helping clients required going to battle on their behalf every day. One day I'd argue motions against an elite team of federal prosecutors on a political corruption case, and the next I'd go toe-to-toe with Chicago police detectives in a street gang investigation. On the outside, my life looked high-profile and exciting; it was the stuff of law and order TV. Yet, on the inside, the truth was, I didn't feel like I fit into this life. Unlike the men I worked with, who were deeply passionate about our work and how we did it, I didn't feel like this competitive dog-eat-dog work environment was truly meant for me.

There is one moment in my legal career when I experienced a different vibe. For a semester in law school, I worked as a student extern for United States Magistrate Judge Nan Nolan. Judge Nolan is the only female lawyer I ever worked under. I had otherwise been trained by and worked exclusively for men. Judge Nolan invited me to sit in on one of her settlement conferences. Her approach was something I had never seen before. Judge Nolan arranged herself and the lawyers at a table. There was no one at the "head" of the room, as judges normally were, and no separate tables for opposing sides. Everyone was gathered together and seemingly equal. Judge Nolan asked questions, took time to listen deeply, expressed compassion, and made sure she understood each side of the case. Once Judge Nolan deeply understood one side, she paused to assist the opposing attorney to also understand what was just spoken. She was like a conductor allowing each side to express their needs and ideas, and then she helped move the energy around so that there was a flow of understanding between the parties. It was clear she was doing some kind of collaboration magic. The parties began to see that they were more similar than separate. She created space for everyone to feel like a winner and like they could truly agree and align in an outcome. I was in awe.

The next time I was exposed to this softer, yet wildly-effective approach in law was nearly a decade later. At home sitting on my couch, I tuned into the documentary "Where to Invade Next" by filmmaker Michael Moore. At the time, I had already left my legal career for other pursuits because I was so disheartened by the daily fight. But then, what I witnessed in this documentary opened me anew. In exploring the systems of law and justice outside of the U.S., Moore discovered "restorative justice," a concept I had never heard of as an American lawyer. In contrast to the aggressive, punitive, and unforgiving U.S. justice system, the key ideas behind restorative justice include: (1) understanding that people make mistakes out of their pain and (2) believing that when nurtured and met with compassion inside an accountability structure, people can be restored to wholeness. True to these ideas, all persons inside a system of restorative justice hold the common goal of maintaining human dignity. Moore drew out examples of this philosophy in practice through interviews with police officers, prison guards, crime victims, and incarcerated persons in places like Portugal and Norway. Police officers spoke about their opinions on guns, that they did not carry guns nor did they believe that would be appropriate. Victims of violent crime shared that they did not seek or believe in revenge. Prison footage showed inmates trusted to roam free on prison grounds with keys to their own private rooms and access to kitchen knives. Inmates spent their days collaboratively creating art or independently learning new job skills. Prison employees too brought a restorative mindset to their job to support inmates to reach their potential. This is best exemplified in the new prisoner orientation process in Norway's maximum security prison. In the orientation video, the prison guards offer hope and encouragement as they flash wide smiles, joyfully play musical instruments, and sing arguably one of the most uplifting songs ever written: "We Are The World."

Watching the documentary, I wept. This is what I had wanted to be a part of as a lawyer, but I had no examples of or language for. I knew I wanted to be a part of this new way of justice. I immediately googled "restorative justice" and "Chicago" to find and connect with Ret. Judge Sheila Murphy, a pioneer and thought leader for the emergence of restorative justice in the U.S. Judge Murphy became my mentor, and generously guided me to fulfill my heart's desires. She showed me the less known places where restorative justice was emerging in my city and so I began to learn and participate in restorative practices such as:

- **Victim-offender peace circles**: an alternative to adversarial courtroom combat where victims, offenders, and community members come together without lawyers to collaboratively resolve criminal matters with an eye toward accountability, compassion, forgiveness, restoration, and making all parties whole again.

- **Re-entry court**: a support structure for formerly incarcerated persons to sit in a circle with judges, case workers, recovery specialists, and community members to receive compassionate understanding and help with resources to make healthy transitions back into society.

- **Student mentoring circles**: a law school student clinic pairing law students with youth in low-income, high-crime communities for mentorship in creatively managing stress and resolving conflict through restorative practices such as relationship-building, storytelling, compassionate listening, empathy, healing, and acceptance.

I had deeply longed, inside law and justice, to share my heart and use the legal system to help people create better lives. Now I have opportunities to do just that, and the beautiful news is that such opportunities in law and justice are emerging more and more every day.

For most of my life, I have known who I am at my core. I am strong, confident, passionate, tenacious, fiercely loyal, undoubtedly empathic, and unapologetically myself. And yet, many of those characteristics have been reduced, muted, and in some cases all but suppressed from existence. Becoming a law student only enhanced the scrutiny on my unique self. I felt like putty, taken and molded however people wanted to see me. And I felt complicit in all of this, because I didn't know how else to be. I have been told that I overshare, I am too honest, I need to tamp down my passion, I need to curb my empathy, and I need to do all of this to be "successful." But these criticisms always felt wrong and deep, deep down in my gut, I never believed any of them.

But as an impressionable legal student, new to the field, I became a sponge, soaking up everything others told me I needed to be: goal-orientated, logical, competitive, and selfish. I changed who I was while internally resisting the change. I became both self-loathing and resentful, hating myself for letting people change me so I could "fit" within the legal system. But I did follow orders. I applied for the jobs people told me to apply for, I enrolled in the classes people told me to enroll in, I wore the clothes people told me to wear. I tried to look the part. *And I was miserable.* The voice in my gut begged me to listen but the influence outside was stronger, telling me to shush that voice, instructing me that the voice was wrong. And I thought to myself: "who am I to disobey orders? These are professionals in my field, all telling me the same thing. I need to listen to them or else I'm doomed. I want to be 'successful.'"

A particularly memorable example of this influence was when I met with a mentor to discuss a piece I was writing for her publication. The discussion was supposed to be about my article but quickly shifted to her inquiry on where I would be working the following summer. This discussion happened in October of my second year of law school. Based on my good grades and strong extra-curricular student history, I had the opportunity at the time to apply to several highly prestigious internships, working for million/billion dollar clients. I knew that the positions required long hours and a rigorous linear work schedule that lacked creativity and often mortality. I was not interested. My mentor was displeased. She questioned my decision not to pursue those opportunities. She used her status, as a very successful female attorney, to explain that I behaved incorrectly on passing on such incredible opportunities. Based on her reaction, I was filled with shame. I meekly told her that I was not interested in the field, making myself smaller right in front of her. This gave her the power to quickly and confidently shut me down. She continued to explain how important it was to capitalize on my status, as a successful female law student, by working in areas which held immense status in the legal world, even if I was not interested. She made me feel ungrateful and that I was not living up to my full potential because I was not taking advantage of opportunities that others would kill for. She told me exactly who she thought I was supposed to be and punished me for the way I knew myself. I left that meeting mentally beating myself up for not applying to the prospective opportunities, even though I knew in my gut I would not find joy working in those fields.

I felt frustrated, shameful, disgusted, and irritated with myself and everyone around me. I felt so miserable that I considered quitting law school all together. Instead of quitting, however, this became a catalyzing moment. I decided to indulge my inner voice. I listened and believed it with unbridled confidence. I did the unthinkable. I unapologetically made decisions based off of my own voice because I had discovered the truth, nothing that was *supposed to* bring me "success" actually did.

At first I felt uncomfortable and awkward. I listened to myself instead of trained legal professionals on how to operate. I was actively and knowingly going against the grain. That did not sit well with me. But I did it anyway. And to my reaffirming surprise, I felt flecks of control and confidence re-enter my life. And *that* brought me back to joy. I continued in school, practicing choosing what I thought was best over what the outside world thought was best for me. I started working for a "less prestigious" state court judge whose values, work-ethic, and conviction I admired. I took classes that were not considered "valuable" because they were not subjects tested on the bar exam, like Critical Race Feminism, Mass Incarceration, and International Human rights. In reflection, I describe these classes as some of the most powerful and influential of my law school experience, clarifying and sharpening my ultimate purpose in the legal world. At the time, choosing these "extra curricular" courses over more traditional ones seemed radical and ill-advised but in review I was taking control of how I wanted to use my legal education.

I didn't have the language or any formal knowledge of what exactly I was doing. But, in my third year of law school that became clear. Inside a class called Restorative Justice, taught by the incomparable Professor Michael Seng and Judge Sheila Murphy, I realized what I was doing by listening to my inner feelings and following them. In doing what felt joyful and dropping what felt unnatural, even if others said it was "wrong" or "crazy," I was being authentic and returning to who I was always meant to be. I was applying restorative practices, the foundations of restorative justice, on myself. And from then on, I began to feel whole and in harmony with my true self.

I learned that there is a reason the guttural voice, speaking my truth, never died. There is a reason that the more I listened to the outside world the stronger and louder and more furious the voice became. I painfully realized that I would always know myself better than anyone else. I just needed to learn how to trust that instinct. Restorative practices brought me back to my whole self, one that is intimately in tune with my inner voice. Trusting the inner voice has cleared the brush from my path, leading me to my purpose in the world. Now I can recognize and indulge in what brings me joy without self-interrogation or restraint.

OUR BREAKTHROUGH IN CLARITY TO PASS ON TO YOU

Upon reflection of our experiences, we see a common theme: the mainstream worlds of law and justice did not validate our innate desires, natural talents, and soulful passions. Our first reaction in noticing that we did not exactly fit in was to think that perhaps we should leave. But eventually, something new emerged. As Stephanie eloquently describes, she validated her feelings and inner voice and began to listen, which allowed her to follow her own true path. And for Gina, she did this too, once she found restorative justice and a mentor who believed in her. And so instead of bowing out, we came to recognize that what we offer to law and justice is valid, deserves a place, and is in fact quite genius.

As two women who care deeply about helping others, we don't want our stories to end with our own realizations and transformations. We desire to pass on the wisdom we gained to you, the next generation, so that you can find your place and your genius in law and justice too. Writing this article has been a reflective exercise for us, and in the journey, we sought out the root causes of our pain and also of our triumph. We arrived at this breakthrough in clarity that can guide your path: *you can easily feel ashamed, like an outsider, and unwanted in the mainstream worlds of law and justice where there exists a nearly exclusive focus on* **masculine genius**, *and you can begin to feel at home, validated, and valuable as you create opportunities in and become free to express your* **feminine genius***.*

Before we begin our analysis to help you see what we see in the legal and justice systems and in ourselves, it is important to begin with a few disclaimers. First, we note explicitly that the masculine/feminine distinctions here are not referring to gender or sexuality. When we refer to the masculine/feminine distinctions we are referring to energies - both archetypal and creative. Second, we do not judge one energy as better than the other. Rather, we offer masculine and feminine as different and complementary. And finally, it is important to note that we all have masculine and feminine energies inside of us - regardless of gender and sexuality. For each of us, we typically recognize that one energy feels more like home, and the other is important to integrate and embrace at certain times in our lives and work.

THE DISTINCTION BETWEEN MASCULINE GENIUS AND FEMININE GENIUS

As the American law and justice systems have amply recognized, there is great genius in masculine energy. Archetypally, the masculine in us represents the warrior and protector whose purpose is to keep those in our care safe during times of danger and an opposing threat. As a natural fighter, the masculine archetype in us seeks to outsmart and dominate adversaries. The masculine is our assertive, giving energy and the qualities of high value include: being physically strong, aggressive and protective; being goal-oriented, intellectual, and productive; and being rational, focused, and controlled. The masculine in us operates from the yang side of yin/yang energy, and we exercise our creative force using the well-known and linear process of "building." Inside masculine energy, we build by applying our logic and intellect to make rational choices that we expect to get us to specific results. You can easily see this archetype and method of creating as dominant in the legal and justice systems. It is represented by the typical lawyer or police officer - whether male or female - known to be tough, aggressive, and protective and who thrives inside linear rules and standards of procedure.

While equally as important, yet not so well-tapped in law and justice, there is also great genius in feminine energy. Archetypally, the feminine in us is the caretaker and nurturer who tends to the needs of the children and home, or from a more expanded view, to the needs of our communities and the planet. Different from the aggressive masculine energy in us, the feminine operates with an inner urge to be compassionate, nurturing, and helpful. Rather than instincts to fight, dominate, and win, the feminine in us approaches a challenge with instincts to listen, collaborate, and create something new that serves everyone. As our open, receptive energy, the qualities of high-value to the feminine are the opposite and complementary to the masculine, such as: being sensitive, feeling-oriented, and intuitive; being nurturing, compassionate, and heart-centered; and and being spiritual, fluid, and collaborative. In our feminine, we operate in the yin side of the yin/yang energy polarities, and exercise our creative force in the less under-stood, mysterious feminine process known as "birthing." Birthing is deeply mys-terious because we reach beyond the limits of our intellect to collaborate with a higher dimension so that we can innovate and create new outcomes. In law and justice, this archetype and method of creating is demonstrated by Gina's telling of Judge Nan Nolan's settlement conference and restorative justice practices. For all parties to come out whole and to birth new outcomes that have never been seen in the past - like in a peace circle or re-entry court - only a soft approach involving compassion, creativity, and collaboration will succeed.

3 GUIDEPOSTS TO EMBRACE YOUR FEMININE GENIUS

Acknowledging masculine/feminine distinctions and masculine energy domi-nance explains why we did not believe we fit in and why we didn't feel free to bring our whole selves to the legal and justice systems. You too have likely been influenced by masculine energy dominance; you need only look at the war analogies throughout our daily language. You too have also likely been taught to devalue or even mock the feminine in yourself or in others; just notice the derog-atory terms often used for that which represents the feminine. As an example, Stephanie was repeatedly told to reduce her feminine qualities of empathy and sharing. Whether you identify as male or female does not matter. The collective human mindset of devaluing the feminine has existed for centuries and likely has influenced you to hide parts of yourself.

If out of reading our stories you too desire to embrace your feminine genius and bring it into your work in law and justice, we offer you 3 guideposts to begin:

Guidepost 1: Follow your feelings of WELLNESS toward your feminine genius. You begin to align with your feminine genius by listening to your feelings and moving toward a state of wellness. When you feel well physically, mentally, emotionally, and spiritually - you know that you are in your right balance of masculine and feminine energy. When you do not feel well, you know that you are out of balance. Beware: the masculine in you will tell you to focus on logic and mask emotions. As such, this guidepost offers you a very real step to embrace the feminine in you as it directly asks you to honor your sensitive, feeling nature.

You can see through our stories, we both felt unwell when forced to fit into a masculine-dominated mold. For Gina, she felt stressed and burned out by the daily mental combat and the demand that she be aggressive, tough, and confrontational to protect her clients. To return to wellness, Gina's feelings guided her to leave the law to pursue more aligned and authentic career opportunities. Later, she was able to return to the law through restorative justice opportunities that felt joyful and called upon her feminine traits like being intuitive, creative, and collaborative. For Stephanie, she felt shame and agony when being pushed into the masculine mold of pursuing prestigious law positions emphasizing financial wars for multi-million dollar companies. She also felt angry about expectations placed on her to be aggressive, tactical and dominating, when she knew her true nature is to be empathetic, nurturing, and sensitive. Seeing no other options, she too thought she had to leave the law behind. That is until she embraced and listened to her feelings which guided her back to wellness and toward her feminine genius.

Guidepost 2: Create supportive ALLIANCES that honor your feminine genius. You become aligned with your feminine genius when you feel supported in expressing your true desires and feminine nature. It is essential to find mentors and colleagues who empower you to follow the desires most true in your heart. On the contrary, mentors and peers who expect you to fit into a stereotypical masculine mold can leave you feeling shameful and wishing you were different. This was true for Stephanie as one of her mentors berated her for choosing to pursue more feminine, purposeful legal opportunities. She became more free and open to embrace her feminine genius upon meeting Judge Murphy and Professor Seng who supported her desires toward social justice work. For Gina too, aligning with Judge Murphy allowed her to thrive in her feminine genius. Judge Murphy's encouragement to pursue opportunities in restorative justice undid the years of masculine-only emphasis on her opportunities in the legal world. For both of us, being mentored and guided by a feminine genius icon like Judge Murphy, and surrounding ourselves with other mentors and peers who honor us for our true desires has created supportive alliances that help us both expand and elevate into our feminine genius.

Guidepost 3: Align with PURPOSE to fulfill your feminine genius. When you align with your innate sense of purpose reflected in your feminine nature to nurture and help others, you fulfill your feminine genius. As in our stories, when we aligned with our natural urges to help others and create positive change in our communities - we returned to a sense of wholeness. For Gina, in restorative justice she joined an area of law that values heart and care for others. She engaged in opportunities to empower people into better lives through peace circles, re-entry court, and restorative mentoring. For Stephanie, she too has more recently followed her purpose and joy to help others within the legal system, and through this has expressed the feminine areas of herself that she loves but had been taught to suppress and demonize.

CLOSING INSPIRATION

By inviting you to learn from our experience, we recognize that we're asking you to follow the less worn path - to accept yourself and stand out in ways that others may not understand. From doing this ourselves, we can offer this Truth: the joy of expressing your genius and full potential far outweighs those initial pains of self-doubt and rejection. We invite you to this transformational journey, not alone, but standing on our shoulders and those of Judge Sheila Murphy and Professor Michael Seng. To inspire your journey we invite you to breathe in the words of poet Amanda Gorman from her 2021 inaugural performance of *The Hill We Climb*: "The new dawn blooms as we free it. For there is always light, if only we're brave enough to see it. If only we're brave enough to be it."

Does the practice of law, or any profession, require one to shed one's personality? Can one be an effective lawyer or professional and still be a decent human being?

Is aggression the most effective way to solve disputes?

To what extent are the feminine qualities described by the authors really human qualities that should be developed in everyone? Is it useful in discussing restorative justice to divide qualities by gender?

What is lost in the practice of law when lawyers do not embrace restorative justice techniques?

DISSENTING FOR MERCY

ALLISON R. TRENDLE

I first decided to go to law school at three-years-old when I decided that I wanted to help people. I grew up on the Southwest Side of Chicago and attended Catholic schools through college, shaping my view of justice through compassion, mercy, and grace. I attended a very small all-girls high school right outside of Chicago, where we were encouraged to have empathy for those who didn't have the privileges we had. The privilege of a good education, positive role models, and boundless opportunities to discover ourselves and succeed in life. After high school, I continued my education at Lewis University in Romeoville, Illinois. I received degrees in Criminal/Social Justice and Psychology, with a minor in Peace Studies. My experience in undergraduate further shaped my views of justice and mercy. There, I began to grasp what those words truly mean. I learned about restorative justice.

Throughout undergrad, my views on our justice system shifted completely. I believed I wanted to be a prosecutor to protect victims, but I learned two important things that changed my future through classes and communicating with incarcerated individuals. First, I learned that our justice system often revictimizes victims. Sometimes our system treats victims as nothing more than a piece of evidence, and that directly contradicted my goals for my future. Second, I learned that offenders are often victims of something: abuse, poverty, community violence, and other circumstances that lead to their crimes. Retributive justice forms the core of our justice system; we lock people away not only for punishment for bad behavior, but for our own, personal revenge. Our system lacks mercy, and by lacking mercy, our society lacks true justice.

With these new ideas, I began my search for law schools during the fall of my senior year. I applied all over Chicago and, that spring, The John Marshall Law School (now UIC John Marshall Law School) sent my acceptance letter and an offer to interview with the dean of the law school for her Dean's Leadership Academy. During that interview, I spoke of my interest in restorative justice. At the time, I thought I wanted to go into juvenile work like one of my favorite professors from Lewis. Juveniles, the most deserving of our compassion and mercy, fall victim to a system that does not care about their past or their development. Restorative justice has begun to take hold in juvenile courts in some states, and I wanted to get involved. After hearing about my interest, the dean told me about John Marshall's Restorative Justice Project, co-chaired by retired Judge Sheila Murphy and Professor Michael Seng. That sealed it for me, and I immediately registered to be a John Marshall student.

I met Judge Murphy Fall 2018 and took Professor Seng's Constitutional Law I course the following spring. I signed up for their Restorative Justice course in Spring 2020 and worked in St. Sabina's on the southside for the spring and summer terms. Fall 2020, a unique semester, I remained on as a student employee for the Restorative Justice Project. I have also completed two judicial internships. One at the Circuit Court of Cook County in the Domestic Relations Division with Judge Regina Scannicchio. This internship sparked my interest in family law and spurred my decision to go into this area of law when I graduate. I also worked for Justice Michael Hyman, who sits in the First District of the Illinois Appellate Court. Justice Hyman taught me many things during my internship, but the most important thing he taught me is that mercy and compassion should inform all aspects of justice and dealing with offenders.

All of my experience in college, law school, and the Project has informed my views on justice and mercy. Judges, including appellate justices, sit in a position that allow them to show compassion to the human beings coming before them. These judges listen to the stories and attempt to understand the background, balancing this information with the needs of the victim and society. These judges are not always in the majority, however, and sometimes, they write dissents to advocate for mercy. Although many judges may take this approach, I spend this chapter focused on three judges who advocated for mercy, and therefore true justice, in every aspect of their judicial careers: Justice Ruth Bader Ginsburg of the Supreme Court of the United States, Justice Seymour Simon of the Illinois Supreme Court, and Justice Michael Hyman of the Illinois Appellate Court.

In federal and state courts, judges on panels who do not agree with the majority opinion sometimes write dissents. Since the 1900s in the Supreme Court of the United States, the Court has seen an increase in the number of dissenting justices, though the justices do tend to vote with the majority most of the time.[1]

---

1   Adam Feldman, *Empirical SCOTUS: Who's in the majority*, SCOTUSblog (Mar. 12, 2019, 11:40 AM),

So, why do judges write dissents? Merely to argue amongst themselves or give law students an extra five pages of reading from their case book? While students might argue otherwise, judges typically do not write dissents for either of these reasons. Judges write dissents, among other reasons, "to facilitate a future change in the law, to invite action from Congress, to provoke public scrutiny of the Court...to limit the scope of a majority decision."[2] A dissent can show that our laws, or at least judges' perception and opinion of the law, are not stagnant and antiquated, but dynamic—evolving as our society does.[3] Dissents also serve the purpose, even outside of the law, to avoid tension and resentment from building up in any unit, particularly a family unit.[4]

Some judges also write for another, related reason. They write not only to encourage a change in the law or invite scrutiny but to encourage to promote treating human beings, often defendants in criminal cases, with mercy. Merriam-Webster defines mercy as "compassion...shown especially to an offender or to one subject to one's power."[5] Judges have power and control over the fates of the people who come before them at all levels. It might be worth noting that all three justices discussed here have a Jewish background, and, although their faith has never been inserted into their dissents or opinions, one must wonder if the building blocks for mercy began with some faith-based teaching. It is not necessary, however, for a judge to come from a particular faith to show mercy when a human being comes before them.

At the trial level, judges make decisions that control the lives of the people who come before them. In criminal trials, judges sometimes decide guilt.[6] Trial judges also impose sentences,[7] giving them the opportunity to show mercy by

---

https://www.scotusblog.com/2019/03/empirical-scotus-whos-in-the-majority/; *see also* Honorable Ruth Bader Ginsburg, Lecture at on the Role of Dissenting Opinions.

2   Michael O'Donnell, *What's the Point of a Supreme Court Dissent?*, The Nation (Jan. 21, 2016), https://www.thenation.com/article/archive/whats-the-point-of-a-supreme-court-dissent/#:~:text=It%20 dissects%20the%20many%20purposes,scope%20of%20a%20majority%20decision (discussing Melvin I. Urofsky, Dissent and the Supreme Court: Its Role in the Court's History and the Nation's Constitutional Dialogue (2017).

3   Frank X. Altimari, *The Practice of Dissenting in the Second Circuit,* 59 Brook. L. Rev. 275, 277 (1993).

4   Email from Judge Sheila Murphy (ret.), UIC John Marshall Law School (Dec. 30, 2020) (on file with author).

5   *Mercy, Merriam-Webster,* https://www.merriam-webster.com/dictionary/mercy (last visited Dec. 14, 2020).

6   *See* Bench Trial, Black Law's Dictionary (10th ed. 2014) (defining bench trial).

7   *See Sentencing,* Legal Information Institute, https://www.law.cornell.edu/wex/sentencing# (last ac-

taking into account an offender's background and the circumstances surrounding the crime. Some assume that the opportunity for mercy, understanding, and compassion stops at this point. Appellate justices do not hear new facts. They must accept the findings of facts made by the trial court. If this holds true, how can appellate justices show mercy – especially when they are not in the majority?

I. JUSTICE RUTH BADER GINSBURG

Most people know Justice Ginsburg from her work with gender discrimination and her 27-year position on the Supreme Court of the United States.[8] During her time on the Supreme Court, Justice Ginsburg wrote over 100 dissents,[9] often marked by her dissenting collar.[10] Between 1993 and 2019, she authored nine cases as the sole dissenter and twenty-one as part of a 5-4 minority.[11] One of these 5-4 dissents, *Ledbetter v. Goodyear Tire and Rubber Company*,[12] illustrates how Justice Ginsburg continued working for gender equality throughout her career and often showed mercy to the parties in front of her as she did.

In *Ledbetter*, Lilly Ledbetter sued for gender discrimination after her employers gave her low performance reviews because of her sex and denied her pay raises because of those low reviews, which left her "[earning significantly] less than her male colleagues."[13] She won at the trial level, then lost on appeal, choosing to take the case up to the Supreme Court of the United States in an attempt to get justice.[14] The Court denied this justice, finding Ledbetter's claim to be

---

cessed December 15, 2020). The discussion of mercy at the trial level will not go beyond this as it goes beyond the scope of this chapter.

8   *Ruth Bader Ginsburg*, Oyez, https://www.oyez.org/justices/ruth_bader_ginsburg (last visited Dec. 27, 2020).

9   *See Ruth Bader Ginsburg*, Ballotpedia, https://ballotpedia.org/Ruth_Bader_Ginsburg (last visited Dec. 27, 2020) (listing the number of dissents authored by Justice Ginsburg between 1993 and 2019).

10   Vanessa Friedman, *Ruth Bader Ginsburg's Lace Collar Wasn't an Accessory, It Was a Gauntlet*, N.Y. Times (Sept. 20, 2020), https://www.nytimes.com/2020/09/20/style/rbg-style.html.

11   *Ruth Bader Ginsburg, supra* note 8.

12   *Ledbetter v. Goodyear Tire & Rubber Co.*, 550 U.S. 618 (2007).

13   *Id.* at 618; *See also Ledbetter v. Goodyear Tire & Rubber Co.*, Oyez, https://www.oyez.org/cases/2006/05-1074 (last visited Dec. 27, 2020) [hereinafter Ledbetter].

14   *Ledbetter*, 550 U.S. at 618; *Ledbetter, supra* note 13.

untimely and leading to Justice Ginsburg's dissent.[15] Showing compassion for Ledbetter, Justice Ginsburg implied that "the majority's ruling [was] out of tune with the realities of wage discrimination."[16] She stated that the majority read the Civil Rights Act in a "parsimonious" way,[17] indicating she was willing to look further, or at least differently, in the Act to give Ledbetter justice. She saw the realities of wage discrimination, discussing how slowly things unfold, when writing her dissent.[18] Without mercy – without seeing the realities of Ledbetter as a human being and an employee suffering an injustice – Justice Ginsburg might not have looked past the wording of the Act, similar to the majority. This risk shortsightedness highlights the important of mercy and compassion in judicial reasoning. While true that judges cannot let their emotions dictate their decisions, objectivity does not necessarily mean a judge must give up all feeling, including mercy, when making a ruling. If a judge sees a case simply as applying law to facts, the judge risks missing the intricacies or, as Justice Ginsburg might say, the realities of someone's life. To see those realities, one must show compassion and mercy; they must continue to recognize the humanness of the parties before them.

II. JUSTICE SEYMOUR SIMON

Justice Simon sat on the Illinois Supreme Court in the 1980s and wrote some of his most well-known dissents during that period, including his dissents in death penalty cases.[19] He graduated from Northwestern University School of Law and worked in Chicago politics before joining the judiciary.[20] During his tenure on the Supreme Court, Justice Simon wrote nearly 200 majority opinions and almost

---

15 *Ledbetter*, 550 U.S. at 632.

16 *Ledbetter, supra* note 13 (citing *Ledbetter*, 550 U.S. at 646 (Ginsburg, J., dissenting)).

17 *Ledbetter*, 550 U.S. at 661 (Ginsburg, J., dissenting).

18 *Id.* at 649-50.

19 Trevor Jensen & Joseph Sjostrom, *Seymour Simon: 1915-2006*, Chicago Tribune (September 27, 2006), chicagotribune.com/news/ct-xpm-2006-09-27-0609270191-story.html.

20 *Id.*

as many dissents.[21] Justice Simon dissented in every death penalty case that the court took during that time period, speaking out about its unconstitutionality.[22]

Justice Simon began this long line of dissents in *People v. Lewis*,[23] a death penalty case for a convicted murderer which had been argued before Justice Simon took his seat on the court.[24] The majority in *Lewis* included three justices who had previously argued that the death penalty statute was unconstitutional.[25] Justice Simon wrote his dissent using that same argument, but the majority upheld the death penalty with a 6-1 vote.[26] Assuming that the three justices still believed that the death penalty violated the constitution, why would they suddenly vote to uphold the statute? They wrote it off as stare decisis,[27] and Justice Simon vehemently dissented.[28] Years later, Justice Simon hypothesized that these three judges drastically changed their argument due to John Wayne Gacy facing the death penalty,[29] but this did not prevent Justice Simon from writing the *Lewis* dissent or any other dissent after. Justice Simon saw the cases not as cases or legal theory, but as real people struggling with real conflict.[30] When you take a step back from a case and look at it as a conflict involving real people, compassion comes easier. With compassion comes mercy, and with mercy comes justice. At times judges and lawyers become so consumed with the law that they no longer see the real people. We search for controlling law and then attempt to fit the law to our case. We can become cold and distance ourselves from the facts – what truly matters.[31] When this happens, we lose sight of the fact that

---

21   *Id.*

22   *Id.*

23   *People v. Lewis*, 430 N.E.2d 1346, 1370-77 (Ill. 1981) (Simon, J., dissenting).

24   Jack M. Beermann, *Jewish Identity and Judging: Seymour Simon of Illinois*, 44 Loy. U. Chi. L.J. 939, 948 (2013).

25   Beermann, *supra* note 24, at 949 (discussing *People ex rel. Carey v. Cousins*, 397 N.E. 2d 809, 815 (Ill. 1979).

26   Beermann, *supra* note 24, at 949 (discussing *Lewis*, 430 N.E.2d at 1363).

27   Beermann, *supra* note 24, at 949 (citing *Lewis*, 430 N.E.2d at 1363-64).

28   Beermann, *supra* note 24, at 949 (citing *Lewis*, 430 N.E.2d at 1371-72).

29   Beermann, *supra* note 24, at 950 (citing Seymour Simon, *Twelve Executions Which Should Not Have Been*, 18 Chi. Bar Ass'n Record 24 (2004).

30   Beermann, *supra* note 24, at 953.

31   Justice Michael Hyman, Presentation at UIC John Marshall Law School for the Judicial Externship Course (Oct. 10, 2019) (stating that the facts matter most in a case).

these characters in the case are human beings deserving of our compassion and mercy. When this happens, according to Justice Simon, there can be no justice. Through his death penalty dissents, he reminded his colleagues and the legal profession that defendants in these cases are human beings and treated them with compassion and mercy by valuing their lives.

Justice Simon did not only dissent in death penalty cases. He also wrote the sole dissent in *People v. Davis*, another criminal case which held that trial court judges need not explain their reasons for sentencing a defendant.[32] In that case, he wrote, "[T]he absence, or refusal, of reasons [for a sentence] is a hallmark of injustice."[33] The majority in that case held that the statute requiring a statement of reasons violated the separation of powers clause,[34] the same argument Justice Simon used when fighting to abolish the death penalty.[35] He wrote that he feared for the future of sentences, where sentencing would appear to be arbitrary and cause injustice.[36]

While Justice Simon sat on the court, his view never became the majority opinion.[37] He clashed with his colleagues[38] but remained firm in his beliefs.[39] Justice Simon sat on the highest court in the state of Illinois. He had power over every human being in every case that came before him; he was often alone in his opinions on the court; but he never failed to act with mercy.[40] It would have been easy to join the majority opinion, especially when he was the sole dissenter.

---

32 *People v. Davis*, 93 Ill. 2d 155 (1982) (Simon, J., dissenting).

33 *Id.* at 163.

34 *Id.* at 162.

35 Beermann, *supra* note 24, at 949 (citing *Lewis*, 430 N.E.2d at 1371-72).

36 *Davis*, 93 Ill. 2d at 168, 163 (Simon, J., dissenting).

37 Beermann, *supra* note 24, at 940.

38 Beermann, *supra* note 24, at 949.

39 Michael B. Hyman, *Justice Seymour Simon*, 20-Oct CBA Rec. 31 (2006).

40 *See* Hyman, *supra* note 31, at 33.

Justice Hyman has sat on the First Appellate District Court in Illinois since his appointment in 2013.[41] He graduated from Northwestern University School of Law and worked in private practice before being appointed to the Circuit Court of Cook County.[42] As an appellate justice in Illinois, Justice Hyman sits on a panel consisting of three justices. He .hears cases on appeal from the Circuit Court of Cook County.

Justice Hyman is unique among his peers because, in his opinions and dissents, Justice Hyman always calls the defendant by name to humanize the person coming before the court.[43] Judges and lawyers often remove the defendant's name to depersonalize the individual – to make them less sympathetic. This practice is taught in law school as a trial technique. It continues in the appellate court where opinions commonly refer to the defendant as "the defendant." Justice Hyman, by giving this person their name back, shows deep compassion for the human being in the case before him. Compassion is at the very core of mercy, and this practice serves as one of the building blocks of the mercy at the heart of Justice Hyman's dissents.

Unlike Justice Simon, however, sometimes Justice Hyman's mercy becomes the majority opinion of the court when he can convince at least one of the two other justices on his panel that his opinion is the right outcome. Sometimes, mercy becomes the controlling law, and this should be the goal of our legal system and our judiciary. Other times, however, the judiciary can regress, and mercy again becomes the dissent. The trilogy of cases in this section shows how mercy depends the timing and panel.

In *People v. Busse*, university police arrested a homeless man found carrying two pieces of wire and loose quarters.[44] The man, who Justice Hyman refers to throughout as Busse, was convicted and sentenced to twelve years in prison

---

41 Michael B. Hyman Biography, http://www.illinoiscourts.gov/appellatecourt/judges/bio_hyman.asp (last visited Dec. 15, 2020).

42 *Id.*

43 Justice Michael B. Hyman, Restorative Justice in the Judiciary (Oct. 23, 2020) (panel discussion at UIC John Marshall Law School). As Justice Hyman's former intern and an attendant at many speeches and presentations he has given, I have heard Justice Hyman encourage the use of the defendant's name in opinions.

44 *People v. Busse*, 2016 IL App (1ˢᵗ) 142941, ¶ 7.

for stealing $44 in quarters from a vending machine.[45] Although Busse's crimes had never been violent, the sentencing judge labeled him a "career thief" and sentenced him from the middle of the sentencing range in order to teach him a lesson.[46] Justice Hyman, writing for the majority in *Busse*, found twelve years for petty theft by a man who had only ever committed low level property crimes to be "grossly disproportionate."[47] Justice Hyman repeatedly stated the "miniscule" amount stolen and the fact that none of Busse's prior convictions had been for violent crimes.[48] Justice Hyman acknowledges that "judges...must follow the law and hold in check their natural sympathies,"[49] but this does not prevent a judge from acting with mercy. Holding in check sympathies means still imposing the consequence that the crime requires – balancing the seriousness of the crime with the surrounding circumstances. A judge can do that while still acting mercifully and not imposing a punishment harsher than what is required. A judge can do that by, like Justice Hyman consistently does, retaining the defendant's humanity and individuality by using their name. Sympathy and mercy are not the same, and while justice requires putting aside sympathies, it also requires acting with mercy – a balance that Justice Hyman strikes in *Busse*.

In *People v. Allen*, Allen, a man with multiple mental illnesses, broke into a truck and stole two packs of cigarettes.[50] When the owner chased him, Allen dropped the cigarettes, which the owner retrieved before waving down the police.[51] The trial court found Allen guilty, and the judge sentenced Allen to 10 ½ years.[52] Justice Hyman, writing for the majority once again, found the sentence to be excessive because of the crime's nonviolent nature.[53] Justice Hyman questioned the point of sentencing Allen over the minimum – struggling to find a reason for a heightened sentence.[54] Comparing Allen to Busse, Justice

---

45   *Id.* at ¶ 1.

46   *Id.* at ¶ 17.

47   *Id.* at ¶ 29.

48   *Id.* at ¶ 31.

49   *Id.* at ¶ 2.

50   *People v. Lundy*, 2017 IL App (1ˢᵗ) 151540, ¶¶ 4-5.

51   *Id.* at ¶ 4.

52   *Id.* at ¶ 7.

53   *Id.* at ¶ 17-18.

54   *Id.* at ¶ 21.

Hyman noted the only difference between the two cases as a broken window, a fact that wouldn't change with a longer prison sentence.[55] Instead, relying on restorative practices which necessarily implies mercy, Justice Hyman suggested the State "[help] Allen to make [the owner] whole, rather than punishing Allen even more severely."[56]

The last case, *People v. Lundy*, shows how just one different justice on the panel can turn a majority opinion into a dissent for mercy. In *Lundy*, a homeless man "attempted to steal four packages of underwear valued at $33."[57] He flicked a pocketknife open in the presence of the employees but didn't point it at them or cause them any fear.[58] This crime earned Lundy a ten year prison sentence after the trial court heavily weighed his prior convictions in favor of a heightened sentence.[59] In his dissent arguing that Lundy's sentence should be reduced to six years, Justice Hyman quoted Nelson Mandela, writing, "A nation should not be judged by how it treats its highest citizens, but its lowest ones."[60] Justice Hyman argued that a ten year sentence "punish[ed] Lundy more for the numerous difficulties brought about by his economic status (impoverished), illness (drug addiction), and condition (homelessness) than for the offense for which he was convicted."[61]

This single paragraph in the dissent shows a great amount of mercy. As a society, we overlook the poor, addicted, and homeless. We push them to the fringes, content to forget about their existence and, when forced to confront the realities of their existence, the legal system dehumanizes them and makes it easier to treat them dispassionately—to only see them as a case. Justice Hyman, unlike the majority, refers to Lundy by his name, humanizing him.[62] With this Nelson Mandala quote, Justice Hyman reminds us that even those that society looks down upon or casts aside deserve compassion and understanding. They deserve to be treated as human, even though they may have committed

---

55 *Id.* at ¶ 22.

56 *Id.*

57 *People v. Lundy*, 2018 IL App (1st) 162304, ¶ 39 (Hyman, J., dissenting).

58 *Id.*

59 *Id.* at ¶¶ 1, 16.

60 *Id.* at ¶ 38 (Hyman, J., dissenting) (quoting Nelson Mandela, *Long Walk to Freedom* 187 (Little, Brown, and Company 1994).

61 *Id.*

62 *See id.* at ¶ 37 (referring to Lundy by name as Justice Hyman did throughout).

a crime. The legal system treats these people, the lowest in our society, with no compassion and no mercy. This speaks wonders about our society and shows the importance of these types of dissents even more. Most judges will not even use a defendant's name, and, if they are unable or unwilling to do that, how can we expect the system to treat them with mercy? Justice Hyman, by inserting this quote into his dissent, shows mercy not only for Lundy, but for all defendants.

Without these judges who show remarkable bravery when going against their colleagues, the law would remain stagnant. The legal profession might be content to continue to distance themselves from the human beings entangled in the facts of the case in front of them. *We* might be content to treat the lowest members of our society – the criminals, the drug addicts, the mentally ill, the poor – with disdain or, arguably worse, utter indifference. Judges like Justice Hyman, Justice Simon, and Justice Ginsburg remind us that defendants are human. They are deserving of mercy and forgiveness. Although these dissents might not be controlling law, they shape the law in their own way. Sometimes, like with Justice Simon's dissents about the death penalty, dissents eventually become law.[63] Dissents keep the law human. They encourage us to hold onto our compassion even while we work to apply the law equally to every person we encounter. We can apply the law equally while still remembering that every human being deserves mercy because without mercy, there can never be justice.

---

63   *See* Christina McMahon, *Illinois Abolishes the Death Penalty*, 16 Pub. Int. L. Rep. 83, 84-85 (2011). George Ryan issued a moratorium on executions in 2000, and Illinois officially abolished the death penalty in 2011. *Id.*

Equal treatment and predictability are essential attributes of justice. Can justice be tempered with mercy without making it appear random and arbitrary?

Is the rationale that allows judges to dissent relevant beyond the courtroom or a formal legal setting? On occasion Presidents have issued statements when they sign bills into law that state why the President disagrees with the Act. In doing so, they signal that they will narrowly interpret or enforce the Act. Are signing statements helpful or harmful? Would society benefit if politicians, policy makers, and others stated their disagreement with official decisions in a structured and respectful manner? If so, how could this be done?

Would our criminal justice system have benefitted if Justice Seymore Simon's dissent that judges should be required to state their reasoning when sentencing a defendant had been adopted as law? Are there other areas were explanations should be required to back up important decisions and why?

Part III
The Death Penalty and Restorative Justice

Death Penalty and the Community of Sant'Egidio[1]

JUDGE SHEILA M. MURPHY (RET.)[2]

The Illinois Supreme Court sent the case of State of *Illinois v. Jimerson* back to the trial court. Mr. Jimerson had been sentenced to death on the voice of only one person. Even in the Old Testament two witnesses were required for execution. There were five defendants, all found guilty and two of the five were sentenced to death. As the Presiding Judge of this case, a motion for DNA testing was sustained on behalf of all the defendants as another Judge in another courthouse refused to give the co-defendant his court DNA.

Sometimes in life you do what others view as absolutely wrong. You do what your conscience tells you, and amazing things happen. When I allowed Mr. Jimerson to leave death row during the pendency of the case, one newspaper headlined, "What is Judge Murphy thinking?" A Journalism Professor, David Protess at Northwestern School of Journalism encouraged his journalism students to reinvestigate the case. They did a masterful job. They were 18 and 19 year old students with courage to do the right thing. In their thorough investigation of the case, they found the real killers and came back with their confession. Several men confessed to the crime of raping and killing two white people, a young man and his girlfriend. After I dismissed the case and freed Mr. Jimerson, I thought the case was over. There was no appeal.

Several weeks later I was visited by two members of the Community of Sant'Egidio. They wanted to meet me and had read about the case of Mr. Jimerson in Rome. I met with them and they explained that the Community of Sant'Egidio is opposed to the death penalty worldwide. Members of the

---

1   *The Community*, The Community of Sant'Egidio, https://www.santegidio.org/pageID/1/langID/en/ HOME.html (last visited March 10, 2021).

2   The author would like to thank University of St. Louis student Maeve Ann Wolff for her great assistance and contributions to this chapter. The author is grateful to Alison Chan, a former Restorative Justice law student and currently an assistant State's Attorney of Cook County, for her efforts and assistance in researching and editing for this chapter.

Community work against the death penalty. They invited me to attend a conference in San Francisco. At the conference, I met a journalist, now a member of the Italian Parliament, Mario Marazziti. Mario was one of the early founders of the Community of Sant'Egidio. He invited me to Rome with law students to learn why the United Nations welcomed only nations who abolished the death penalty. I came with law students and we learned that in Europe the death penalty is looked upon as cruelty and horror. In Rome, they had enough of it with lions eating people while people thought it was sport.

Members of the Community of Sant'Egidio visit death penalty prisoners in North America. One of the prisoners they visited, Dominique Green had no family or friends to visit him. He wrote a postcard to a Roman newspaper and asked for "friends." He received over a 1000 replies. Members of the Community began to visit him and were impressed with his intelligence and goodness. The Community, represented by Mario, asked me to help Dominique. I did so, with a young law student Andy Lofthouse. Andy and I worked on Constitutional areas with other lawyers. Andy also found witnesses. His Mother Pat Lofthouse found the family of Andre LaStappe. This wonderful man was shot and killed. His family spoke of his love for the Sacred Heart. His wife told Archbishop Tutu. I was so pissed off when Dominique was found guilty. His sons Andre and Andrew later befriended Dominique. Dominique was condemned to death by an all white jury and a Judge who allowed a defense lawyer to sleep during another death penalty case.

A member of the Sant'Egidio Community from New York, Mr. Thomas Cahill, came to Texas to meet Dominique.[3] He was so impressed with the young man who had already forgiven everyone who hurt him, including the prosecutors, lawyers, prison guards...even his Mother. Dominique had been gifted with the book, "No Future without Forgiveness." Dominique developed a great feeling of peace through forgiveness. He then communicated with others on death row and helped them learn to forgive.

He told Mr. Cahill all this not knowing that Mr. Cahill was a dear friend of the author of the book, Archbishop Desmond Tutu. Archbishop Tutu came from South Africa to death row in Texas. I was nearby when they were visiting. I heard the most wonderful laughter coming from the little room. It reminded

---

3   Author Thomas Cahill wrote *A Saint on Death Row: How a Forgotten Child Became a Man and Changed a World* unfolding Dominique Green's life and tragic death where Dominique was wrongly accused and then executed.

me when Pierre Teihard de Jardan[4] said, "Laughter is proof of the presence of God." At a later mass at a church, Archbishop Tutu told how he met the family of the deceased over the phone. Dominique was taught friendship and love by the Sant'Egidio Community. He quickly learned to give back friendship to other prisoners. With funds from Sant'Egidio Dominique's first and only love came to visit him, now a medical doctor.

Dominique made friends with everyone. In his short life he knew how to honor them. On his last day of life, he did, during his short life, receive great friendship. He became a friend to all including Andre and Andrew La Strappe, sons of Andrew Lastrappe, who believed in Dominique's innocence. Dominique gave them each a prayer book given to him by Archbishop Tutu. The Community of Sant'Egidio hired a detective to find Dominique's soulmate, now a practicing physician. It was joy that shone in both their eyes.

His Mother for the first time, mentally ill, she testified against him at the trial and fell asleep on the benches. He forgave her and quietly asked me to sit with the two of them, "So my mother can learn how to talk to her child. She never knew kindness as she was never shown it." On his last night on earth, he asked Andy and myself to help children who had no friends, no hope.

Dominique was the founder of the Restorative Justice class at University of Illinois, Chicago (UIC), John Marshall Law School. Each student is given a book written by Thomas Cahill, "A Saint on Death Row." The law students study Restorative Justice that is taught by many guests who are living restorative practices. Our law students may not have fully developed compassion before they came, but they have it when they leave. They also know what it is to listen to the children they help. The very children that Dominique asked us to help. He said, "Just keep up the struggle." The Editors of this book teach right now. It is all about saving children and being true to ourselves as well.

Dominique Green had been represented by many lawyers before I was called upon to help him.[5] He also had an investigator who left when I interviewed the trial attorney so there was no witness! The investigator told me later about how he had collected gold teeth from men on death row. He said this matter-of-factly, as though it was a good thing. I had represented clients in the past before

---

4   Pierre Teilhard de Chardin was a French theologian, French Jesuit priest, scientist, philosopher, teacher, and paleontologist who educated his life working on understanding Darwinism.

5   Sheila M. Murphy is forever grateful to the law firm of Rothschild, Barry and Myers for encouraging me to represent Dominique Green and helping in countless ways, including hiring Andy Lofthouse and Ruth Lofthouse, two brilliant law students, now splendid lawyers.

I became a judge on capital cases, and I knew how important investigators are. Dominique got the best investigators when we came into his life. Only it was too late. Andy Lofthouse was a law student when I met him and he was an unusual one. After graduating from the University of Colorado School of Journalism, Andy worked for a newspaper in Summit County, Colorado. Reporters make wonderful investigators, and Andy was the best. He contributed greatly to the legal research and the strategy for the appeal. The only defense witnesses found in this case were found by Andy and his Mother, Pat Lofthouse, a filmmaker. Years had passed before we came into the case so evidence that could have been used to prove his innocence was gone. No DNA evidence was possible as the samples were apparently not saved. Dominique's fingerprints were never found on the gun and the fingerprints that were on it were never identified. The video surveillance tape of the premises that Dominique was sure would show that he had not been the one to shoot the victim never surfaced.

Andy and his Mom found the family of the man who was shot, Mr. Andrew Lastrapes, Jr. a black truck driver who stopped at a convenience store and was robbed. His wife Bernatta said that his back pocket was torn off which would suggest a scuffle. Mr. Lastrapes always carried a knife and he had puncture wounds on his hands. No scientific evidence was turned over by the prosecutors at trial.

Why was Dominique convicted? Dominque was black, poor, and without a lawyer who had ever tried a death penalty case. The system saw to it that the jury was all white. Dominique's case was heard by Judge Shawer, the presiding judge who was used to sending black men to Death Row even if one of their lawyers fell asleep during the trial.

Dominique's mother, who was a diagnosed schizophrenic and suffered from multiple personality disorder, told the jury to do whatever they had to do. Mr. Lastrapes' widow, however, was heartbroken when the jury convicted Dominique of her husband's death. She was horrified to see Dominique's mother asleep during the trial. Mr. Lastrapes was a man of faith who knelt when he prayed. He would not want anyone executed on his behalf. During the trial, it was clear to the family that Dominique was innocent. Mrs. Lastrapes told us that there were two black young men and one white man who testified against Dominique. One of the black defendants' mother was a teacher, and her son had a good lawyer. The white man was not charged. The prosecutor forbade the teacher's son from coming to court on the day the white man testified as the prosecutor feared that he would bring forth Dominique's innocence. "If you are black and poor you are at a huge disadvantage," says David Atwood, founder of the Texas Coalition to Abolish the Death Penalty. The courts rolled right over his Constitutional rights and even denied Dominique on his last day in court his right to allocution. His written speech was stolen but he was prepared to give it anyway!

In Texas, Dominique's paternal grandmother was the last person who was good to him. She died when he was eight years old. After she died, at nine years old, Dominique was in second grade and was raped by a priest. His mother began beating him until she saw the blood. She eventually turned against him, and at one time held his hand over a gas stove . . . just like her mother had done to her. He left home as often as he could, but when he did come home he watched out for his younger brothers and took them out of the house whenever he could get away from their mother. He rented space in a storage shed and took his brothers with him so they would be safe. As a juvenile he was arrested and placed in detention. He was repeatedly sexually abused in his childhood. No one came to pick him up when he was allowed home visits. Other parents would pick up their child, but Dominique was left there to be raped by the guards. At a young age, he drew pictures of blood coming out of his eyes. No one noticed or cared until he met the Italians of the Community of Sant' Egidio and then Andy and me.

Had Dominique's mother's medical needs been met, she could have been a good mother. Dominique's Dad had problems as well and his medical needs were not addressed. Dominique's grandmother loved him and showed him love. The school did not refer him for counseling then or when he later was the victim of a petophile priest and acted out. He could have remained in school, or with his brilliance been a scholar at a boarding school. Juvenile detention centers attracted pedophiles. His trauma went untreated. Dominique was 18 at the time when he was charged with murder. Now we know that the frontal lobe, the decision making part of the brain, is not fully developed until young people are approximately 25 years old.[6]

Andy Lofthouse married his law school sweetheart whom he met at Rothchild Barry and Myers law firm. He practices law with his Dad, Wayne Lofthouse, while his wife, Ruth Lofthouse is an Assistant State's Attorney in Lake County. Ruth also assisted in Dominique's case. Pat Lofthouse, Andy's

---

6   Mariam Arain et al., *Maturation of the adolescent brain*, Neuropsychiatric disease and treatment vol. 9 (2013): 449-61. doi:10.2147/NDT.S39776.

mother, has become a remarkable film maker and continues to assist people she met long ago in Texas.

I learned that not every county in Texas is not like Harrison County and not all courts are conducted like the ones there. In Harrison County, the prosecutors look upon convictions as gold if they want to become judges. So there was little or nothing that a black young man without funds or friends could do. At least Dominique was given friends by the Community of Sant' Egidio in Rome. Another man on Death Row whose name was also Green felt sorry for Dominique and told him to write a postcard to a newspaper in Italy and say that he had no family or friends. Members of the Community started writing to him and then took up a collection for his defense. His Italian "family" made a film of his life so that the world could see the madness of killing this brilliant young man.[7] He read the Archbishop Desmond Tutu's book, *No Future without Forgiveness*, and he forgave everyone who had harmed him. He helped others on death row to forgive and he transformed their lives. And he came to love his friends from Sant 'Egidio. "I finally got a family," he told me over and over. My husband, Patrick and my son, Patrick Murphy-Racey, also became his friend, and Patrick took photos of Dominique in his telephone space on Death Row. He was smiling. The Archbishop even came to Death Row to meet this amazing young man. There were no tears, only laughter. The African prayer books given to Dominique by the Archbishop were given to the sons of Andrew Lastrapes on Dominique's last day of life when the young men came to say goodbye.

On the last night of his life, Dominique was actually helping us. He spoke of helping children so that they could be loved by someone even if their parents could not take care of them. When Dominque was executed, lightning appeared in the sky that was seen by all of his friends standing vigil outside ... and then they knew ... that Dominique's life ended October 26, 2004.

Years later, Andy and I defended another young black man, Kenneth Foster. He was driving a car when a passenger asked him to stop so he could talk to a girl. The boyfriend came out and was shot. Texas law of parties holds all parties equally liable. This was the law in the U.K. Two young men were on the roof and one shot and killed someone. The young man with him had no weapon or intent to kill anyone. He was the last one hanged in Britain. Later Parliament and the Queen pardoned him posthumously.

---

7   Dominique's Story (Rai-TV 2010), https://vimeo.com/ondemand/16256. This documentary was created by Mario Marazziti and Giulia Sirignani with narrating voice of John Turturro (dubbed by Flavio Insinna).

Mr. Foster's petition for Certiorari was denied. Our brief was presented to the Governor of Texas. Several hours before the execution, Governor Perry went with the judges who dissented. Mr. Foster is serving life without parole. We felt as if Dominique was guiding us to protect life as he had once protected his little brothers' lives.

Love is what the Sant'Egidio Community practices. Dominique left this world praying for others. He had hope. At the moment of his death lightning struck on a clear night. In Rome, they were on their knees praying. Dominique's ashes are near the children's room of Sant'Egidio.

Since Dominique's tragic death, 25 states still have the death penalty, 22 have abolished it and 3 states have a governor-imposed moratorium.[8] What was the U.S. Justice Department thinking when they petitioned the United States Supreme Court to kill 12 men and 1 woman in 2020-2021?

The federal government reinstated the death penalty in 1988. The Trump administration put to death 13 convicted murderers over a span of six months. These averages to more than four times the number of federal executions since the death penalty was reinstated. The urgency to execute this many individuals before the transfer of power shows that justice was rushed. We may never know the true reason why these executions were rushed before Trump's exit, but Justice Sotomayor states that the execution of these thirteen people "is not justice" and it is a shame that her colleagues allowed these "expedited sprees of executions."[9] It is troubling that the government bypassed the Court of Appeals and went straight to the Supreme Court knowing that the Supreme Court majority would rule in their favor with little to no reasoning. The lives and executions of the thirteen federal death row individuals are as follows.

On January 15, 2021, 48-year-old, Dustin Higgs was executed by lethal injection. Higgs did not kill any of his victims. His co-defendant, Willis Haynes, shot the victims after being instructed by Higgs. Higgs did not threaten or force to shoot Haynes to kill the victims. Hayes got a life sentence, while Higgs got the death penalty. Higgs was convicted of a 1996 kidnapping and murder of three young women in the Washington D.C. area. Higgs' attorneys appealed to delay

---

8   *State By State*, Death Penalty Information Center (last visited Mar. 14, 2021), https://deathpenalty-info.org/state-and-federal-info/state-by-state.

9   Raul A. Reyes, *'This is not justice': Justice Sonia Sotomayor offers fierce dissent in death penalty case*, NBC News (Jan. 17, 2021), https://www.nbcnews.com/news/latino/not-justice-justice-sonia-soto-mayor-offers-fierce-dissent-death-penalty-n1254554.

the execution due to Higgs' COVID-19 diagnosis and his low IQ.[10] Another major issue is that Higgs was being sentenced to death in a state that does not have the death penalty.[11] Higgs was federally convicted and sentenced in the state of Maryland. However, because Higgs was sentenced in 2001, the death penalty would still apply and, since the death penalty is currently abolished in Maryland, another state would need to be designated to carry out the execution. An emergency petition was filed with the Supreme Court before the Fourth Circuit Court of Appeals had a chance to rule on the merits.[12] The Supreme Court voted, 6-3, to vacate the state issued by the U.S. Court of Appeals for the Fourth Circuit. The government petitioned the Supreme court to grant a certiorari before judgment[13] in order to ensure the execution was going to be on time.[14] The Supreme Court majority supported the government's appeal but did not give reason behind the decision aside from dissenting opinions from Justices Sotomayor, Breyer, and Kagan all dissented that they would have denied the Government's petition to vacate the lower court's stay.[15]

---

10 Higgs' attorney stated that the execution would "substantially interfere with his attorneys' ability to have meaningful contact with him during these critical days before his scheduled execution" and said it proves "reckless disregard for the lives and safety of staff, prisoners, and attorneys alike." Paul LeBlac and Rachel Janfaza, *2 federal death row inmates test positive for Covid-19*, CNN (Dec. 17. 2020), https://www.cnn.com/2020/12/17/politics/dustin-higgs-death-row-covid-19/index.html.

11 Maryland abolished the death penalty in 2013. *Supra* note 8.

12 David Cole, *A Rush to Execute*, The New York Review (Feb. 25, 2021), https://www.nybooks.com/articles/2021/02/25/trump-supreme-court-execution-spree/#:~:text=In%20six%20months%2C%20the%20Trump,in%20the%20previous%20six%20decades.&text=Over%20the%20last%20several%20months,in%20days%20or%20even%20hours.

13 Petition for Writ of Certiorari, *United States v. Higgs*, 141 S.Ct. 645 (2021) (No. 20-927).

14 A Certiorari before judgement is "a rarely used power that enables the Court to rule on the merits of a case without allowing for a normal briefing, argument, or ruling to occur at the appellate level. Certiorari before judgment has been described as an extremely unusual maneuver with obscure standards used to leapfrog normal judicial order. Justice Sotomayor's dissent asserted that these petitions are ordinarily only granted "upon a showing that the case is of such imperative public importance as to justify deviation from normal appellate practice and to require immediate determination in this Court."" Annika Russell, *Justice Sotomayor's Dissent in United States v. Higgs Rebukes Supreme Court Practices During Federal Execution Spree*, American Bar Association (Feb. 9, 2021), https://www.americanbar.org/groups/committees/death_penalty_representation/publications/project_blog/justice-sotomayor-higgs-dissent/.

15 Justice Sotomayor stated, "This is not justice. After waiting almost two decades to resume federal executions, the Government should have proceeded with some measure of restraint to ensure it did so lawfully. When it did not, this Court should have. It has not. Because the Court continues this pattern today, I dissent." *Higgs*, 141 S.Ct. at 657 (Sotomayor, J., dissenting).

On January 14, 2021, 45-year-old, Cory Johnson was executed by lethal injection.[16] Johnson suffered from intellectual disability related to physical and emotional abuse he experienced as a child. His drug addicted mother abandoned him when he was 13-years-old to a residential facility for children with intellectual and emotional impairments. Johnson was convicted of murdering seven people, relating to his involvement with the drug trade in Richmond, Virginia. Johnson was diagnosed with COVID-19 and his attorneys argued that damage in his lungs from COVD-19 would make the execution "more likely to be unusually painful."[17] Johnson's attorneys also attempted to reduce his sentence via the First Step Act of 2018[18]. But, the district court denied the motion, the Fourth Circuit court denied the rehearing, and the Supreme Court executed Johnson without an appellate court ruling.

On January 12, 2021, 52-year-old, Lisa Montgomery was executed by lethal injection. Montgomery was the first woman executed on federal death row in nearly 70 years. Montgomery suffered horrific sexual and physical abuse for most of her life and had been diagnosed with numerous mental illnesses that included but not limited to, bipolar disorder, psychosis, and traumatic brain injury. Montgomery was convicted of kidnapping resulting in death. On December 16, 2004, Montgomery drove to Skidmore, Missouri, where she strangled a pregnant woman named Bobbie Jo Stinnett. Montgomery sliced open Stinnett's belly and took the baby home. The federal court of appeals for the D.C. Circuit stayed the execution with a 5-4 vote. However, the Supreme Court vacated the stay, once again without giving reason.[19]

On December 11, 2020, 56-year-old, Alfred Bourgeois was executed by lethal injection. Bourgeois had an intellectual disability. An earlier execution date was stayed by a federal judge but overturned in October. Bourgeois was convicted of torturing and abusing his 2-year-old daughter to death. Justice Sotomayor

---

16 *Federal Government Executes Corey Johnson, Who was Likely Intellectually Disabled, Withou Nay Judicial Review of His Eligibility for the Death Penalty*, Death Penalty Information Center (Jan. 14, 2021), https://deathpenaltyinfo.org/news/federal-government-prepares-to-execute-corey-johnson-who-is-likely-intellectually-disabled-without-any-judicial-review-of-his-eligibility-for-the-death-penalty.

17 Russell, *supra* note 14.

18 *S.756 - First Step Act of 2018*, Congress.gov, (last visited Mar. 14, 2021), https://www.congress.gov/bill/115th-congress/senate-bill/756

19 Russell, *supra* note 14.

stated that Bourgeois is considered intellectually disabled[20] and therefore, the court is not allowed to execute individuals with intellectual disabilities under the Federal Death Penalty Act (FDPA) provision.[21] The federal court in Texas denied Bourgeois' claim of intellectual disability with no valid evidence.[22] Then, the federal district court in Indiana ruled in March 2020 that Bourgeois made a "strong showing" of intellectual disability and granted him permission to litigate the claim. The Supreme Court then never reviewed his claim of intellectual disability before sentencing him to death.

On December 10, 2020, 40-year-old, Brandon Bernard was executed by lethal injection. Bernard was the youngest offender executed by the federal government in nearly 70 years. Bernard was convicted at age 18 for carjacking and murdering a couple visiting Texas. Bernard's claims never got the chance to be heard on its merits. Bernard alleged that the government violated *Brady v. Maryland* because exculpatory evidence[23] was kept from the defense. The Fifth Circuit's reasoning for withholding the hearing was based on the general bar on second-or-successive habeas petitions.[24] The Supreme Court declined to hear Bernard's case again without reason and executed him. Bernard never had the opportunity to argue the merits of his claims in court and now never will.

On November 19, 2020, 40-year-old, Orlando Hall was executed by lethal injection. Hall's attorneys argued that racial bias played a role in his sentencing and raised concerns about the execution protocol and other constitutional issues. Hall was convicted of a 1994 kidnapping and rape of 16-year-old Texas girl, Lisa Rene, before dousing her with gasoline and burying her alive. On September 24, 2020, 40-year-old, Christopher Andrew Vialva was executed by lethal injection. Vialva was the first black man put to death under Trump's federal execution spree. Vialva was convicted of carjacking and the murder of two youth ministers, Todd and Stacie Bagley, when Vialva was 19. On September

---

20　At 45 years old, his achievement test scores ranked at an elementary school level; A study conducted by the Death Penalty Information Center showed more than 130 deaths sentences were reversed as a result of intellectual disability and more than 80% of death row prisoners who had their death sentence vacated were persons of color and ⅔ were African American. *Supra* note 16a.

21　Pursuant to FDPA provision 18 U. S. C. §3596(c), "[a] sentence of death shall not be carried out upon a person who is [intellectually disabled].

22　*Supra* note 16.

23　The prosecution had expert evidence that Bernard was a low-level follower and not a gang leader, but never disclosed it to the defense. When this evidence was discovered by Bernard's attorney's the lower courts ruled that it was too late. Cole, *supra* note 12.

24　Russell, *supra* note 14.

22, 2020, 50-year-old, William Emmett LeCroy was executed by lethal injection. LeCroy was a former U.S. soldier who was obsessed with witchcraft and that led him to kill. LeCroy was convicted of murder of a Georgia Nurse. On July 17, 2020, 52-year-old, Dustin Lee Honken was executed by lethal injection. Honken ran a meth drug ring where he killed federal witnesses. Honken's attorneys did not argue any mitigating circumstances, but filed appeals to cancel or stay the execution, but were denied. Honken was convicted of murdering five people in Iowa in 2005, two of whom were his children. On August 28, 2020, 45-year-old Keith Dwayne Nelson was executed by lethal injection. Nelson was convicted of a 1999 kidnapping, sexual abuse, and murder of 10-year-old girl, Pamela Butler, who he abducted whole she has rollerblading in front of her Kansas home. Nelson confessed to raping Butler and strangling her with a wire. Butler's attorneys filed multiple legal challenges including that the use of the drug pentobarbital violated the Food, Drug and Cosmetics Act, but was unsuccessful.

On July 16, 2020, 68-year-old Wesley Ira Purkey was executed by lethal injection. Purkey had been raped by his mother and struggled with mental illnesses. At the time of execution, he was suffering from Alzheimer's disease, schizophrenia, and brain damage, which left him unable to understand why he was sentenced to death. Purkey believed that his execution was intended as retaliation by the federal government for his frequent complaints about prison conditions, according to his attorneys. Purkey was convicted of a 1998 murder of 16-year-old teenage girl, Jennifer Long. The government bypassed the appellate process and went directly to the Supreme Court, who ordered the execution without reason.[25]

On July 14, 2020, 47-year-old Daniel Lewis Lee was executed by lethal injection. Lee was a white supremacist who played a lesser role in the murder of a family but was sentences to death while the killer who orchestrated the crime received a life sentence. Lee was scrapped to the execution gurney for over four hours. His attorneys challenged the ongoing controversy of the federal government's lethal injection protocol. Hours before, the Supreme Court issued the final go-ahead, ruling in a 5-4 split decision in the dead of night that the federal government's single-drug execution protocol was constitutional. There was also an appeal to delay the execution by the family of Lee's victims due to safety concerns of the coronavirus pandemic, which were denied by the Supreme Court. Lee was convicted of murdering a family of three.

---

25   Russell, *supra* note 14.

Nelson's, Purkey's and Lee's attorneys argued that the use of pentobarbital, the lethal injection, violated his Eighth Amendment rights because the drug causes fluid to accumulate in the lungs rapidly. The federal district court issued the stay in favor of all three individuals but the Supreme Court vacated the injunction on the grounds that the last-minute state would be inappropriate based on the government's expert testimony.

On August 26, 2020, 38-year-old Lezmond Mitchell was executed by lethal injection. Mitchell was the only Native American on death row. This was the only time in modern history where the federal government pursued the death penalty over the objection of a tribe when the crime was committed on tribal land. This was pursuant to sovereignty concerns related to the Navajo Nation. There were multiple appeals to stay or cancel the death sentence but were all unsuccessful. Mitchell was convicted of a 2001 murder of 63-year-old Alyce Slim and her 9-year-old granddaughter, Tiffany Lee, in Arizona.

If the Supreme Court were with these 13 individuals and upheld the 17-year hiatus in federal executions, where would they be? Over the last six months, the Supreme Court overturned 14 separate stays of execution from appellate and federal district courts with little to no reasoning.[26] Many states have already abolished the death penalty and not only for reasons of those who were able to prove their innocence, but because it is wrong to kill anyone. Current loopholes, however, make it possible for those who were sentenced in an abolished state to still be executed in another "designated state," so is the death penalty truly abolished? Lastly, what could the community have done to save Dominique? Dominique could have been any of us. Dominique could have grown up to become a doctor, scientist, professor, bricklayer, carpenter, pipefitter, teacher, priest, minister, rabbis...etc. How can we save the future Dominiques? Abolish the death penalty because it is plainly wrong.

---

26 Cole, *supra* note 12.

In the courts, Dominique could not prove his innocence. Would it have helped to have hired a public relations agency to assist him?

Dominique died in 2004. Would social media have assisted him in his fight against death?

If Facebook had existed at that time and witnesses had come forth who observed the shooting, would they have made a difference?

How can the film about this case be used to abolish the Death Penalty?

For years prosecutors told us that the Death Penalty reduces homicides. Why are there so many homicides in states that have the Death Penalty?

Why did the United States Supreme Court rush to kill 13 people in 2020-21 without hearing their motions? Why did the Justice Department bypass all Circuit Appellate Courts in death penalty cases in 2020-21 and deny hearings in those Courts?

CRITICAL ISSUES AT THE INTERSECTIONS OF RESTORATIVE JUSTICE, RACIAL JUSTICE, INDIGENEITY, AND HEALING

FANIA DAVIS

INTRODUCTION

In this chapter, I invite students of restorative justice to explore four critical questions in their learning journey. First, how might we view and practice restorative justice as a social service to transform individuals impacted by harm *and* a social movement to transform social systems that enact harm? Second, in what ways does restorative justice call us to engage in both justice-making and healing? Third, how important is it for restorative justice practitioners to develop and pursue mind-body awareness practices that allow us to transform ourselves as we transform the world? And fourth, how important is it for practitioners to co-create collective healing and learning spaces where we embody who we need to "be" to bring forth the transformation we seek.

PRACTICING RESTORATIVE JUSTICE THROUGH A RACIAL AND SOCIAL JUSTICE LENS

For almost 35 years, the United States' restorative justice community had no racial justice consciousness to speak of, viewing itself more as a social service to spur individual transformation than as a social movement to catalyze social transformation. Further, the restorative justice movement, like the Peace, Women's, Environmental and so many other North American movements, has been shaped, or misshaped, by the white supremacy and systemic racism that are so totalizing in our nation, permeating and pervading all our institutions, structures, cultural domains and collective consciousness, leaving nothing and no one untouched.

Beginning about 2012, however, practitioners of color in the U.S. and their allies strategically and intentionally began influencing the U.S. restorative justice community to adopt a restorative justice theory and praxis that center racial justice and honor its indigenous roots. As a result of this organizing, the restorative justice community in the third decade of the 21st century involves more people of color, youth, more LGBTQIA persons, more formerly incarcerated persons, and more members of historically marginalized communities generally than ever. We are also seeing increasing numbers of programs, publications, convenings and conferences that address the intersections of racial and restorative justice. Much more work remains, but there is a growing realization within our movement of the importance not only of addressing harm between and among individuals but also of transforming social structures and institutions that are themselves purveyors of incalculable harm.

The restorative justice community's emerging self-image as a *social justice* movement, a modality of both systemic and relational transformations, occurs within an ecosystem of surging social justice activism, whether Black Lives Matter, indigenous rights, transformative justice, LGBTQIA, Dreamers, #MeToo, anti-Islamaphobia, abolitionism, gun violence, climate and environmental justice, food justice, electoral politics, economic justice, white anti-racism, truth-telling, reparations, anti-slavery and anti-lynching memorialization and more. The groundswell of activism as we move into the third decade of the 21st century is mind-boggling, without equal in history. Restorative justice is in the mix, transforming and being transformed.

Yet much more is needed. The responsibility for continued transformation falls on the shoulders of white restorative justice practitioners. In these times, white practitioners are being invited to step up to the plate in a big way as models of anti-black racism. White people cannot continue to rely on restorative justice practitioners of color to do this work.

History's waves are offering a big assist. In the wake of the 2020 George Floyd killing –in truth, a public lynching – we're seeing an historically unprecedented awakening among white people in general about racism. All the police terror protests after Trayvon Martin in 2012 and Mike Brown in Ferguson in 2014 were overwhelmingly black. The majority of protesters during demonstrations against police killings after George Floyd, however, were white. Also, during the summer and fall of 2020, polls showed more than 67% of Americans supported

Black Lives Matter, including 60% of white people.[1] White Republicans were even marching in Black Lives Matter demonstrations. Legislators wore traditional African kente cloth in Congress. Major thoroughfares were renamed after Black Lives Matter. The words "white supremacy" and "reparations" moved from margin to mainstream. White individuals and scores of predominantly white universities have begun unearthing long buried truths about their forebearers' complicity with slavery, the slave trade, genocide and land theft. Monuments to slavery and slave trade are coming down. Memorials to those enslaved and lynched are coming up. Reparations were debated by 2020 presidential candidates. Systemic racism has become virtually a household term. Reparations initiatives are being launched by hundreds of jurisdictions in the nation[2]. Calls to defund the police, reimagine public safety and engage in truth and reconciliation are ringing from shore to shore. Additionally, nearly 80 institutions of higher learning participating in the rapidly growing Universities Studying Slavery consortium are unearthing long buried truths about their complicity with slavery and the slave trade, taking responsibility for the harm, and making reparations.[3]

Associated with this leap in the consciousness of white people and predominantly white institutions about systemic racism is a bourgeoning of anti-black

---

1   Kim Parker, Juliana Menasce Horowitz & Monica Anderson, *Amid Protests, Majorities Across Racial and Ethnic Groups Express Support for the Black Lives Matter Movement*, Pew Research Center (June 12, 2020) https://www.pewresearch.org/social-trends/2020/06/12/amid-protests-majorities-across-racial-and-ethnic-groups-express-support-for-the-black-lives-matter-movement/   ("[Sixty-seven percent] of Americans say they strongly...or somewhat...support the Black Lives Matter Movement."). This includes 60% of white people: https://www.pewresearch.org/social-trends/2020/06/12/amid-protests-majorities-across-racial-and-ethnic-groups-express-support-for-the-black-lives-matter-movement/.

2   *See Black residents to get reparations in Evanston, Illinois*, Brit. Broad. Corp. (Mar. 23, 2021), https://www.bbc.com/news/world-us-canada-56497294 ("Hundreds of communities across the US are considering reparations to black people, including the state of California, Iowa City and Providence, Rhode Island.").

3   https://slavery.virginia.edu/universities-studying-slavery/. Georgetown University established a $100 million reparations funds for descendants of enslaved persons sold to keep the university afloat. Brown University acknowledged long silenced truths about its complicity with slavery, and engaged in acts of repair including a reparations fund and establishing a Center for the Study of Slavery. University of Virginia along with Yale, Harvard and Princeton are engaging in acts of truth-telling, memorialization, renaming and reparations initiatives spurred by student activism. Much of the national reckoning underway today touches on the four elements of restorative justice accountability: 1) recognizing harm—truth-telling (2) taking responsibility for harm—public apologies and acknowledgments (3) making reparations proportional to the harm—restitution, reparations funds, memorialization initiatives to honor victims and (4) preventing recurrence—narrative change, public re-education, releasing white supremacist systems and reimagining them.

racism resources. There's the growing field of critical whiteness studies, including but not limited to such works as Robin DiAngelo's *White Fragility*[4] and *What Does It Mean to be White?*,[5] Debby Irving's *Waking up White Finding Myself in the Story of Race*,[6] Nell Painter's *The History of White People*,[7] Ibram X. Kendi's *How to be an Anti-Racist*[8] and so many others. There are also ground-breaking anti-black racism affinity organizations of white people that spiked in membership both after November 2016 and June 2020 like Showing Up for Racial Justice (SURJ),[9] White Awake[10] and Coming to the Table (CTTT).[11]

Restorative justice titles on the subject of racial and social justice include *Listening to the Movement*,[12] *Colorizing Restorative Justice*,[13] my *The Little Book of Race and Restorative Justice*[14] and *Restorative Justice in Urban Schools*.[15] For restorative justice practitioners working in educational settings, *Rethinking Schools*[16] is a leading grassroots magazine on racial and social justice in education with abundant resources on Black Lives Matter in schools.

Concerning lexicon, the emphasis on practicing restorative justice through a racial and social justice lens leads me to prefer the term "restorative *justice*" whether we're referring to work in schools, communities, workplaces or the

---

4   ROBIN DIANGELO, WHITE FRAGILITY: WHY IT'S SO HARD FOR WHITE PEOPLE TO TALK ABOUT RACISM (2018).

5   ROBIN DIANGELO, WHAT DOES IT MEAN TO BE WHITE?" DEVELOPING WHITE RACIAL LITERACY (2012).

6   DEBBY IRVING, WAKING UP WHITE, AND FINDING MYSELF IN THE STORY OF RACE (2014).

7   THE HISTORY OF WHITE PEOPLE, NELL IRVIN PAINTER (2011).

8   IBRAM X. KENDI, HOW TO BE AN ANTIRACIST (2019).

9   SHOWING UP FOR RACIAL JUSTICE (SURJ), https://www.showingupforracialjustice.org/ (last visited May 5, 2021).

10 WHITE AWAKE, https://whiteawake.org/ (last visited May 5, 2021).

11 COMING TO THE TABLE, https://comingtothetable.org/ (last visited May 5, 2021).

12 TED LEWIS, LISTENING TO THE MOVEMENT: ESSAYS ON NEW GROWTH AND NEW CHALLENGES IN RESTORATIVE JUSTICE (Carl Stauffer ed. 2021).

13 COLORIZING RESTORATIVE JUSTICE: VOICING OUR REALITIES (Edward C. Valandra & Waŋbli Wapháha Hokšíila eds. 2020).

14 FANIA E. DAVIS, THE LITTLE BOOK OF RACE AND RESTORATIVE JUSTICE (2019).

15 ANITA WADHWA, RESTORATIVE JUSTICE IN URBAN SCHOOLS (2017).

16 RETHINKING SCHOOLS, https://rethinkingschools.org/ (last visited May 5, 2021) ("Rethinking schools is...dedicated to sustaining and strengthening public education through social justice teaching and education activism. [The] magazine...promote[s] equity and racial justice in the classroom.").

justice system, rather than "restorative *practices*". Nomenclature is important. Language reflects one's worldview. Ours is a nation born in the blood of genocide, land theft, slave trade, slavery, racial capitalism, heteropatriarchy, white supremacy and structural racism. Because these unspeakable injustices and their legacies are ever present and ubiquitous, our intention as restorative justice practitioners in the U.S. must *always* be to do justice, no matter the setting, whether in educational institutions, workplaces, communities or justice systems.

INDIGENOUS ROOTS OF RESTORATIVE JUSTICE

In *The Little Book of Race and Restorative Justice* I wrote the following about the indigenous roots of restorative justice:

> While the emergence of U.S. restorative justice in the late 70s did not explicitly acknowledge indigeneity as its birthright...this began to shift by 2000....Navajo Nation Supreme Court Chief Justice Robert Yazzie began speaking and writing about Navajo Peacemaking Courts since the 1980s [as an ancient expression of contemporary restorative justice]. Since the 1990s, Dr. Morris Jenkins had published about the African-centered justice practices of the Gullah, an African-descended people living in the Carolinas and Georgia who preserved African lifeways.[17] Having revived traditional peacemaking circles and successfully collaborated with Judge Barry Stuart in their use in Yukon criminal sentencing processes, Harold and Phil Gatensby and Chief Mark Wedge of the Tglingit First Nations were key to the dissemination of the peacemaking circle process across the United States and Canada in their role as initial trainers. Kay Pranis's *The Little Book of Circle Processes* affirms and explores the indigenous teachings and values that comprise the foundations of the circle process and of restorative justice more broadly. Pranis acknowledges it was the Tlingit and Tagish people of Canada who taught her—and authorized her to teach—the peacemaking circle process. The indigenous roots of restorative justice refer not just to the origins of the circle technique, says Pranis, but perhaps "more importantly, the roots are in the world view of indigenous people—the understanding of

---

17   Davis, *supra* note 13, at 19-20.

interconnectedness and the dignity of all parts of creation ... [This is] an evolving concept ... [that] has grown in importance over the years."[18]

It is noted that to emphasize the indigenous ethos of restorative justice is not to sanction cultural appropriation. If restorative justice facilitators seek to incorporate indigenous elements of another culture in their circle practice[19], for example, respect requires, at minimum, fully understanding and explaining to circle participants the meaning of the cultural practice and identifying the individual who shared it and authorized them to use it. That said, every human being has indigenous roots, including white people, and all restorative justice practitioners might consider unearthing the healing and peacemaking ceremonies and practices of their own ancestral traditions to incorporate into their restorative justice practice.[20]

EMBRACING THE INNER HEALER AND WARRIOR –
TRANSFORMING OURSELVES AS WE TRANSFORM THE WORLD

There is so much injustice in the world – injustice caused by colonialism, racial capitalism, slavery, slave trade, land theft, genocide, structural racism, heteropatriarchy, mass incarceration, xenophobia, and climate catastrophe. We need justice.

---

18 Davis, *supra* note 13, at 19-20

19 Leading Circle theorist and practitioner Kay Pranis identifies five basic structural elements of the Peacemaking Circle: Circle keeper, talking piece, values, consensus, and ceremony. The Circle keeper acts as a servant leader. They don't run the Circle, but intentionally create a space where the Circle can run itself. The talking piece allows all voices to be heard. Whoever holds it is the only one speaking, and they speak with respect and from the heart. Everyone else listens with respect and from the heart. At the foundation of Circles are values that nurture good relationships and allow us to bring forth the best version of ourselves. Consensus means everyone owns Circle decisions but it doesn't require 100% agreement, so long as everyone can live with the decision. Ceremony might be a simple quote, breathing or movement exercise, or it might draw on such explicit indigenous practices as drumming, dance, smudging or ancestral libations. This element marks the Circle as a deeply communitarian space where everyone gets to meaningfully connect and share with one another in ways we don't often get to do. Circle is a profoundly relational process. When we come together to address a specific issue in Circle, we spend at least half the Circle time on relationship-building and story-telling before moving on to address the issue and solutions.

20 Davis, *supra* note 13, at 19. WHITE AWAKE, supra note 9. White Awake offers guidance to white people seeking to recover peacemaking and healing ways from Sap'mi, Celtic, and other European indigenous cultures.

And for centuries, down through the generations, these iniquitous systems have enacted and continue to enact unrelenting, unfathomable trauma to our mind-bodies, our families, our communities, and our earth. We need healing.

Not one or the other. Not just justice. Not just healing. If we are to move into a future, this is a both/and, a non-binary proposition.

Further, these inequitable systems of domination, hierarchy and colossal harm live both inside and outside of us. This reality then requires us to pursue self and collective awareness practices that enable us to transform ourselves as we transform the world. Transform persons and relationships as well as transform social systems and structures. Walking our talk is important. Are we embodying restorative justice values of radical respect, radical rationality, radical responsibility, and radical healing in our daily lives?

Many who identify as healers might bring more warrior energies into their lives. Others who identify as activists might invite more healing energies into theirs.

Trauma science tells us that if we do not process and heal trauma, we will perpetually reenact it by hurting ourselves or hurting others—by acting in or acting out. If we are to disrupt the nation's cycle of reenacting history's pain and move into a new future, we must be both warriors and healers. To clarify, I use the term "warriors" in the warrior-sage sense and not in its militaristic, combative valence. I use "healer" to refer broadly to healers of the social body.

On the need to transform ourselves as we transform the world, when I first learned about restorative justice, I didn't fully realize how deeply disruptive restorative justice is, not only to punitive justice systems outside of us but to ways those punitive systems live *inside* us. Disruptive to ways we are socially conditioned to be present to ourselves, to one another, and to the earth. I didn't realize at the outset the implications of the manner in which restorative justice invites us to create the best version of ourselves possible – whether interacting with others in restorative justice peacemaking circles or interacting with others in the course of life itself. Restorative asks us to embody values rooted in the world's wisdom traditions, living deeply into our interidentity and interrelationality with one another and the earth. Ultimately, we might say it invites us to re-imagine what it means to be human.

This internal work restorative justice calls us to do requires cultivation of a high level of mindfulness and self-awareness skills, whether we're talking about building the capacity of white people to discern and eradicate the often nuanced ways they as individuals perpetuate structural racism or capacity to notice and transform the ways we all reproduce punitive and harmful ways of being present to one another and the earth.

IMPORTANCE OF CREATING DECOLONIZED HEALING SPACES

Restorative justice is justice re-envisioned. This paradigm shift in the way we think about and do justice has been dawning on the stage of human history for only a few decades. Yet, its roots are ancient. Predating and challenging the slave trade, genocide and racial capitalism, restorative justice is inspired by a vision of justice decolonized. It is rooted in indigenous insights affirming humans' equal moral worth and dignity and their interidentity and reciprocal responsibility to one another and the earth. One of the more powerful things we can do today is cultivate and participate in intentional community spaces that are grounded in values of radical respect, relationality, and responsibility; spaces that exemplify shared, visionary, and futuristic leadership. Spaces that also challenge racism, heteropatriarchy, racial capitalism and other systems of domination. Restorative justice, particularly the peacemaking circle model, offers a framework to create these communitarian spaces. These are counter hegemonic spaces. These are healing spaces. These are liberated spaces. These are maroon spaces.[21]

Restorative justice also invites us to augment the old social movement paradigm query, "What do we need to do to bring forth the transformation we seek?" to ask, "Who do we need to be to bring forth transformation?" How do we transform ourselves and our environment in ways we wish to transform our world? Oakland's Movement Strategy Center says, "We accelerate change by embodying and manifesting the values we seek in the world right here and now." It's a form of time travel. The future is now. Embodying the future means being strategic about creating laboratories within our movement that engender decolonizing structures and approaches that supplant existing systems of domination, particularly racial capitalism, white supremacy, punitive justice, heteropatriarchy, sexism, elitism, ageism, ableism, and human supremacy. Embodying the values of radical relationality and radical healing and creating maroon spaces

---

21   Africans who escaped slavery established their own communities, known as Maroon Communities, and created their own systems of governance, health, and education as free persons. Lynn Brown, *The Obscured History of Jamaica's Maroon Societies*, JSTOR DAILY (Aug. 31, 2016), https://daily.jstor. org/maroon-societies-in-jamaica/. These communities, which existed across the Americas, blended the various cultures of the freed African and the indigenous people of the area and became their own cultures. *Id.*

or liberated zones in schools, communities, prisons, families and other settings that, expanding geometrically in number, will reach a tipping point, break loose from being contained within small populations and give way to new cultural patterns and norms. Restorative Justice peacemaking Circles are a kind of liberated zone or maroon space where we plant the seeds of our future now. In these spaces we go beyond railing against what we don't want to reimagine and rebuild anew.

CLOSING

Restorative justice is justice re-imagined. It is a holistic, collaborative justice that allows impacted persons to recognize harm, take responsibility for harm, repair harm and prevent recurrence. An inclusive accountability process led by those most negatively impacted and pursued by radically respectful, democratic, and relational means. A forward-looking justice that creates new futures. One that challenges systems of domination that live outside of us as well as those that live inside of us. Restorative justice-informed processes rooted in anti-racial capitalist, anti-heteropatriarchal values and in indigenous wisdoms about humanity, collectivity, responsibility and the earth are our North Star.

What is the difference between viewing restorative justice as a social service and viewing it as a social movement?

How might it look to practice restorative justice through a racial justice lens?

In what sense may restorative justice Peacemaking Circle spaces be considered maroon spaces?

In what ways do they call forth a new future?

In what sense is restorative justice a justice decolonized?

How does restorative justice invites us to re-imagine what it means to be human?

Law and Order?

KATHLEEN M. BANKHEAD

John F. Kennedy said, "The cost of freedom is always high, but Americans have always paid it. And one path we shall never choose, and that is the path of surrender, or submission."

Black Americans have paid that high cost in spades, but, when it comes to our liberty, we are relentlessly condemned for refusing to surrender or submit. I pray we never will!

I was blessed to have been born during the best time in recorded history for a black child in the United States. I know that my great great grandparents or maybe even my great grandparents were born into the savagery of the US foundational institution called slavery. There have been civil rights struggles and sacrifices since African peoples were kidnapped from their homes and exported to unthinkable cruelties far away. I was born in the late 50s and grew up during the civil rights movement of the 60s, but was too young to have to sacrifice my body or future for the sake of black folks' liberty and America's soul. Nonetheless, and gratefully, I reaped the benefits of those who did sacrifice even with their lives so that I might live freer. And I did.

Now, in 2021 and for some few years prior, a new generation of blacks, other people of color and white allies, are demanding equity and equality. They are marching, protesting, so called "rioting" and "looting" and sacrificing their bodies, their futures, their very lives for that ideal. Now, I am too old, too settled, too scared to participate in the streets.

Listening to the anguished voices of those repulsed by the "violence" to buildings and property - the same voices that were silent and implicitly, or explicitly championed all the iterations of the violence against black people - I was soul sick. My hopes for a final, lasting empathetic change in the hearts and minds of whiteness dashed against the reality that black existence is still slave to the feelings of whiteness, I resigned myself to the lived reality that black lives still don't matter to our fellow Americans or our country and neither equity or equality will ever happen for my people. Then when I heard the unmitigated cries for "law and order" from those privileged enough to engage in lawlessness with impunity, I snapped! This essay, this truth was my healing, I hope it helps you too.

Law and Order? Law and Order? The protection of Law and Order is desired by no other group more than black people. Law and Order is what black people have been screaming for, praying for, fighting for and dying for for hundreds of years.

When the African continent was exploited, looted and colonized for its diamonds, gold, oil, natural gas, uranium, silver, platinum, copper, cobalt, iron, bauxite and cocoa beans, palm oil, wood and tropical fruits the people probably coveted the protection of a moral law and order.

When African men women and children were chased and kidnapped, forced aboard commercial ships and stuffed into cargo holes for months long journeys across the Atlantic Ocean I'm sure they prayed that they'd be rescued by law and order.

"For the captive Africans aboard a slave ship, the voyage to the New World was a passage of nearly unimaginable horror. The slave deck itself was a living nightmare - only a few feet high, the African captives were shackled together lying down, side by side, head to foot, or even closer. Deaths from suffocation, malnutrition, and disease were routine on the slave deck, as were arbitrary torture and murder by the crew. The closeness, the filth, and the fear delivered many into madness, and suicide attempts were common. Other ships could smell slavers from far away, and Portuguese sailors called them *tumbeiros*, or floating tombs.

Those who were not killed by conditions on board were often permanently disabled by beatings or disease. Many slaver captains threw sick or injured Africans overboard so that their losses would be covered by insurance." [Oh! The lawlessness! The looting of black bodies!]

"On more than 300 voyages, the captives on the slave deck attempted to overthrow the crew," [and in several cases they triumphed.]" https://www.loc.gov/classroom-materials/immigration/african/journey-in-chains/

Was that struggle to gain freedom, lawlessness? Was that the rioting? Was that the looting? Should the kidnapped have remained peaceful? Revolted in a different way? Been patient and waited for the arc of morality to lean their way? ...hundreds of years later we are still waiting...

When the Africans arrived at various locations along the route and were sold to other humans as slaves; When their children, husbands, wives, mothers, fathers, brothers, sisters, family and friends were sold away from them; When they were beaten, raped, maimed, dehumanized, humiliated, tortured, worked to death; killed for various affronts or no reason at all; when they escaped but were caught and returned to be made an example, taught a lesson, to send a message they pleaded for their liberation by law and order.

When a black man stood up for this nation's freedom and was the first killed in the Boston "riot" for America's independent existence he sacrificed his life for law and order.

When the enslaved filed lawsuits and continued to file lawsuits to gain their freedom in the courts they sought law and order.

When they were whipped, hobbled or killed for daring to learn to read, they moaned for law and order.

When the Emancipation Proclamation was signed they anticipated law and order;

When they fought in the civil war and won they rallied for law and order;

When the 13th Amendment was ratified, they waited on law and order;

When the Civil Rights Act of 1866 was passed and the 14th Amendment was ratified, they expected law and order;

When the 15th Amendment was ratified they envisioned law and order;

When the Civil Rights Act of 1871 was passed prohibiting violence against black people they ached for law and order;

When almost 85 years later a 14 year old boy was kidnapped at gun point from his helpless family's home and the men that tortured and murdered him were set free they yearned for law and order;

When Civil Rights Act of 1875 was passed and when separate but equal was never equal they hoped for law and order;

When they against all odds with without straps, boots, or a fishing pole and little to no help from the government built thriving cities and those cities were burned and destroyed and they were murdered in the streets and had bombs dropped on them they migrated for law and order

When they marched peacefully and were spat upon, attacked by dogs, had hoses turned on them, were beaten with batons, hauled off to jail they wailed for law and order;

When they braved sitting at lunch counters, refused to sit at the back of the bus, and when they walked to work for over a year, they stood for law and order

When Brown vs. Board of Education was decided in favor of equal education and the Civil Rights Act of 1964 was passed they dreamed of law and order

When they had to guess how many jelly beans, pay poll taxes and take rigged literacy tests, they marched for law and order

When the Civil Rights Act of 1965 was passed they imagined law and order

When men and women were kidnapped and had nooses placed around their necks and they were mutilated and burned alive while their assailants celebrated their souls cried out for law and order;

When the Civil Rights Act of 1968 was passed they dared to count on law and order;

When they couldn't get a VA mortgage loan or any loan to buy a house; When they couldn't rent an apartment in their desired neighborhood; when they couldn't get money to start or build a business; When they had the money but couldn't live in the neighborhood of their choice; when they were redlined and not protected by the thin blue line they clamored for law and order

When around this country school funding was based on property values ensuring the underfunding and consequent inferiority of black schools they struggled for law and order;

Whey they had crosses burned on their lawns they seethed for law and order

When a teenaged boy was walking home from the store with some candy and pop and was followed, chased and assaulted by a grown man he fought for law and order;

When a 12 year old child was playing with a toy gun in the park and the police pull up and kill him within seconds he screamed for law and order

When a young man was casually shopping in Walmart in an open carry state while carrying a toy rifle offered for sale in the store and police ambush him he had no chance for law and order

When a black man that was a passenger in a car announced that he had a concealed carry permit and was killed in front of his girlfriend and a small child for legally possessing a gun, he tried to invoke law and order.

Over and over and time and time again, no law has ever led to racial equality or economic justice for black people; and when every law on the books that privileges white Americans has been applied to the disadvantage of black Americans all we've ever marched for, sat in for, rioted for, looted for, burned for and deserved just like every other American but still haven't received is law and order!

Because we alone bear the burden of America's racism, greed and inhumanity, we still long for, long awaited, law and order.

As long as there are more temporary and ineffective civil rights laws, continuing abuses of power, baked in inequality and human rights tragedies to tell, than there is time to tell them; until law and order is purposed to protect black, red and brown people, the only law and order I want to hear about is the law and order that serves and protects blacks and other people of color. Only then will there be law and order!

DISCUSSION QUESTIONS:

How does our society address the cry for "law and order?"

How does reciting history help us heal the wounds inflicted by slavery and the Jim Crow era?

What practical steps can individuals or society take to alleviate the pain caused by centuries of segregation and discrimination?

How does poetry (and the other Arts such as music, drama, and painting) help us heal?

POLICE AND RESTORATIVE JUSTICE

PATRICK MURPHY-RACEY

People across the country call the police a lot. In Knoxville, Tennessee, people call 911 for domestic disputes every 21 minutes, on average. The way this works is typical of most places in that the vast majority of the calls for help with "domestics" happen in the evenings from 6pm till around 1am. So, in just 6 hours each evening in my small town, Knoxville 911 dispatchers send officers to investigate 68 calls exclusively for domestic disputes. The problem is there are many other calls that are coming in all at the same time. They respond to burglar alarm calls to businesses and homes, disputes between neighbors, for shoplifting, missing children, Alzheimers patients that walk off, downed trees, and truancy calls when kids simply refuse to go to school. And then there are the next level calls for people who die or commit suicide, traffic accidents with injuries, drug deals gone bad, reports of child or elder abuse, house-fires, opioid overdoses, custodial interference, drunk drivers, armed robberies, shootings, and stabbings. On weekends when the weather is good or on holidays, the calls increase as people just spend too much time together.

If this all sounds crazy, then welcome to modern policing where people call 911 for just about everything. Today, for instance, I heard dispatch try to send an officer to a pawnshop where the owner called 911 because an employee was being rude to her and refused to wear a mask. That call was cancelled by a supervisor, as was another when a person called police to complain that their next door neighbor's leaves were being blown into their yard by the wind.

To be a police officer on patrol in any city in the country is a massive test of patience. Officers that can keep up with the call volume and sprint through every shift often fail and quit. Only those that can run a marathon have a chance in the career. The pay is mostly terrible, the benefits are often lack luster, and the pensions that allow cops to work for 20 years and then retire are disappearing by the day. Why do they do it? I've asked them. Most say that they always wanted to be an officer. Some offer that it's "the family business." About half are veterans of our military who just couldn't figure out how to make a 9-5 work for them or they are simply interested in serving. I will offer you an answer for most of them as to why they do it. I believe most feel an overwhelming sense of calling even if they can't always identify that for themselves.

Officers patrol smaller areas of their cities and counties called zones, usually given numbers. Each zone has its own characters that call 911 all the time because they are lonely or have mental issues. I've been to one older man's home on different occasions with different shifts. He calls 911 and tells dispatch there is someone trying to get into his house. They talk to him using his first name and tell him units are responding (because they have to). He literally calls sometimes as often as twice a week. We always end up doing a check of the house, then officers go inside and check on his food supply. If it's not too busy, some officers will actually open a can of ravioli and make him dinner before they leave. If it's really slow, officers will go by when he doesn't call to visit with him and do a welfare check. The man is on in years, in bad health, and is poor. I have witnessed officers bring him food on occasion when he looks too thin. This happens all over the country but officers don't often talk about the good they do. I know of an elderly woman that gets visits once a week or so by officers on patrol. If they don't visit, she calls 911. If they visit often, she doesn't call in. It's a simple compact and each side understands their role. These stories never hit the news but they happen all the time and in every department, and in every city.

I don't know all this because I read a book or looked up the stats on a website; I sit in the right seat of patrol cars about 100 hours a month; I see all this first-hand. I am a law enforcement chaplain. I am "on call" regularly, to respond to death scenes, to do death notifications, and to assist families in their first hours of violent grief when they lose a grandmother, husband, sister, or child. I also minister to officers who sometimes have difficulty dealing with a particular call that they responded to.

The more I ride with officers, the more I am amazed that anyone would want to do this work. They work in rotating shifts so that they may not see their kids for days at a time. Because they make so little, most also have to work side jobs to make ends meet, especially if they have families. Because of what they see every day, many first responders suffer from both Cumulative and Situational Post Traumatic Stress Disorder (PTS) and/or moral injury at least once or twice in their career. Most officers see dead people on a regular basis, due to natural causes, overdose, and suicide. If they are really unlucky, then throw in a dead child, the horrific results of suicide, or a body undiscovered for a month or more.

I know officers that have had to pick up body parts in the road after an "ejection" from a car wreck often caused by people not wearing seat belts. Officers are called upon to guard bodies as they wait for detectives to investigate, the medical examiner, crime technicians to document, and eventually, funeral directors to transport. Each time officers encounter violence, death, potential and real threats to their lives, these experiences build, one on another, and over time. My respect and awe for what police officers risk and do every day increases each time I ride.

When George Floyd was killed by Minneapolis Police Officer Derrick Chauvin, our nation erupted with both justified protests as well as unjust violence. Probably like you, I've seen all the footage. The anger, frustration, and injustice of what happened prompted demonstrations in Minneapolis and throughout the country. I supported the protests. Floyd's murder at the hands of Chauvin, was simply that. Even when other officers right next to him asked if they could move him so he could breathe, Chauvan refused. It was terrible. But the property damage, looting, and danger to communities I cannot support.

I should point out that I am a middle-aged white man. I am a part of what Elizabeth Wilkerson coined "the ruling caste." I am writing this chapter based on my observations about what I have seen in my many hours of riding along with officers on patrol, and not to justify what happened in Minneapolis or anywhere else where police actions have resulted in the deaths of people of color. Black Lives Matter is not the equivalent of Blue Lives Matter, or even of All Lives Matter. To become a law enforcement officer is a decision that any motivated individual can make. Law enforcement is first a job that later resolves into the officer becoming part of a family of officers that includes men, women, white, black, yellow, brown, straight, gay, and otherwise. Within that family are officers that are prejudiced, bigoted, and homophobic, in ways that can sometimes limit their ability to be fair, balanced, and impartial officers of the law. Officers flow mostly from the communities in which they grow up.

Blue Lives Matter is different from Black Lives Matter. Being black in America is not a choice. You can't quit your race like you can leave law enforcement. Jim Crow is still alive, and there are very real pressures on people of color. People of color endure discrimination and prejudice every day in ways that those of us that lack color would never dream of. Those who were born into Wilkerson's "lower caste" cannot simply quit their jobs and leave their family... Being black in America is something you simply are; it is not a choice.

It's often difficult for those of us that lack color to understand some of the many challenges that face people of color. Our son turned 16 and started driving just seven months ago. I taught him to drive and spent a lot of time in the passenger seat forming his skill set for the road. When he got his license, I was terrified to see him drive off to his friend's house by himself. I thought of him getting into an accident as I watched his little truck disappear around the corner in our subdivision. I worried most about someone hitting him or speed being involved in a wreck. What never entered my mind was his being shot and killed by police on a traffic stop—because it's so unlikely. My son is white and drives a car with no dents in it, the tires all match, all the lights work, and the tag is valid. His little truck is 23 years old but it is not what most officers on patrol would consider a "good stop."

As a relatively new student of restorative practices, there is so much space in which RJ can invade. In 2020, law enforcement is fat, ripe, and ready for restorative training for officers. Simply locking up people is clearly not the answer and seems to just cost us all more money in the long run. Putting social workers at extreme risk and asking them (or making them) respond to violent calls rather than police will get more well meaning and innocent people killed. But giving officers CIT (critical incident training) does not do enough to deal with mental health issues, people off their meds, and addicts "geeking" at the end of an angry binge. There are many strong currents at work under the asphalt, massive societal ills working against the police, children raised to stare at phones, and dockets filled every day with deep-rooted issues that the law cannot reach.

So what needs to change?

Police academies could provide military veterans entering law enforcement with unique training that might assist them to abandon a battlefield mentality and better prepare them for how to deal with trauma, officer safety, and the protecting side of being an officer rather than the warrior side. Often non-military trainees defer to their military trained beat partners when things become sticky and dangerous. All officers need to re-center on their original mission: to serve and protect. They can be helped in this mission through learning about restorative justice and restorative techniques.

George Floyd is an icon of what is wrong with those officers who do not heed the police mission to serve and protect. And it is not just to serve and protect some; it is to serve and protect all. As Floyd says over and over again, "I can't breathe," one of the officers with Chauvin asks him, "Should we turn him over?" Chauvin says no twice, when he's asked the same question again by his beat partner. The two officers with Chauvin had done their training under him and had just recently completed the four phases of "patrol training." The junior officer was asking the right question, but he was unwilling to challenge a senior officer. Admittedly, there has to be a chain of command for things to work in law enforcement, but when someone in charge is doing something wrong, it presents the younger officers with a problem and officers should be trained on how to resolve it, especially in situations that recur constantly. As George Floyd lay dying at their feet, clearly this was not an example of healthy chain of command.

Legalizing marijuana at the federal level would be extremely helpful in emptying our jails and prisons and keeping young black men out of them in the first place. If you take away pot offenses altogether, many more black males will not be in prison because police won't be able to use "probable cause" to arrest them for simple possession.

There are huge chunks of mantle that need to be shifted and moved in order for "black lives" to feel safe around my blue family. Very little so far has done the trick, even when black officers don a uniform. I believe strongly that restorative practices are the only thing powerful enough to move these plates around so that real justice can be served by the police, the parole system, and the courts. An embrace of restorative justice is gravely needed to get people not only to hear, but actively to listen to each other. If we can begin to truly listen and understand each other better, we can become sensitive to actual justice in its raw and pure state rather than a nominal and fake justice that fails to restore those who have been injured. It fascinates me that it's possible our court system actually hears cases without the victim being present. If the victim cannot meet face to face with their accused, how will either party ever be healed or made whole again?

The Black Lives Matter movement has generated many conversations. This dialog, if it continues, will help us find each other in the tumult of these times filled with violence, pandemic, shut downs, the 2020 presidential election, unemployment, and distance learning. Our country is a mess right now and restorative practices are about the only thing that can help us emerge as a nation trying to find its more authentic self. Racism harms not only African Americans; it harms whites as well. Robin Diangelo's book, "White Fragility," agrees with the growing recognition that "racism is a white problem." There is great wisdom in this truth and one I have been thinking about a great deal lately.

Former FBI Director James Comey was addressing the International Association of Chiefs of Police in 2016 when a man in uniform stood up. "He told me his name and then he said, 'I'm Jewish.' That confused me, but he went on. 'I was one of the first there [Pulse Nightclub] that night, and as I ran toward the sound of gunfire, at my side was a Muslim officer. We were Jew and Muslim and Christian. We were white and black and Latino and Asian. We ran to help people we didn't know and we didn't care what they looked like. We ran toward the danger because that's who we are, that's what we do. I thought you should know that. I think people should know that.' And then he sat down. That is the true heart of law enforcement. We are flawed. We must—and we will—work to get better. But we are good people from all walks of life who have chosen service over self. I know that. I think all people should know that."

I will now pass the talking piece to the next chapter author and prepare to listen.

DISCUSSION QUESTIONS:

Why are police officers themselves the victims of trauma and how can they be healed?

Should the social service activities described by Mr. Racey be performed by the police or should they be assigned to a separate social service agency?

Is there something in being a law enforcement officer that causes individual officers regardless of their race, color, ethnicity, gender or class to associate more with the police as an institution than with the communities they come from? What kinds of emotions or trauma can these divided loyalties lead to and how can they be diminished?

Should cities and governmental units devote more resources to hiring counselors, chaplains, social worker and other like professionals to work with police officers? Is the answer defunding the police or providing new and additional funding for the police? If these services are needed, are they better provided within the police agencies or through separate agencies with specific missions?

Practically, how can one convince people of color who have suffered harm by the police and police officers to engage in meaningful dialogue that does not result in one or the other of the parties walking out of the room and making matters even worse?

Is it possible to create a better relationship between the police and the community? Is having community members ride along with police officers while they perform their duties a practical solution? What are other ways that police-community relations can be improved?

Are military veterans an asset or a hindrance to police reform? Once the "shoot to kill" is embedded into someone's psychic, how can it be removed? Do policing experiences indicate that maybe we should relook at how the military trains soldiers?

Segregation, Violence, and Restorative Justice –
Restoring our Communities

MICHAEL P. SENG[1]

I. INTRODUCTION – VIOLENCE IN OUR CITIES – CHICAGO AS AN EXAMPLE

American headlines in the past several years have reported tragic cases of shootings of young persons and innocent bystanders in many of our cities largely resulting from gang and other acts of random violence. Perhaps no city has received greater publicity and has been hit harder by this type of thoughtless violence than Chicago. Every day one reads about small children, innocent teenagers and seniors being shot down in the line of fire on Chicago's streets. Most of the violence occurs in impoverished and low-income communities of color.

Along with private acts of violence, we hear of the shootings and deaths because of questionable police actions. These actions are also largely confined to impoverished and low-income communities of color. Most prominent are the deaths of civilians by police that have occurred in Ferguson and Baltimore, as well as Chicago. The spate of police killings beginning with the strangulation of Floyd George in Minneapolis in 2020 demonstrate that that this is a national crisis that cannot be swept away as has happened after innumerable incidents in the past.

What is going on in Chicago and other major American cities is not isolated. Violence, whether perpetrated by private individuals or groups or by those in public authority such as the police, is not acceptable at any level. Violence simply begets more violence. What is happening is closely related to other social and economic ills. Persons often resort to violence when they have nothing else

---

1   This chapter is reprinted from The John Marshall Law Review, v. 50, p. 487 (2017). The Law Review has given permission for the reprinting of the article. Minor updates have been added to bring the chapter current.

to lose. Violence as perpetrated in our cities today is closely tied to a lack of jobs, lack of educational opportunity, lack of political power, and a feeling of utter and complete hopelessness.

Traditional remedies such as hiring more police or locking up the perpetrators are not working and are done at considerable cost to society. Often these remedies exacerbate problems rather than alleviate problems. Having more police officers on the street can perpetuate the siege mentality that is experienced by persons in low income segregated communities, especially if the officers are not well trained to handle the resentment their presence inevitably brings. Convicts return from imprisonment with a chip on their shoulder. The prison environment only reinforces their bad habits. They return to their communities with criminal records that make it more difficult for them to find decent employment or housing. They become estranged from their families. Rather than preparing persons to reintegrate positively back into society, incarceration does exactly the opposite.

Society is more and more moving to solutions offered by restorative justice. Restorative justice offers a holistic approach to the effects of violence. It recognizes that focusing only on the perpetrator does little good. Victims must be restored, but a victim-centered approach is insufficient. Crimes of violence affect the entire community. The community must be restored, but restoration does not mean returning to the status quo. The community, as well as the offender and often the survivor, must be transformed so that bad behavior is discouraged and not seen as the norm. Racism, classism, and other impediments to reintegrating the individual and the community must be expunged. The community itself provides the environment where the anti-social behavior occurs, and the community must be part of the solution. We cannot ignore the causes that lead to the antisocial behavior. To do so will only exacerbate it. The task is immense, but the cost of inaction is too great to ignore.

This article will explain why restorative justice is an effective remedy in resolving the social and economic problems that plague our communities. A narrow approach will not succeed. Restorative justice solutions require participation by the entire community; nothing less will work.

Many explanations can be offered for the problems of violence in our cities. Urban violence is not new. Violence has been around as long as persons have congregated in urban areas. Street gangs were in existence in American cities in the 19th and 20th centuries.[2] Police misconduct has existed ever since the establishment of modern police forces.

Nonetheless, the level of violence that we are experiencing today, whether greater or less than that suffered in the past, is disturbing and is unacceptable. The loss of even one life is a tragedy. The loss of more than 760 lives in one year due to violence, as has occurred in Chicago, is a major catastrophe.[3] The loss of these lives did not happen through a force of nature; it happened because of the failure of our institutions. We can do better.

Three reports were issued in the City of Chicago in 2017 that provide explanations for the violence that is occurring there: The Justice Department Report on Police Misconduct in Chicago issued on January 13, 2017;[4] the Great Cities Institute at the University of Illinois at Chicago Study on Youth Joblessness in Chicago;[5] and the Metropolitan Planning Organization's study on The Costs of Segregation in Chicago.[6] None of these studies in itself offers a complete explanation, but each is helpful in pointing out problems that must be corrected if the shootings in Chicago are to be reversed. I cite them in the order that they were published.

---

2   Evan Andrews, *7 infamous gangs of New York* (June 4, 2013) http://www.history.com/news/history-lists/7-infamous-gangs-of-new-york. James C. Howell & John P. Moore, *History of Street Gangs in the United States* (National Gang Center, USDOJ, May 2010) https://www.nationalgangcenter.gov/Content/Documents/History-of-Street-Gangs.pdf. One of the most popular American musicals, West Side Story, is about gang violence in New York in the 1950s.

3   *Trump again puts spotlight on violence in Chicago*, CHI. TRIB., Mar. 29, 2017, p. 7

4   *Investigation of the Chicago Police Department*, United States Department of Justice and the United States Attorney's Office Northern District of Illinois (January 13, 2017) https://www.justice.gov/opa/file/925846/download.

5   *Abandoned in their Neighborhoods: Youth Joblessness amidst the Flight of Industry and Opportunity*, Great Cities Institute, University of Illinois at Chicago, (January 29, 2017) https://greatcities.uic.edu/wp-content/uploads/2017/01/Abandoned-in-their-Neighborhoods.pdf.

6   *The Cost of Segregation*, Metropolitan Planning Council (March 31, 2017) http://www.metroplanning.org/uploads/cms/documents/cost-of-segregation.pdf

a. The Department of Justice Report finding a lack of police training and accountability in Chicago

On January 13, 2017, the United States Justice Department (DOJ) published its investigation of the Chicago Police Department.[7] The report was issued in the final days of the Obama Administration. The new Trump administration has announced that it will not enforce the reforms against police departments recommended by the previous administration.[8] The Chicago mayor and police chief have taken the position that they will implement the reforms whether or not required to do so by the federal government but perhaps not through a consent decree.[9] Regardless of how the recommendations are implemented, the report details major deficiencies in the police department that stand as unchallenged at the present time.

The investigation was initiated to determine if the Chicago Police Department (CPD) was engaging in a pattern and practice of police misconduct and, if so, to identify systemic deficiencies that lead to that misconduct.[10] The investigation focused on officer use of force, including deadly force, and on officer training, reporting, and accountability.[11] It also focused on disparities, including race and ethnicity.[12]

The investigation concluded that Chicago police officers "engage[d] in a pattern or practice of using force, including deadly force, that is unreasonable."[13] It found that this was attributable to the fact that:

"[The CPD] has not provided officers with adequate guidance to understand how and when they may use force, or how to safely and effectively control and

---

7   *Supra*, note 4. The Justice Department did similar reports on Ferguson, Missouri, Cleveland, Ohio, and Baltimore, Maryland.

8   *Sessions move muddies cop reform*, CHI. TRIB., Apr. 5, 2017, p.1, c.1.

9   *Ibid.* The long-term effectiveness of consent decrees has been questioned. What is needed is an on-going dedication to police reform, the momentum of which is often very difficult to sustain especially given changes in the political environment. *The Rise and Fall of Federal Efforts to Curb Police Abuse*, N.Y. TIMES, Apr. 10, 2017, p. A12. *Chicago, get that consent decree*, CHICAGO TRIBUNE, July 6, 2007, p. 18.

10   *Supra*, note 4, at 21.

11   *Ibid.*

12   *Ibid.*

13   *Id.* at 5.

resolve encounters to reduce the need to use force. CPD also has failed to hold officers accountable when they use force contrary to CPD policy or otherwise commit misconduct. . . . [T]hese failures result in officers not having the skills or tools necessary to use force wisely and lawfully, and they send a dangerous message to officers and the public that unreasonable force by CPD officers will be tolerated."[14]

Some of this failure was attributable to the quality or quantity of training given to police officers.[15] Indeed the report recited that interviews with recruits who had recently graduated from the training academy revealed that only one in six recruits came close to properly articulating the legal standard for use of force.[16] It found that post-academy training was equally flawed.[17]

The report further found that officer wellness and safety was ignored.[18] Officers understandably face acute distress and this is manifested in how they interact with local citizens. Officers that are under stress are more likely to overreact in confrontations with community residents. The report cited "officer alcoholism, domestic violence, and suicide" as manifestations of the trauma suffered by members of the CPD.[19] The report articulates how stress can impact on the officer's performance.[20] It found that "high levels of unaddressed stress can compromise officer well-being and impact on officer's demeanor and judgment, which in turn impact how that officer interacts with the public."[21] The effects of such trauma manifest themselves when the officer is both at home and at work creating a vicious cycle that is not easy to interrupt.

The report found that CPD officers "expressed discriminatory views and intolerance with regard to race, religion, gender, and national origin in public social media forums, and that CPD takes insufficient steps to prevent or

---

14   *Ibid.*

15   *Id.* at 10.

16   *Ibid.*

17   *Ibid.* The report finds that post-academy training fails to provide probationary police officers with appropriate training, mentorship, and oversight and lacks any long-term plan or strategy.

18   *Id.* at 11.

19   *Ibid.*

20   *Id.* at 118.

21   *Ibid.*

appropriately respond to its animus."[22] Furthermore, "the raw statistics show that CPD uses force almost ten times more often against blacks than against whites."[23] The report concluded that:

> "[T]he City must address serious concerns about systemic deficiencies that disproportionately impact black and Latino communities. CPD's pattern or practice of unreasonable force and systemic deficiencies fall heaviest on the predominantly black and Latino neighborhoods on the South and West Sides of Chicago, which are also experiencing higher crime. Raw statistics show that CPD uses force almost ten times more often against blacks than against whites. As a result residents in black neighborhoods suffer more of the harms caused by breakdowns in uses of force, training, supervision, accountability and community policing."[24]

Of particular interest to restorative justice advocates is the way that the City handled citizen's complaints against the police. The report states that rather than investigate complaints, the Independent Police Review Authority (IPRA) disposed of complaints through a process it called "mediation."[25] "Mediation" according to the IPRA basically meant a quick bargaining process where the officer who is under investigation agrees to a sustained finding in exchange for a reduced punishment.[26] The complainant and the community are excluded from the process.[27] Even apart from the appropriateness of the solution, this procedure does not satisfy community feelings of injustice and lack of power. It also ignores the positive input that all participants can have on the final outcome.

The complaint process furthered feelings of unequal treatment in black and Latino communities in Chicago. The report found that "complaints filed by white individuals were two-and-a-half times more likely to be sustained than

---

22 *Ibid.*

23 *Id.* at 145.

24 *Id.* at 15.

25 *Ibid.*

26 *Ibid.*

27 *Id.* at 54.

complaints filed by black individuals, and nearly two times as likely to be sustained as complaints filed by Latinos."[28]

The report explains the breakdown in police-community relations in Chicago and how, at best, the police are ineffective, or at worse, how they contributed to the violence and unlawful behavior that plagues some of Chicago's residential communities.[29]

b. The Great Cities Institute Report on youth joblessness

On January 29 2017, the Great Cities Institute of the University of Illinois at Chicago issued a report that, with the DOJ report, is relevant to violence in Chicago's neighborhoods.[30] The report directly ties youth unemployment to violence. The report summarizes a series of hearings where young people testified that they wanted work and that they connected joblessness and crime in their neighborhoods, and how securing a job, even a summer job, created pathways for life changing opportunities.[31] The report supplements these testimonials with data and provides analysis and context to these concerns.[32]

The report demonstrates that youth joblessness is disproportionately felt by young people of color and especially black males and that it is concentrated and chronic.[33] The problem is tied to the emptying out of jobs from neighborhoods and concentrating jobs in Chicago's downtown, where whites are employed in professional level services.[34]

The report found that among 20 to 24 year old men, nearly half were neither working nor in school and that these low rates were spatially concentrated in racially segregated neighborhoods.[35] In a cluster of communities that were predominantly African-American, the unemployment rate for 16 to 19 year olds was over 90 percent and in predominantly Hispanic areas on the Southwest or

---

28   *Id.* at 68

29   *Id.* at 144.

30   *Supra,* note 5.

31   *Id.* at i.

32   *Id.* at ii.

33   *Id.* at iii.

34   *Ibid.*

35   *Ibid.*

Northwest sides it was between 80 and 90 percent.[36] The unemployment rate for young people in Chicago, both male and female, was extremely high compared to New York and Los Angeles.[37] The statistics showed that the employment rate for young people in Chicago was worse in 2015 than in 1960. This was the opposite from the experience in the rest of Illinois and the United States.[38]

These statistics were further enhanced by the fact that among the employed, the percentage of black and Hispanic youth working in relatively high paying manufacturing jobs declined since 1960.[39] During that period, the percentage of black and youth working in low paying service jobs increased, while white youth increased employment in professional and related fields.[40] The study also showed that most jobs had moved away from areas of the city with heavy black and Hispanic concentrations to the Loop and the North Side, where there were larger concentrations of whites.[41]

The executive summary of the report concluded that:

"[J]oblessness disproportionately persists for young people of color and is geographically concentrated. Its roots are structural and have an impact on young people, their households, and their neighborhoods. Reflecting long-term impacts of segregation, racial disparities and economic restructuring, joblessness is a function of structural changes in the economy that date back several decades and was compounded by the 2008 global recession that exacerbated conditions and isolated people even further."[42]

Ultimately, the report suggested that the lack of economic opportunities increases stress and a feeling of hopelessness in young people, which can then lead to lawlessness and violence.[43]

---

36   *Id.* at 51.

37   *Ibid.*

38   *Id.* at v.

39   *Id.* at xiv and xv.

40   *Ibid.*

41   *Id.* at xxiii.

42   *Ibid.*

43   *Ibid.*

c. The Metropolitan Planning Council's Report on the cost of
segregation in Chicago

On March 31, 2017, a third report was issued by the Metropolitan Planning
Council in partnership with the Urban Institute that focused on the cost of segregation in the Chicago region.[44] In many ways, this report confirmed the self-
evident. The report found that:

> "Economic and racial segregation has strangled opportunities for millions of
> people. Disinvestment has devastated entire city neighborhoods and suburban
> villages, towns and cities. Lack of diversity also hurts affluent communities,
> where limited housing options often mean that young people cannot afford
> to return when starting their own families, retirees cannot afford to stay and
> valued employees are priced out."[45]

The report estimated that incomes for African-Americans would rise by an
average of $2,982 per person per year if economic and racial discrimination in
Chicago were reduced to the national median.[46] Income and racial inequality
compound and exacerbate each other's effects.[47]

The report further found that segregation results in lost lives and that in 2016,
the homicide rate in the region would have dropped by 30 percent if the level of
segregation had been reduced to the national median.[48] Noting that the number
of African American homicides was over 17 times the number for whites,[49] the
study concluded that reducing segregation would have a significant impact on
the violence and murders that occurs in Chicago. Not only is the effect in lost
lives. The study traced a nexus between the homicide rate and residential real
estate values, which in 2010 would have increased by at least six billion dollars
if segregation was reduced to the national median.[50]

---

44 *Supra*, note 6.

45 *Id.* at 3.

46 *Id.* at 4.

47 *Id.* at 5.

48 *Id.* at 6.

49 *Id.*at 7.

50 *Ibid.*

The report also found a strong link between segregation, school quality, and college preparedness, which translated into further inequality and its social and economic consequences.[51]

Significantly, the report details that the negative effects of segregation are not only felt in low-income, racially segregated neighborhoods, but everywhere in the region because taxpayers pay the costs of segregation in higher taxes for criminal justice and public health systems. The cost is also reflected in lower long-term economic growth.[52] In 2021, the Metropolitan Planning Council issued Part II of its study that recommended steps to reduce the disparities and inequities by race and income in the region. Included in the recommendations is reforming the criminal justice system.[53]

These three reports while not covering the entire field document the strong link between racial discrimination and segregation and violence. Each of these reports contains important recommendations to address the root causes of discrimination and violence, and the recommendations should be implemented. However, none of these reports offers a holistic solution that addresses the individuals whose lives are affected by the social and economic issues addressed in these studies.

The factual findings in these reports are supported by similar findings nationwide. Many recent studies detail the growing wealth gap in the United States,[54] and the crucial link between greater income and wealth inequality and a widening racial wealth gap.[55] As well stated by Thomas Shapiro in his recent book, *Toxic Inequality*, "[r]esidential segregation bakes inequality into the lives of families by reproducing parents' disadvantages for their children."[56] These inequalities breed the sense of hopelessness that is so prevalent in many

---

51   *Id.* at 8, 9.

52   *Id.* at 16.

53   *Our Equitable Future: A Roadmap for the Chicago Region*, Metropolitan Planning Council (2021) https://www.metroplanning.org/uploads/cms/documents/cost-of-segregation-roadmap.pdf.

54   THOMAS PIKETTY, CAPITAL IN THE TWENTIETH CENTURY (Harvard 2014); ROBERT REICH, SAVING CAPITALISM (Knopf 2015); JOSEPH STIGLITZ, THE PRICE OF INEQUALITY (W.W.Norton 2012).

55   THOMAS M. SHAPIRO, TOXIC INEQUALITY: HOW AMERICA'S WEALTH GAP DESTROYS MOBILITY, DEEPENS THE RACIAL DIVIDE & THREATENS OUR FUTURE (Basic Books 2017), p. 15.

56   *Id.* at 198.

residents of our most neglected neighborhoods.[57] Shapiro urges a combination of wealth building and racial justice to remedy the situation.[58]

III. TRUMP'S SOLUTION – "SEND IN THE FEDS"

The studies outlined above are admirable because they look at the broader social and economic forces at work that create the environment where violence occurs. They are a step ahead of the traditional response to violence, which is to call for tighter law enforcement and stronger penalties and punishment for the offenders. Citing the socio-economic factors that lead to crime has traditionally been tantamount to being soft on crime. The way to be tough on crime is to make offenders accept responsibility for their bad actions. This approach is not absolutely wrong, but it is only part of the solution.

Former President Donald Trump provoked alarm in Chicago by saying if Chicago does not get a handle on its murder problem, he will "send in the Feds."[59] If by this, he meant, as most persons assume he meant, sending in troops or other federal law enforcement personnel, he was constitutionally and politically in trouble. Constitutionally, because there would appear to be little constitutional basis for the federal government to intervene in local law enforcement by sending in federal personnel to perform peace-keeping functions.[60] Also,

---

57   *Id.* at 216.

58   *Id.* at 185.

59   *Trump tweets about Chicago gun violence, threatens to "send in the Feds,"* CBS News (January 24, 2017); Liam Ford, Trump *tweets about Chicago 'carnage,' says he may 'send in the Feds!' if not fixed,* Chi. Trib. Jan. 25, 2017. http://www.chicagotribune.com/news/local/breaking/ct-trump-chicago-carnage-tweet-20170124-story.html.

60   There is precedent for a president sending troops into Chicago to stop violence and the disruption of commerce in President Cleveland's response to the Pullman Strike. In re Debs, 158 U.S. 564 (1895). However, that decision was undercut by the Supreme Court's invalidation of President Truman's seizure of the steel mills to prevent a nationwide strike. Youngstown Sheet & Tube Co. v. Sawyer, 343 U.S. 579 (1952). Nor do the sending of troops by Presidents Eisenhower and Kennedy to enforce federal court orders in civil rights cases provide precedent. The Supreme Court has held that the Fourteenth Amendment does not give persons a right to federal protection if their right to life or liberty is taken through the inaction of state officials. DeShaney v. Winnebago County Dept. of Soc. Servs., 489 U.S. 189 (1989). Similarly, the Court's recent jurisprudence interpreting the Commerce Clause provide strong precedent against federal intervention when individual rights are at stake. United States v. Lopez, 514 U.S. 549 (1995); United States v. Morrison, 529 U.S. 598 (2000); National Federation of Independent Business v. Sibelius, 132 S. Ct. 2566 (2012).

Later after disturbances in 2020, Trump compromised with Chicato Mayor Lori Lightfoot so that federal law enforcement authorities worked with City and State officials to track and prosecute violent offend-

depending upon how it is done, sending in federal troops could violate the Posse Commitatus Act, which forbids the use of the military in domestic operations.[61] Politically, because his own political party and his own rhetoric did not favor federal intervention in matters that have been traditionally of state or local concern. If he meant that he will give Chicago money to fight violence, this is, of course, allowed through Congress' constitutional power to spend money for the general welfare.[62] How that money would have been spent and whether it would have further escalated the problem or provide a solution as proposed by the three studies above is not clear.

What is clear is that the Trump administration failed to curtail violence by police or in the community as demonstrated by the police murder of George Floyd and others throughout the United States in 2020 and 2021 and the protects that followed.

IV. CHICAGO AND THE NATION DID NOT JUST GET THIS WAY – LONG ESTABLISHED PROBLEMS

Chicago did not just wake up one day and find itself to be segregated. Segregation in Chicago, like in much of the rest of the country, resulted from intentional policies and practices over the years. Even when the policies and practices were not overtly intentional, they were often followed without any consideration of their effect in perpetuating segregation.

Chicago is among the top five or six most segregated cities in the United States.[63] Chicago experienced the great migration of African Americans to the

---

ers. https://www.justice.gov/usao-ndil/pr/us-attorney-s-office-provides-update-federal-prosecutions-and-strategies-combat-violent.

61 18 U.S.C. §1385. See United States v. Dreyer, 804 F. 3d 1266 (9th Cir. 2015).

62 U.S. Constitution, Art. 1, Sec. 1, cl. 1. While the federal government can give the states money for law enforcement and social programs, it cannot compel them through threatening the loss of non-program funds to initiate programs that they find objectionable. *Sibelius*, 132 S. Ct. 2566 (2012).

63 This section is recycled from my chapter, Michael P. Seng, *Restorative Justice and Housing Discrimination*, in RESTORATIVE JUSTICE IN PRACTICE – A HOLISTIC APPROACH (Murphy & Seng, editors, Vandeplas Pub., 2015). Much of this section is based on a study undertaken by The John Marshall Law School Fair Housing Legal Support Center. John Marshall L. Sch. Fair Hous. Leg. Support Ctr., *Segregation in the Chicago Metropolitan Area – Some Immediate Measures to Reverse this Impediment to Fair Housing* (May 1, 2013) http://www.jmls.edu/fairhousing/pdf/2013-chicago-segregation-study.pdf.

North in the first half of the 20th century.[64] African Americans found defined boundaries where they could live. Some of these boundaries were set through official action, such as through policies followed by the Chicago Housing Authority,[65] and others were set privately, especially through the use of restrictive covenants.[66] Segregation defined Chicago's neighborhoods, and it carried over into commercial life, job opportunities, schools, and political representation.

Chicago's neighborhoods were further defined by religion and ethnicity. Nicknames given to communities that reflect their ethnicity still carry over today even though the religion or ethnicity of the neighborhood has changed.[67] When neighborhood boundaries were breached this was met with resistance and sometimes by violence. Because of market restrictions, African Americans were subject to fraud and exploitation.[68] Lending and insurance practices, policies followed by the Federal Housing Administration, and the actions of brokers, appraisers, and homeowner's associations all combined to keep Chicago segregated and African Americans confined to deteriorating areas.[69]

Thus, segregation in Chicago was carried on over the years through both private and public action. Segregated housing patterns once established are not easy to erase. Indeed, many of the neighborhoods that were redlined or subject to restrictive covenants retain their racial identity today.[70]

---

64 ALLEN H. SPEAR, BLACK CHICAGO: THE MAKING OF A NEGRO GHETTO (U. Chicago Press 1967); NICHOLAS LEMANN, THE PROMISED LAND (Vintage Books 1991); ISABEL WILKERSON, THE WARMTH OF OTHER SUNS (Random House 2010); JOE ALLEN, PEOPLE WASN'T MADE TO BURN (Haymarket Books 2011).

65 *See* Gautreaux v. Chicago Housing Authority, 501 F.2d 324 (7th Cir. 1974) (Chicago and the federal government were accused of creating segregated housing patterns through their siting of housing developments.)

66 *See* BERYL SATTER, FAMILY PROPERTIES: RACE, REAL ESTATE, AND THE EXPLOITATION OF BLACK URBAN AMERICA (Metropolitan Books 2009); RICHARD R. BROOKS & CAROL M. ROSE, SAVING THE NEIGHBORHOOD (Harvard U. Press 2013).

67 For instance, the Czech Pilsen neighborhood has become Mexican, and Little Italy is now the site of the University of Illinois in Chicago campus.

68 *Ibid*; Clark v. Universal Builders, 501 F.2d 324 (7th Cir. 1974) (the "contract buyers" case).

69 NATALIE MOORE, THE SOUTH SIDE (St. Martin's Press 2016); Satter, *supra* note 66.

70 An excellent study connecting redlining with contemporary predatory lending practices in Sacramento is Jesus Hernandez, *Redlining Revisited: Mortgage Lending Patterns in Sacramento 1930-2004*, 33 INT'L J. OF URBAN AND REGIONAL RESEARCH 291 (June 2009). *See also,* Jesus Hernandez, *Race, Market Constraints, and the Housing Crisis: A Problem of Embeddedness*, 1 KALFOU, A Journal of Comparative and Relational Ethic Studies 29 (Fall 2014). (discussing the high concentration of unsustainable mortgage products in predominantly non-white neighborhoods that have a history of racialized credit lending practices.)

It was not until 1968 that federal law was clarified that private housing discrimination was illegal. The Supreme Court reexamined the Civil Rights Act of 1866[71] and held that Congress meant what it said. The Court held that all persons had the right to own or lease real property free of both private and public racial discrimination and that the Thirteenth Amendment was the source of Congress' power.[72] For the first time, the Court recognized that racial discrimination was a "badge or incident of slavery" for which Congress could provide a remedy under Section 2 of the Thirteenth Amendment.[73]

Also in 1968, Congress passed the Fair Housing Act that broadly prohibited many, but not all, discriminatory housing practices based on race, color, religion, and national origin.[74] Later Congress amended the Act to add sex[75] and, in 1988, familial status (defined as families with children under the age of 18) and handicap (or disability) as protected classes.[76] The Fair Housing Act reaches private discrimination as well as discrimination through governmental action.[77] It prohibits intentional discrimination as well as policies and practices that have a discriminatory impact.[78] The Department of Housing and Urban Development has adopted a regulation implementing the disparate impact standard.[79] Even before the Supreme Court's decision in June 2015 finally upholding the impact standard, all the federal courts of appeal had held disparate impact to be an appropriate theory of liability under the Fair Housing Act.[80]

---

71   42 U.S.C. §1982. The present codification of §1982 reads: "All citizens of the United States shall have the same right, in every State and Territory, as is enjoyed by white citizens thereof to inherit, purchase, lease, sell, hold, and convey real and personal property."

72   Jones v. Alfred H. Meyer Co., 392 U.S. 409 (1968).

73   *Id.* at 443.

74   Pub. L. 90-284, 82 Stat. 73 (1968), 42 U.S.C. § 3600 *et seq.*

75   Pub. L. 93-383, §808(b), 88 Stat. 633, 729 (1974).

76   Pub. L. 100-430, 102 Stat. 1619 (1988).

77   42 U.S.C. § 3603.

78   Texas Department of Housing and Community Affairs v. Inclusive Communities Project, 1335 S. Ct. 2507 (2015). The case concerned how the State of Texas allocates Low Income Housing Tax Credits. Justice Kennedy recognized that once established, segregated housing patterns are not easily eradicated. Therefore, policies that perpetuate segregation and that are "artificial arbitrary and unnecessary barriers" to housing choice are illegal.

79   Implementation of the Fair Housing Act's Discriminatory Effects Standard, 78 Fed. Reg. 11460-01 (Feb. 15, 2013).

80   Texas Department of Housing and Community Affairs v. Inclusive Communities Project, 135 S. Ct. 2507 (2015). Important earlier opinions adopting the disparate impact standard included Metropoli-

Chicago and Illinois played an important role in bringing about the passage of the Fair Housing Act. A report by the National Advisory Commission on Civil Disorders that was appointed by President Johnson and headed by Illinois Governor Otto Kerner described America as moving toward two separate and distinct societies divided by race.[81] Also, Congress passed the Fair Housing Act as a memorial to Dr. Martin Luther King following his assassination in April 1968. It was through Chicago that Dr. King became an advocate for fair housing. In 1966, Dr. King led an open housing campaign in Chicago. It was his first civil rights initiative outside the South. He met with both official and private resistance. He allegedly remarked that he had never experienced such manifest racial hatred as he saw in Chicago.[82]

However, the passage of civil rights laws did not reverse the legacy of segregation in Chicago. The city remains segregated today as demonstrated by the recent study of the Metropolitan Planning Council.[83]

The economic meltdown and the foreclosure crisis that began in 2007 has only exasperated the problem. Because many African Americans—even African Americans who were qualified—were shut out of the prime lending market and steered to subprime loans, the foreclosure crisis hit them particularly hard.[84]

Additionally, many renters in Chicago are minorities, and many have been displaced because the properties they rented went into foreclosure.[85]

---

tan Housing Development Corp. v. Village of Arlington Heights, 558 F.2d 1283 (7th Cir. 1977), *cert. denied*, 434 U.S. 1025 (1978) and Huntington Branch, NAACP v. Town of Huntington, 844 F.2d 926 (2d Cir. 1988), *aff'd, per curiam*, 488 U.S. 15 (1988).

81 REPORT OF THE NATIONAL ADVISORY COMMISSION ON CIVIL DISORDERS (1968) https://www.ncjrs.gov./pdffiles1/digitization/8073ncjrs.pdf.

82 DAVID GARROW, BEARING THE CROSS (William Morrow 1986); ALAN B. ANDERSON & GEORGE W. PICKERING, CONFRONTING THE COLOR LINE: THE BROKE PROMISE OF THE CIVIL RIGHTS MOVEMENT IN CHICAGO (U. Georgia Press 1986); JAMES R. RALPH, JR., NORTHERN PROTEST (Harvard U. Press 1993); TAYLOR BRANCH, AT CANAAN'S EDGE: AMERICA IN THE KING YEARS, 1965-68 (Simon & Schuster 2006).

83 *The Cost of Segregation*, Metropolitan Planning Council (March 31, 2017) http://www.metroplanning.org/costofsegregation/default.aspx?utm_source%2fcostofsegregation

84 *Ibid. See* Christine Vidmar, *Seven Ways Foreclosures Impact Communities* (NeighborWorks America 2008) (available at http://www.nw.org/network/neighborworksprogs/foreclosuresolutions/reports/documents/7ForeclosureImpacts.pdf; Lawyers' Committee for Better Housing, *Three Year Impact Assessment: Apartment Building Foreclosures and the Depletion of Rental Housing in Chicago – Fact Sheet*, http://lcbh.org/wp-content/uploads/2012/07/LCBH-Three-Year-Impact-Assessment-Apartment-Building-Foreclosures-and-the-Depletion-of-Rental-Housing-in-Chicago_Fact-Sheet.pdf. (Outlining the negative effects that foreclosures have on the broader community).

85 Rebecca Burns, *The house that Jim Crow built*, THE CHICAGO READER (March 2, 2017); James H. Carr

This contributes to the cycle of diminishing the supply of housing available to minority residents, who often are forced to live with family members or in shelters. The foreclosure crisis has effectively stripped the wealth from minority communities.[86]

Because it took many years to reach where Chicago is today and because much of Chicago's segregation is due to intentional discrimination, or at best indifference toward people of color and lower income individuals, affirmative steps will be necessary if Chicago is ever to achieve any real integration. We cannot ignore history. Nor can we believe that by simply following neutral policies in the future, the effects of the past will be undone.[87] What is true of Chicago is true for most of America.

V. REMEDIES – THE STRUCTURAL LAWSUIT; NON-VIOLENT PROTEST; AND RESTORATIVE JUSTICE

Three important remedies are available to fight segregation and discrimination. Two of them originated during the civil rights struggle in the 1950s and 1960s, and one is quite new, at least in the civil rights context.

First, Thurgood Marshall and the NAACP Legal Defense Fund pioneered the structural lawsuit to secure civil rights in the United States.[88] The structural lawsuit came into its own in *Brown v. Board of Education*,[89] which held that education is perhaps the most important function of state and local government, that children cannot get an equal education in a segregated school, and that segregated schools are inherently unequal.

& Katrin B. Anacker, *White Paper: Long Term Social Impacts and Financial Costs of Foreclosure on Families and Communities of Color* (Nat'l Cmty. Reinvestment Coalition 2012)

http://www.ncrc.org/images/stories/pdf/research/wp_aecf_final10312012.pdf. Maya Dukmasova, *South Shore is Chicago's eviction capital*, THE CHICAGO READER (April 17, 2017)

86 *Ibid.*

87 Texas Department of Housing and Community Affairs v. Inclusive Communities Project, 135 S. Ct. 2507, 2525 (2015).

88 MICHAEL P. SENG AND F WILLIS CARUSO, *Achieving Integration Through Private Litigation*, THE INTEGRATION DEBATE: COMPETING FUTURES FOR AMERICAN CITIES (Chester Hartman & Gregory D. Squires, eds. Routledge 2010); Owen Fiss, *The Supreme Court 1978 Term: The Forms of Justice*, 93 HARV. L. REV. 1 (1979); Abram Chayes, *The Role of the Judge in Public Law Litigation*, 89 HARV. L. REV. 1281 (1976).

89 347 U.S. 483 (1954).

While the objective of *Brown* has not been achieved in public education in Chicago,[90] the structural lawsuit has been used successfully not only to fight racial discrimination,[91] but to secure equal rights for women,[92] persons with disabilities,[93] and the LGBT community.[94] It provides a path to protect immigrants and refugees. The structural lawsuit has been under attack since it was first used, and since the 1960s, United States Supreme Court opinions have weakened but not destroyed its impact.[95] Nonetheless, civil rights litigation still offers a means to change society. Indeed, America's resort to the courts for justice is an example for the world.

A second means to achieve change is through protest movements. Martin Luther King and the Southern Christian Leadership Conference developed non-violence as a technique for peaceful protest.[96] Non-violence played and continues to play an important role in securing civil rights in the United States and inspiring peace movements around the world. Non-violence has been attacked as unrealistic and naïve, but it offers hope and sanity and a prospect for permanent change.

A third movement is underway. The restorative justice movement takes inspiration from Archbishop Desmond Tutu and the Peace and Reconciliation Commission in South Africa.[97] Restorative justice offers a comprehensive solution to antisocial actions, including civil rights violations, by focusing on the relationships between individuals and on their relationship to the community.

---

90 Ronald Brownstein, *Why Poverty and Segregation Merge at Public Schools*, THE ATLANTIC (Nov. 12 2015) https://www.theatlantic.com/politics/archive/2015/11/why-poverty-and-segregation-merge-at-public-schools/433380/. Steve Bogira, *Trying to make separate equal*, THE CHICAGO READER (June 13, 2013).

91 Michael P. Seng, *The Cairo Experience: Civil Rights Litigation in a Racial Powder Keg*, 61 U. ORE. L. REV. 285 (1982).

92 United States v. Virginia, 518 U.S. 515 (1996).

93 City of Cleburne v. Cleburne Living Center, 473 U.S. 432 (1985).

94 Obergefell v. Hodges, 135 U.S. 2584 (2015).

95 Missouri v. Jenkins, 515 U.S. 70 (1995); Seng, *The Cairo Experience, supra* n. 83; ERWIN CHEMERINSKY, CLOSING THE COURTHOUSE DOORS: HOW YOUR CONSTITUTIONAL RIGHTS BECAME UNENFORCEABLE (Yale U. Press 2017).

96 Martin Luther King, Jr., *Letter from a Birmingham Jail* (April 16, 1963) https://www.africa.upenn. edu/Articles_Gen/Letter_Birmingham.html.

97 DESMUND TUTU, NO FUTURE WITHOUT FORGIVENESS (Doubleday 1999), MINOW, BETWEEN VENGEANCE AND FORGIVENESS: FACING HISTORY AFTER GENOCIDE AND MASS VIOLENCE (Beacon Press 1998); Sarah Ester Maslin, *El Salvodor's Ghost Town*, THE NATION, p. 20 (April 17, 2017).

The restorative justice movement seeks techniques to transform individuals and communities by repairing the harm done by criminal and anti-social behavior.

Thus, restorative justice is the ideal tool to confront the problems associated with violence in Chicago. The restorative justice tool does not reject the possibility of a structural lawsuit, and indeed, the threat of a structural lawsuit may well be a motivating force to activate the restorative justice process. Ultimately, a voluntary, bottom-up remedy specifically designed to implement restorative justice may be more efficient in achieving the dismantling of segregation than a top-down federal court injunction.

Similarly, restorative justice is a form of nonviolence that is structured to achieve a lasting solution. The South African Truth and Reconciliation Commission and similar efforts aimed to transform society through a peaceful, non-violent process. Restorative justice is the natural fulfillment of the litigation and protests against civil rights violations that were initiated in the 1960s.

VI. THE RESTORATIVE JUSTICE TRIANGLE

Restorative justice remedies have been successful because they seek a holistic solution. Restorative justice is frequently described though a triangle. On one side is the perpetrator; on the second side is the victim, often described as the survivor; and on the third side is the community. All are parties to a restorative justice solution.

a. The perpetrator

Restorative justice focuses on the offender, or the perpetrator.[98] It looks to the root of the misbehavior and demands accountability. It sets up a plan for the offender to repair the harm done.

---

[98] In discussing the discretion given to federal judges when imposing a sentence under the Federal Sentencing Guidelines, the United States Supreme Court held that a district judge may consider evidence of the defendant's postsentencing rehabilitation and adjust the sentencing guidelines downward. Pepper v. United States, 131 S.Ct. 1229, 1239-40 (2011). Justice Sotomayer stated that the federal tradition has allowed the sentencing judge "to consider every convicted person as an individual and every case as a unique study in the man failings that sometimes mitigate, sometimes, magnify, the crime and the punishment to ensue." In making this determination, judges have "broad discretion to consider various kinds of information." 18 U.S.C. § 3577.

Our current criminal justice system looks at the perpetrator from a strictly punitive perspective.[99] We too often equate prison time with punishment, and the focus is how long? Rehabilitation has ceased to have any meaning in our criminal justice system. Similarly, if the purpose of our criminal justice system is deterrence, we are not accomplishing that goal very well either. Even outside the criminal realm, our focus in the civil area is not very creative. We seldom move beyond trying to pin a dollar amount on the damages caused by a tort-feasor.

Policies that seek only to punish offenders have been singularly unsuccessful. They are not only ineffective; they are costly. The overwhelming subjects of our criminal justice system are persons of color. These findings are presented in a number of recent books.[100] These books differ about the causes for the increased incarceration of persons of color, but they agree that our current system is broken and is not subject to easy repair. Michelle Alexander in her bestselling book, The New Jim Crow, largely places the blame on racism and the war on drugs.[101] John Pfaff in his recent book, Locked In, places the blame on tough political talk and prosecutorial discretion.[102] James Forman, Jr. reminds us that much of the push that resulted in the current crisis came from a tough on crime movement that originated in black neighborhoods that were affected by crime.[103] Once someone is involved in the criminal justice system that person is disabled for life, finding it difficult to secure a job or a home and sometimes disqualified from exercising his or her political rights as well.[104]

---

99   The United States Supreme Court has recognized that the adoption of a penological theory is a matter of choice for the legislature. Ewing v. California, 538 U.S. 11, 25-26 (2003). In upholding California's Three Strikes and You're Out" law, Justice O'Connor stated that "Recidivism is a serious public concern in in California and throughout the Nation" and that "incapacitation and deterrence" were proper rationales for recidivism statutes.

100 MICHELLE ALEXANDER, THE NEW JIM CROW (The New Press 2012); TA-NEHISI COATES, BETWEEN THE WORLD AND ME (Random House 2015); JAMES FORMAN, JR., "LOCKING UP OUR OWN: CRIME AND PUNISHMENT IN BLACK AMERICA" (Farrar Straus Giroux 2017); CHRIS HAYES, A COLONY IN A NATION (W.W.Norton & Co. 2017); JOHN F. PFAFF, LOCKED IN: THE TRUE CAUSES OF MASS INCARCERATION AND HOW TO ACHIEVE REAL REFORM (Basic Books 2017); BRYAN STEVENSON, JUST MERCY (Random House 2014).

101 ALEXANDER, supra n. 100. See also, STEVENSON, supra n. 100; COATES, supra n. 100.

102 PFAFF, supra, n. 100.

103 FORMAN, supra n. 100.

104 The impact of criminal charges on persons of color and other classes protected by the Fair Housing Act, 42 U.S.C. §3601 et seq., has been recognized by the United States Department of Housing and Urban Development in its recent guidance against imposing blanket restrictions making housing

Our present system breeds resentment and not responsibility. Restorative justice holds perpetrators responsible for the consequences of their actions. It makes perpetrators see the harm that they have done and ideally requires them to work out a solution to repair that harm. Restorative justice does not mean that there is no punishment. What it does mean is that the perpetrator must acknowledge the wrong and make amends, when possible. Accountability is thus the byword. Restorative justice is creative and it is healthy. It does not seek to stigmatize the offender. It places the crime and the offender in context and seeks to restore the offender to a good, productive life.

b. The victim or survivor

Restorative justice also focuses on the victim, or the survivor. The history of American criminal law is to exclude the victim from the equation except as a witness. The parties in a criminal case are the perpetrator and the state. However, victims have demanded to be heard and the strength of restorative techniques is that the victim is brought into the process.

Identifying the victim is an important part of the process. Restorative justice does not view the object of the crime as being the only victim. Victims may be family members and others who are affected by the anti-social actions of the perpetrator. For example, the perpetrator's children who will be left without parents if the perpetrator is sent away to prison are true victims of the offense.

How to make someone whole is not always readily apparent. One cannot undo a murder, for instance. Nonetheless, consideration must be given to the victim's or survivor's feelings and some type of pay-back will be required even if it is general community service. This payback is not only important to making the victim whole, it is important to making the perpetrator whole. It helps remove the stigma and shame that can be poisonous and that can weigh on the perpetrator and lead to further antisocial conduct.

Perhaps the most difficult question when confronting restorative justice is whether forgiveness of the perpetrator by the victim is necessary. Forgiveness is certainly the ideal. Forgiveness should be the aim of all restorative techniques. Forgiveness completes the circle. It makes the victim whole by removing

---

unavailable to ex-offenders. Office of General Counsel Guidance on Application of Fair Housing Standards to the Use of Criminal Records by Providers of Housing and Real Estate-Related Transactions (April 4, 2016).

resentment from the victim's heart. To the extent possible, the parties should work toward forgiveness.

But forgiveness is hard and often takes considerable time to achieve. Forgiveness should not hold up the process. It is unfair to punish indefinitely a perpetrator who wishes to make amends simply because the victim cannot find the heart to reach out to the perpetrator. I do not believe that forgiveness is absolutely necessary in such circumstances. But I do believe it must be the goal of the process. A more important part of the process is that perpetrators must forgive themselves in order to move on. The shame must be removed to restore the offender to full health. But we must view restorative justice as not only an end, it is a process. We work toward forgiveness even if we do not achieve it.

The classic journey to forgiveness is told by Jean Bishop, who forgave her sister's and brother-in-law-s murderer and ended up visiting him in prison.[105] This was not an easy journey, but it is the ideal that restorative justice seeks.

Another classic example is Lisa D. Daniels, whose son Darren was shot in a drug-related murder in Chicago. Ms. Daniel read her victim impact statement at the sentencing hearing of the young man who plead guilty of second degree murder over her son's death. Her statement expresses the ideals of restorative justice:

> "Bishop Desmond Tutu is quoted as saying: 'my humanity is bound up in yours, for we can only be human together.' I believe that statement to be true. I believe that we are all connected by our humanity and I cannot speaker for my son's humanity without speaking for the same humanity of the man who, by one really bad decision, took his life."

Ms. Daniels told the court what her son meant to her and to his children. She said that her hope was that her son would not be remembered for his worst mistake and that she recognized that the result of the encounter could just as easily have been reversed so that her son would have been the defendant and the defendant would have lost his life. She ended her statement by asking the judge to show leniency.

In pronouncing the sentence, the judge altered the originally agreed 15 years sentence to 7.5 years plus time served. As he left the courtroom, the defendant

---

105 Jeanne Bishop has written accounts of her journey. JEANNE BISHOP, CHANGE OF HEART (Westminster John Knox Press 2016); Jeanne Bishop, *The Shock of True Forgiveness*, RESTORATIVE JUSTICE IN PRACTICE: A HOLISTIC APPROACH (Murphy & Seng, editors, Vandeplas Pub., 2015).

turned to Ms. Daniels and looked into her eyes and said, "Thank you." She burst into tears but one month later she wrote him a letter assuring him that she meant what she said and that she would assist him in his re-entry process. Ms. Daniels has now started the Darren B. Easterling Center for Restorative Justice that will serve as a trauma recovery center on the South Side of Chicago to help young people avoid the fate of her son and his shooter.

This is the ideal that restorative justice aims for and sometimes achieves. The survivor is made whole to the extent possible by reaching out in forgiving the perpetrator. The perpetrator is made whole by making amends for his or her misconduct.

c. The community

Restoration between the offender and the survivor will only take us so far. We must also recognize the responsibility of the community and ensure that the conditions that led to the antisocial behavior are corrected. This means confronting discrimination and violence and working to change the environment that produced them whether it be in the areas of employment, education, housing, law enforcement, health care, or political representation.

Community itself is a flexible concept. It may be a circle of family or friends or neighborhood residents. Hawaii does 'Ohana conferencing where in juvenile cases the entire family is brought into the process – parents, grandparents, aunts and uncles, and whoever else is part of the extended family. They discuss the situation and together come up with a solution that generally involves the entire group.[106] The process respects Hawaiian culture and provides an extended sounding board for reaching a solution. Because everyone is involved in making the plan a success, the group is more likely to achieve the results agreed upon.

In school settings, participation may be extended to include teachers, administrators, staff, or other students – whoever has a stake in correcting the misbehavior. If the injury affects the neighborhood, involving those who live or work in the neighborhood may be helpful if done in a respectful and restorative

---

106 Wilma Friesema, *Restoring Connections: Hawaiian Values and the EPIC 'Ohana, Inc. Programs that Serve the Children and Families in Hawaii's foster Care System*, RESTORATIVE JUSTICE IN PRACTICE: A HOLISTIC APPROACH (Murphy & Seng, editors 2015); *See also* Martha Mills, *Why Restorative Justice? And, Less Straightforward, How Did I Get There?* RESTORATIVE JUSTICE IN PRACTICE: A HOLISTIC APPROACH (Murphy & Seng, editors 2015) (discussing how restorative justice was used to solve a dispute between teenagers who destroyed a fish house and the owners of the fish house and the community.)

manner and not just to shame the offender. Involving police and other public officials may be important to bring them into the solution and also to educate them about the problems in the community and the personal situation of the offender. If the offender acted because he or she did not have a job or had an addiction problem, involvement of the entire community may be necessary to assist in changing the environment that produced the conduct.

Furthermore, lawyers should be educated in restorative justice. Lawyers should be familiar with restorative justice techniques as a form of alternative dispute resolution. Lawyers can also bring unique insights into the process, and when structural impediments stand in the way of achieving a just solution, lawyers are trained how to remove those impediments whether by filing a lawsuit or advocating for change in a legislative or administrative forum.[107]

Restorative justice cannot be separated from civil rights, and sometimes the two can be effective partners in establishing enduring and healthy relationships.

Restorative justice thus may lead to truly effective ways to confront neighborhood problems, especially if the demands are taken to city hall or to the local school board, or if local residents band together to sue a property owner who is allowing vacant property to be used for illegal purposes. Restorative justice cannot be successful in a vacuum. It requires community involvement, and if something is standing in the way of the community and its residents from achieving their potential, then the restorative justice process provides an ideal forum to discuss the solution to the problem and a springboard for action.

The community itself is benefitted by the reform of the offender and the restoration of the victim, but the community must accept its own responsibility in producing the offense, and if the causes of violence and misbehavior come, at least in part, because of conditions in the community, the community must take action to correct the situation. Communities have real personalities, and they cannot be neglected in the restorative justice process.

VII. IMPLEMENTING RESTORATIVE JUSTICE IN CHICAGO

In many respects, Chicago is taking a lead in implementing restorative justice, which makes it an interesting time to be practicing law in Chicago. Other cities

---

107 A number of legislative and administrative reforms are suggested by SHAPIRO, TOXIC INEQUALITY, *supra* n.55.

are likewise creating innovative solutions to solve the problems created by violence and similar anti-social activities. Now is not a time for despair. Now is a time of opportunity to advance new agendas.

Restorative justice provides a unique opportunity to create solutions from the bottom up. Restorative justice focuses on the immediate problem in a specific context, and it allows those affected by the problem to provide solutions. We do not have to look to Washington. Often we do not even look to State government. Restorative justice remedies rely upon local communities for implementation. The remedies fit local needs and the work being done by private and faith-based organizations located in the neighborhoods.

Chicago has established a Restorative Justice Community Courts in the West Lawndale, Englewood, and Avondale neighborhoods. These courts allow youth involved in non-violent offenses to appear before a judge to seek a restorative solution.[108] The judges, public defenders, and prosecutors are all trained in restorative justice techniques. The purpose is to divert cases away from the criminal court and to give those accused of offenses an opportunity to become productive members of society free from the stigma of a criminal record. The courts started as a pilot project, but they have led to establishing similar courts in other neighborhoods. These courts will supplement some of the work already done in specialized courts that focus on addiction problems, prostitution, and veterans.

Local federal judges have initiated a reentry program, the James B. Moran Second C.H.A.N.C.E. Program, where persons released from federal prison elect to participate.[109] Participants meet in bi-monthly sessions with a federal judge, federal prosecutor, federal defender, a representative of the parole service and a trained counselor to discuss the problems they are having in reentering society after serving time in prison. The sessions are very therapeutic and encouraging. Participants share their experiences in confronting social, employment and other challenges. They set individualized goals and that encourage them to follow a crime-free, drug-free lifestyle and these goals are enforced by positive

---

108 Mary L. Datcher, *Cook County Circuit Court Wins Grant to Create Community Court*, CHICAGO DEFENDER (April 4, 2014) https://chicagodefender.com/2016/04/14/cook-county-circuit-court-wins-grant-to-create-community-court/. The courtroom was dedicated on July 20 and was set to open on August 31, 2017. CHICAGO SUN TIMES (July 21, 2017, p. 10).

109 Joan Gottschall & Molly Armour, *Second Chance: Establishing a Reentry Program in the Northern District of Illinois*, 5 DEPAUL J. FOR SOC. JUST. 31 (2011); Martha Neil, *2 Federal Judges Work with Ex-Cons in Chicago Re-Entry Program*, ABA JOURNAL (August 16, 2012), http://www.abajournal.com/news/article/federal_judges_work_with_ex-cons_in_chicago_re-entry_program/.

and negative consequences. Persons who complete the program participate in a "graduation" ceremony. The program provides an encouraging bridge between incarceration and return to society.

Several years ago, the Chicago public school system made restorative justice an official policy of the Chicago public schools.[110] Restorative justice has not been implemented evenly in all schools, but at least some schools have implemented restorative programs to deal with truancy and disciplinary problems. The Chicago Department of Public Health recognizes that violence and the trauma it produces is a public health concern and, therefore, impacts on student performance in school.[111]

Community organizations have formed restorative justice hubs in the neighborhoods.[112] The hubs create a safe and healthy space where youth are welcomed and supported. The hubs are especially important because they serve those young people who are no longer in school.

Colleges, universities and law schools are teaching restorative justice to their students. The UIC John Marshall Law School has initiated a course in restorative justice and as part of the course students are required to do an externship in the community.[113] The majority of these law students are going into neighborhoods noted for their gang activity and violence and are working with elementary and high school students on truancy and disciplinary issues. The results are not only changing the lives of the neighborhood residents but redirecting the goals and lives of the law students.

The Interfaith Committee of the Chicago Bar Association has been sending attorneys into Chicago schools to teach restorative techniques to teachers,

---

110 The Purpose section of the Student Code of Conduct for the Chicago Public Schools states that "Chicago Public Schools is committed to an instructive, corrective, and restorative approach to behavior. If behavior incidents arise that threaten student and staff safety or severely disrupt the educational process, the response should minimize the impact of the incident, repair harm, and address the underlying needs behind student behaviors. In accordance with the SCC, all disciplinary responses must be applied respectfully, fairly, consistently, and protect students' rights to instructional time whenever possible". http://policy.cps.edu/. *See also*, MAYOR'S COMMISSION FOR A SAFER CHICAGO, STRATEGIC PLAN FOR 2015, pp. 37-41.

111 MAYOR'S COMMISSION FOR A SAFER CHICAGO, STRATEGIC PLAN FOR 2015, pp. 31-35. A research letter in the Journal of the American Medical Association states that "Between 2004 and 2015, gun violence research was substantially underfunded and understudied relative to other leading causes of death, based on mortality rates of each cause." JAMA (January 3, 2017) http://jamanetwork.com/journals/jama/article-abstract/2595514.

112 Community restorative justice hubs, https://rjhubs.org/. Robert Koehler, *Restorative justice and the rebirth of Chicago*, CHI. TRIB., January 1, 2015. http://www.chicagotribune.com/news/columnists/.

113 The John Marshall Law School Restorative Justice Project, http://www.jmls.edu/restorative-justice/.

administrators and students.[114] The Catholic Lawyers' Guild along with other faith based legal groups successfully drafted and lobbied the Illinois legislature to pass a bill that provides a privilege in restorative justice practices. Significantly, the new law "encourages residents of the State to employ restorative justice practices, not only in justiciable matters, but in all aspects of life and law."[115] Also, the Catholic Lawyers Guild is working to introduce new restorative justice programs in some of the Catholic elementary and high schools.[116]

Each of these programs is making a contribution and together they will have an impact.

VIII. CONCLUSION

Restorative justice provides a promising answer to the violence and anti-social behavior that seems to be gripping our social institutions. It is the obvious successor to the social movements that started with the civil rights struggle in the mid-Twentieth Century.

What is so healthy about restorative justice is its focus. It is not narrowly focused on the offender. Nor is it narrowly focused on the victim. It is a community based movement that seeks to transform the entire community. The focus on individual responsibility is not lost, but it is kept in perspective.

Restorative justice offers promise that we can have a more harmonious society where everyone feels interconnected and where we feel safe, but also confident that we are seeking fairness along the way. Restorative justice provides us with a path that we can use on our journey to assure civil rights to all human beings.

---

114 Letter from the President of the Chicago Bar Association (May 23, 2013). http://www.metrocorp-counsel.com/letters/23953/letter-president-chicago-bar-association.

115 SB 64 and HB 3248 were approved by both chambers and were sent to the governor for his signature on May 20, 2021. https://www.ilga.gov/legislation/102/HB/PDF/10200HB3248.pdf.

116 CLG Restorative Justice Project, http://www.clgchicago.org/restorative-justice-project/.

How does segregation affect each of our daily lives today regardless of who we are or where we live?

To what extent is each of us personally responsible for the social problems that exist in our society today?

What can each of us do to provide a remedy for the social problems that exist in our society that are the result of a long history of racist and discriminatory practices?

In *Grutter v. Bollinger*, 539 U.S. 306 (2003), the United States Supreme Court opinion upheld the University of Michigan Law School's policies that used race as a criteria for admission. In her opinion for the Court, Justice Sandra Day O'Connor stated that she expected "25 years from now [2028], the use of racial preferences will no longer be necessary to further the interest approved today [diversity in higher education]." Were Justice O'Connor's expectations reasonable for society-at-large or even for higher education?

How can we successfully use restorative justice techniques to mitigate racism and violence in our society?

How do we persuade the diverse sectors of our society to come to a circle as equals and civilly share their stories and interests and seek accord?

ALISON'S STORY: THE ROAD TO EMPOWERMENT AND SELF-AWARENESS

ALISON CHAN

THE BEGINNING

My parents immigrated to the United States from the beautiful island of Taiwan in 1992. My father was able to come over on a sponsored work visa. He arrived first to get settled, then my mother followed. Their American Dream led them to the Midwest, specifically, the suburbs of Chicago, Illinois. My parents did not know any English and picked their names randomly. I always wondered why my parents did not have Asian names like their friends and my mom said she wanted to be different. Their journey to assimilating into the American life began before they even arrived in the United States. My mom adopted the name Judy while she was in Taiwan and I am not too sure about my dad, but they are just two letters different – Andy and Judy.

Growing up, I had the quintessential American home: the white picket fence, the single-family house in the suburbs, with a dog and a happy family. I am fond of the memories my family created for me. I first learned Mandarin Chinese to communicate with my parents and simultaneously learned English watching TV and attending school to communicate with other kids my age. My parents learned English on TV and from the lessons my brothers and I learned from attending school to make their own transition into their new lives easier. We worked hard to learn English and were always taught to focus on academics, music, and sports. This work ethic was instilled in my brothers and I at a very young age. Being raised in the suburbs had its pros and cons. While we were one of approximately only 4-5 Asian families in our predominantly white neighborhood. I grew up playing with kids that did not have the same color of skin or experiences as me. However, it was not always easy to navigate through these differences. Throughout my years, growing up in this environment made me feel ashamed of my ethnic background because I was too different.

WHAT IS RACISM? I DON'T KNOW, BUT I WENT THROUGH IT.

There are specific instances of racism that I encountered from a very young age and still continue to experience in the present day. For example, I distinctly remember when I was in third grade and a white classmate made a weird gesture. He took his fingers and pulled the outer corners of his eyes in a slanted motion and made sounds like "ping dang dong." I knew deep down he was making fun of me. I do not remember what I did, but I do remember going home and telling my mom what happened – very confused. The next day, my mother went to talk to the teacher and the principal. My teacher talked to the class on how inappropriate the gesture was, and the boy apologized to me. To be honest, I did not remember my mother talking to the school nor the little boy apologizing to me. But I just remember knowing *what* he did was wrong but did not know *why*. While I knew that I was a victim of othering and discrimination, I didn't know at the time that this systemic phenomenon had a name: racism.

As the years went by and I continued navigating through the American education system, I felt the need to keep my head down, do well in school, sports, and any other extracurriculars in order to feel successful. I always knew I was different and couldn't act like the other students but did not really understand why. Specifically, I remember walking into art class in high school and this white male student would greet me saying, "Nagasaki, Mitsubishi, Suzuki, Konichiwa…" so on and so forth. I did not know what to do so I just laughed nervously and found my seat. This dragged on the entire semester. I remember feeling so belittled that I just kept my head down as I waited for the bell to ring to signal the end of class.

> "Asian-Americans, with their "solid two-parent family structures," are a shining example of how to overcome discrimination." – Andrew Sullivan

In 2008, my parents divorced, which is looked down upon in Asian culture. No matter what once you marry, you need to stay married. It does not matter the circumstances. If one divorces, the divorcee has a "stain" on their back. Little did I know back then, but my mother lost her close and only Asian friends once she divorced. They abandoned her at her lowest. I look back at the pictures and see how skinny and sad my mother was. I only wish I could have supported her and been a better daughter rather than rebelling because my parents were divorced.

In 2011, my mother remarried and moved us to San Francisco, California where she still lives. Little did I know, the Bay Area is very diverse compared to the Northwest suburb I grew up in. The majority of the population were people of color – specifically of Asian ethnicities. Although I looked like the student sitting next to me in class or the person at the grocery store, I felt extremely out of place. I felt very uncomfortable and that was when I realized that I was experiencing cultural shock. There was no one making fun of me at work or in the classroom. But now, I was fighting an inner battle because I still did not share the same experiences growing up as my peers. I looked like them, but I did not feel like I was Asian enough to fit in with our differences. My local high school was majority Asian, but the neighborhood we lived in, once again, was dominantly White, furthering the narrative that I did not belong anywhere. While I guess my mother just felt more comfortable in predominantly White neighborhoods, I never quite got to the same level of comfort as her.

A WHOLE NEW WORLD

I graduated from the University of Illinois, Urbana-Champaign in 2017. I was a transfer and prior to that, I attended community college in a predominantly white community. I knew no one when I arrived on campus and I signed a lease at a private, Catholic dormitory on campus. The community at the dormitory was once again predominantly White. It is weird, right? Although, I did not fit in growing up in a predominantly white neighborhood, I felt some sort of comfort bring in the same environment at the dormitory. Yet I felt like I did not fit in in the Bay Area when I looked like the person next to me. No matter where I was, I still did not feel like I completely fit in. It seemed like I was stuck in between the two worlds.

I majored in Psychology with a minor in Asian American studies—this minor was added later on due to a personal identity epiphany I experienced. My major was not diverse when it came to the race and ethnicity of the students. Once again, it was a predominantly white major. I tried to make friends but was not successful. No one seemed interested, except one girl (who was white) who I still talk to this day. We actually ended up working together to be trained as social justice paraprofessionals and we connected because we were both transfers. As mentioned, I later chose to minor in Asian American Studies in order to sit down and intentionally learn more about my ethnic roots in a way I haven't had the opportunity to before. My parents would not talk about Taiwan's history or Taiwan politics. I later learned it was because Taiwan was under martial law for 38 years (longest in the world) and it was a very traumatizing and sensitive period in Taiwan. I had to seek out other paths to learn more about the history of where my family came from. I minored in Asian American studies to really understand the Asian American history—which is often skipped over or reduced to a single paragraph in America's traditional history curriculum, and I attended an international conference during the summer where I had the opportunity to visit Taiwan and learn about its history and culture.

During my time at the University of Illinois, Urbana-Champaign, I tried to make friends by rushing for Panhellenic sororities—or what the students would call the "White sororities." Our campus had cultural sororities which were sororities for persons of color i.e. Asian, Latinx, etc. Truthfully, the experience of rushing the "White sororities" was a humiliating experience. No one wanted to talk to me and even if they did come up to talk to me, it did not feel genuine. No one took the time to try to get to know me. I felt like I had to put on this façade in order for at least one girl to like me because it was so visibly obvious that I was different from everyone else in the room. In order to try to cover this up, I just ended up being someone I was not. Putting up this constant manufactured act was emotionally taxing, so I decided to not finish the process and dropped out the second round. When I shared this experience with one of my friend's friend, she suggested that I rush an Asian sorority. Immediately I was like, "whoa whoa whoa, what?" That was definitely out of my comfort zone. But as we talked, I realized that I had to be open to new experiences, even if they scared me, or I would be spending the next two years alone on a campus with over 35,000 students.

Shortly after, I was connected with one of her sorority sisters and there was already a clear difference in the experience—and it seemed hopeful. She was very nice and took me out to dinner and took the time to get to know me on a personal level. I *finally* felt a bit welcomed. It was even more comforting when she gave me advice to be myself and not to worry about trying to impress the sisters. While I still felt that I did not exactly fit in with the sisterhood, I at least didn't feel like I had to hide every element of myself when rushing. The process was very hard, but I stuck with it until the end because I knew this was an opportunity I should not give up. Unfortunately, I did not receive a bid, but I still came out very thankful because that was the door that I was waiting to open – the door that led me to seeing what other opportunities existed in the rest of the large Asian American community on campus. This open door led me to not only meet my best friends, but also opened the door to exploring and embracing my identity as an Asian American woman, and one that was now prepared to fight injustice and racism. I was smarter now—I had the vocabulary to identify and combat the racism that I, and so many others, experienced and still continue to experience.

LAW SCHOOL? ME? NO WAY!

I never thought that I would want to be a lawyer. At a young age, my parents wanted me to be a doctor, lawyer, or something in STEM. This is stereotypical of the Asian culture because the myth of meritocracy gives the illusion of security in the form of a well-respected and high paying profession. I discovered early on in my life, I was horrible at math and science, but was always a good writer and reader. I started college majoring in Biology, and it was such a miserable experience. I struggled through pre-calculus. I remember having multiple break-downs and felt hopeless. I remember when I met with my school counselor to plan out my classes, all I saw in my future was math and science. I was terrified. I knew that I would be completely miserable and knew that I would not survive. I was raised to challenge myself and never give up, but I knew that there was a line that needed to be drawn. I drew that line. I took a break from school, went back to community college, and later graduated from University of Illinois, Urbana-Champaign.

As I was studying Psychology, I soon realized that I like to talk and argue, but resented research. I remember being a research assistant for a professor and he had me code with a program called "R." I remember studying late in the library for hours on how to use the program and still would not be able to grasp the pro-gram. Then, I had to perform tests for the professor to collect data for research. It was extremely boring and unmotivating. I was a year out from finishing my major, and it was pretty much time to decide what I would do after graduation. I had no idea what to do so I applied for the Peace Corps. I love to travel and give back to the community. I made it through the interviews, but unfortunately was not chosen to be a Peace Corp.

This is where the panic stepped in. Everyone around me knew what they were going to do after graduation and all I knew was that I did not know what to do. This was a very anxious period of time because I am a planner so having no plan or idea of a plan was very stressful. I called my mother panicking and she suggested that I go to law school. I laughed. As I got older, I always tried to do the opposite of what my mother wanted. I do not remember what led me to pursue law at that time, but before I knew it, I enrolled in a summer LSAT course and then took the LSAT that September of my senior year of undergrad. And the rest is history.

LAW SCHOOL CHANGED MY LIFE.

People say to treasure your four years in undergrad because they are the best years of your life. I look back to those years and I see what they mean. On the other hand, law school was like boot camp, but also the best three years of my life. I am going to be graduating in May and then start to prepare for the UBE Bar Exam. It seemed like the past three years flew by. The first year was the hardest. My friends and I joke that the first year brought out the worst in everyone. We were anxious, competitive, had low confidence, experienced major imposter syndrome, and had to learn a new language pretty much – the legal jargon.

Before starting law school, I worked at a law firm and volunteered at the first legal non-profit in the nation that serviced Asians and Asian Americans. Unfortunately, I did not get the score I wanted in the LSAT. So, I decided to take a year off to work in the legal field and study for the dreadful exam. During this time, I still continued my work in activism for the Asian and Asian American community while I was at the non-profit. While working at the law firm, I worked directly with injured clients. They were in a vulnerable and painful period in their life. They were worried about money and since they were not able to work, worried about how they would survive in the Bay Area. Specifically, I remember a few incidents we had at the law firm. Clients would be verbally abusive towards the office manager, paralegal and me. The office manager is Asian, and the paralegal is Latinx. Whenever the clients would be angry, they would yell at us saying that we do not understand them and cannot speak English. Then, they would request to speak to the attorney, who is White. It was an exhausting experience because clients reacted with their impulsive emotions which led them to act with bias against us because we appeared to be different and therefore in their eyes, incompetent. While the office manager would always try to take the hits for me and the paralegal, I knew this was wrong and unacceptable behavior to receive from clients. I guess the way I dealt with it was reminding myself that they are in a vulnerable position and frustrated. But, on the other hand, I tell myself that it is not okay to treat or talk to someone in such a demeaning manner.

Throughout law school, I do not recall specific traumatic incidents where I experienced racism. However, the media was full of incidents of racism. There was the Black Lives Matter Movement, #MeToo Movement, attacks on the Asian American community, immigrants at the border, and overtly racist President, and the list goes on. But I found myself not being able to take the time to reflect on what was going on around me. I was in my own bubble and I had the choice whether or not to react to it. It made me feel guilty because during my years at the University of Illinois, Urbana-Champaign, I found a passion for advocating for communities of color and injustices in the local community. I found a passion educating the AAPI community, my family, and my friends about how to address and identify microaggressions, recognizing their bias and how to be a better human being. I remember talking to my mentors and community leaders expressing how guilty I felt, but they always told me "it is okay," "you are just taking a break for yourself," etc. But I could not help feeling that if others are out there fighting for their lives and I could join them, why can't I? Law school is an all-encompassing experience. You have limited time for friends and family outside of law school. At least for me, I lost some friends along the way, but still had supportive friends that understood the journey I was taking.

During my last year of law school, a group of students, faculty, and staff felt the need to create a task force in response to the murder of George Floyd and other murders of Black youth and individuals in recent years. The Race & Justice Task Force was then established. This was the first time in my law school career that I finally felt like I came out of my bubble. I had a platform to address injustices and educate my local legal community. I was able to organize events and workshops to have a dialogue on recent events. I found it to be extremely rewarding and refreshing. It seemed like I was bottling all the racist events happening in the world and did not have a place to release the frustration and talk it through. The Race & Justice Task Force gave me that release. It seemed like my fellow students, professors, faculty and staff all felt some sort of relief during our dialogue. They all did not have a place organized for everyone to come together and just address the injustices in the world and in their lives.

I saw how important it was to listen to one another and how easy it was just to create a safe space for all to speak their minds.

Due to the pandemic, I was able to take a class on Restorative Justice at the University of Illinois in Chicago John Marshall Law School. This class, which I am still taking, provided me with the tools and reflection to be a better advocate and better human being. I aspire to be a criminal prosecutor and have been able to see how restorative justice can and does play a role in the criminal justice system. We have to learn to forgive and work together to move forward for the better of everyone. Help one another where it is needed. Educate and lead those for a brighter and hopeful future. As a law student and soon to be attorney, it feels as if there is not one solution to fight against systemic racism and it can get overwhelming. I know that these racial and systemic injustices will not be solved overnight, but I have a personal and community duty to continue to educate, build, and push through these barriers as a daughter of immigrants, Asian American woman, and soon to be attorney at law.

I will leave you with an inspiring quote from a woman I look up to and respect. She was an Asian American civil rights activist who worked with the Black Panthers to address injustices in the Black and Asian American community. Her name was Yuri Kochiyama.

> *"Remember that consciousness is power. Consciousness is education and knowledge. Consciousness is becoming aware. It is the perfect vehicle for students. Consciousness-raising is pertinent for power, and be sure that power will not be abusively used, but used for building trust and goodwill domestically and internationally. Tomorrow's world is yours to build."*

How have stereotypes and perceptions of others, both intentional and implicit, had an impact on me and on my relationships with others?

What can each of us do to ease the insecurities of others and to be sure that they feel welcome and included?

How can we educate and influence young children to be more sensitive and aware of the insecurities of others and to be more inclusive with those with different backgrounds?

To what extent are our own perceptions influenced by the backgrounds and traumas suffered by our parent and elders and how do we respect our legacy while breaking free from the shackles that are imposed on us by our families and immediate environment?

How can we burst our own "bubbles" and partake in the richness of our surroundings?

What are the similarities and differences between the Asian experience in the United States and that of other minority groups? Are they susceptible to similar solutions?

A Healing Journey: The Road to Reunification

WILMA FRIESEMA, EPIC `OHANA, INC.

When we think of restorative justice, we often think of a practice that brings reconciliation, fairness, and dignity back to relationships that have been damaged. Here in Hawai'i, the Hawaiian culture's restorative justice practice is called Ho'oponopono. Ho'o means to make something happen, and pono means righteousness and balance. Righteousness refers to rightness, integrity, and virtue, and balance to harmony within oneself, with others, the land, and with life. To repeat pono in the word ho'oponopono shows the importance of the righteousness and balance that is to be restored.[1]

In essence, ho'o points to an active process: we're coming together to return to righteousness and balance, but we're not there yet. It will take work; it will take effort. Similarly, we can think of restorative justice as restoring justice – an active, on-going process that will take time, commitment, and energy on everyone's part. Many restorative justice practices are, in truth, part of a longer journey, a healing journey, that participants travel in order to reach their destinations of dignity and well-being.

For parents engaged in the Child Welfare System (CWS), the healing journey of reunification is often a long, arduous undertaking that involves multiple restoring justice efforts. The road to reunification is not easy, and while each family has their own story, there are commonalities. This past year a Storytelling Committee, here at EPIC 'Ohana, Inc., looked at the reunification process in-depth and identified six stages that parents go through. While each parent's journey may not go in a straight line through these stages, understanding the stages, and the challenges and opportunities within each, can help restoring justice practitioners recognize the types of practices and support that will be most beneficial.

---

1 Thank you to Kehau Pe'a for sharing her knowledge of ho'oponopono.

Vivian Kim Seu was a teen when she gave birth to her first daughter, and was just 22 when her first two children were taken into foster care. Because her father had died when Vivian was nine, she, her mother, and her children were living at her grandmother's house. Young Vivian loved her daughters, but she was headstrong and searching for a love that was elusive. When CWS entered the picture, she didn't have a clue that she was about to begin a journey – a healing journey – which, despite its many twists and turns, would result in the sober and meaningful life she has today.

Brittney Mahelona and Kyle Masuda blindly embarked on their journeys as well. Brittney was incarcerated on drug related charges when she learned that her two girls had been taken into foster care and were placed with her parents. Likewise, Kyle Masuda, a dad of six boys, was in jail when his boys were separated from their mother and taken into care. It was the heartache of those losses, however, that fueled the determination for these three parents to get their children back.

EPIC's first identified stage of the reunification process starts at the very beginning, before CWS involvement. This is when the family unit is still intact. We call this phase: *The Journey Begins*. For our three parents, and others like them, life may not be perfect, but the family is together, attachment is growing, and there are moments and days that create lasting memories. For Kyle, the bonding started from day one with the life changing experience of his first son's birth. For Brittney, it grew through the precious daily interactions she shared with her daughters. For Vivian, treasured moments were days at the beach with her children and extended family. As with all families, it's the countless shared experiences, both large and small, that weave together a family's rich tapestry of love.

For restoring justice practitioners, taking the time to learn about the family's positive experiences prior to CWS involvement can help set the tone and foundation for the work ahead. This is true for whatever stage they, as a practitioner, enter the family's reunification process. Not only does learning about their positive history honor the bond the parent has with his or her children, it conveys the message that the practitioner see the parent as much more than their problems. It reminds them of what they've done right as a parent, as well as the joy and wonder of being a parent. This is especially important if they are unable, in that moment, to fully be a *safe* parent.

The second stage is entitled: *Tripping, Falling, and Stepping Back*. This is when CWS first steps in. The connection and love in the family is still there, but its stability has been usurped by the parent's struggles and personal issues. It's during this stage that life has taken a turn for the worse, and the challenges are now a crisis. For parents, this stage can begin months or years before CWS involvement.

For our three parents, drug addiction was the derailing factor; for others it can be mental health issues, domestic violence, poverty, a history of trauma and abuse, or a lack of adequate parenting skills. As CWS's intervention shines a light on the family's safety issues, many parents feel angry, overwhelmed, and defensive. This second stage is a very destabilizing time. For parents, the steps they are required to take are rarely easy, even if they are clarified in a Family Group Decision Making process such as Hawai'i's 'Ohana Conferences. For the family, life has been upended and it can feel overwhelming to move forward into new and unfamiliar territory.

For Vivian, this stage lasted a long time. As she describes it, it was like a rollercoaster. During this phase she hated her social worker and was determined to live life the way she wanted. She went through the motions of doing her services and would have short periods of sobriety, but she kept returning to using drugs to fill an inner void, to forget about reality. As a result, CWS got involved in her life four times.

Kyle was in prison in Florence, Colorado when he heard that his boys were taken into foster care. Feeling disheartened and disempowered by his circumstances, he was ready to give up. But it was his cellmate, Donald, another man from Hawai'i, who encouraged him to fight to get his kids back. Without Donald's consistent encouragement and belief in him, Kyle would have succumbed to despair. Likewise, Brittney was upset and felt like a failure when she heard her girls were taken into care, though she was relieved to learn they were placed with her parents.

During this stage, it is important for restoring justice practitioners — whether they be social workers, Guardian Ad Litems (GAL), or other service providers — to recognize and understand the vulnerability underneath the defenses and resistance, and to not take the resulting behaviors personally. It's important to engage with the parents as respectfully and collaboratively as possible, and to focus on identifying the parent's strengths. Practitioners want to be curious about what might be driving the parent's behavior, and explore the natural supports that they have in their lives. It's their natural supporters, after all, who may be able to convey a belief in the parent that strikes an inner chord which professionals just can't reach. For Kyle, it was someone from his own culture, his home, that could talk in a way he could really hear. Donald's belief in Kyle gave him strength to persevere against some very tough odds.

With time, patience, and support, parents can face the reality of their situation and move on to the third stage which we named: **Regaining Balance and Taking Steps Again.** During this stage parents are acclimating to the change and finding their footing. Their determination to get their children back is growing. For our three parents, parenting classes, drug treatment programs, transitional housing, and the Family Wrap Hawai'i program[2] were especially helpful. Those services, and many more, support the message that Hawai'i's CWS strives to give to all parents: CWS's foremost goal *is* for families to be reunified. During this stage, however, parents often have a hard time believing that's truly CWS's intent. They often have difficulty believing in themselves too, but seeds of hope and encouragement are being planted, even if relapses and setbacks occur.

While in prison, Brittney was enrolled in Drug Court, a restorative justice practice that actively works with drug offenders. Through the program, participants are eligible for an early release and are provided supportive services to help them get their lives back on track. Drug Court also holds participants accountable. If a parent relapses while in the program, he or she will be sent back to jail.

Brittney's judge agreed to release her to Bridge House, a rural clean and sober residential program located on Hawai'i island. Unfortunately, Brittney relapsed two weeks after entering the program and returned to jail for 20 days. However, after that second jail stint, she returned to Bridge House and was able to maintain her sobriety. The program's isolated location, daily classes, support groups, and gardening projects helped Brittney to clear her head and build her spirit. Her mom brought her girls up on weekends and they spent their days playing games, working in the garden, doing arts and crafts, and having makeup sessions. Bridge House gave her the time and safety she needed to get on steadier ground.

Vivian also participated in Drug Court. As she put it, "They broke me down and built me back up." For Vivian, the structure and support were what she needed to aid in her fight for sobriety and to reunify with her children. It helped her set a boundary in a new relationship too. Instead of chasing love she stated, up front, to her new potential partner, Randy, that her priority was getting her

---

2   Family Wrap Hawai'i is a wraparound program that seeks to address the underlying unmet needs of parents. The team meets monthly, and gives intensive emotional and practical support to the parents who are on theirreunification journey.

children back. Randy could get on board with that or he could leave, she said. He chose to stay and actively support her reunification efforts. They've been together now for eleven years.

It took Kyle six weeks to get into a parenting class, but when he attended his first session he felt great. It was such a relief to finally be doing something proactive for his kids. Through the class he began to understand, more deeply, how to be a good dad and care for and nurture his children. For Kyle, it was an eye-opening experience that further fueled his determination to keep fighting for his boys.

During this third stage, restoring justice practitioners are highly engaged with the parents. Services are provided, and there's frequent interaction with the parents both to provide support and to track how they're doing. Are the services helpful and effective? Are there new issues that need to be addressed? Becoming sober, or changing entrenched ways of living, is rarely easy. Throughout, but especially in this phase, it's important for restoring justice practitioners to recognize and nurture that spark of initiative and drive within the parent, even if they do stumble and fall. When Brittney relapsed, for example, her Drug Court caseworker continued to give encouragement and support. Yes, there were consequences, but her stumble was also a learning opportunity. For practitioners to believe in the parent, and to let them know that they see the deeper intentions that exist below the parent's insecurity and self-doubt, is vital during this stage. Parents are just starting to believe a better life is possible; mirroring a reflection of confidence and trust in their inner spirit can make all the difference.

The fourth stage is entitled: **Finding Your Stride.** This is when those seeds of self-confidence begin to spout and parents become more focused and determined. They're fully engaged in services and are acquiring new skills that will help them be healthier parents and wiser adults. For Kyle, the support of his roommate and his own relentless determination to speak before a judge on his *own* behalf, fueled his efforts to excel in his classes. In addition to the parenting classes, he signed up for a nine month/500-hour drug rehabilitation program. He graduated and, upon receiving his certificate of completion, learned that a year had been shaved off of his sentence. He was so thrilled! With that reduction, his heart was filled with hope. He just might be released in time to return to Hawai'i and personally speak to the judge to request a stay order on the termination of his parental rights.

For Vivian, her trust in her social worker changed dramatically. Now her social worker, Noe, was an ally who helped her get the support and services she needed. For Brittney, after she left Bridge House, the Family Wrap Hawaii team's belief in her helped her secure housing and take steps towards independence that she didn't think were possible.

In this stage, the collaboration between the parents and the restoring justice practitioners in their lives is starting to blossom. Parents continue to turn to the practitioners for support, but they are also starting to take more control of their situation. While they still are in an active stage of learning, that learning is being integrated into the way they see themselves and the world. They are starting to believe, more deeply, in their own capacity to make positive things happen in their lives. For restoring justice practitioner, it's helpful to remain attentive and supportive, but also to give some space for the independence and self-determination that is emerging. During this stage parents start to make more independent choices. Some of those choices will work out, some won't, but it's their ability to make those choices and recover from disappointments that's important to recognize and celebrate. This is especially true when it comes to their relationship with their children, and their efforts to reestablish a trusting bond with them.

In the fifth stage, **Almost Home**, the parent's hard work is coming to fruition. The end of the journey is finally in sight. Unsupervised visits are standard during this phase, and skills learned in previous stages are more fully put into practice. Life has changed, and a new, healthier way of living is becoming the "new normal." The parent's trust *in* themselves and their team of supporters, and the trust in the parents *from* their supporters, reaches full bloom and feels nearly effortless.

While the future looks promising and the end of CWS involvement is growing closer, this stage has its challenges too. Reconnecting with their children and transitioning to being an active parent in their children's daily lives is not easy. It's an adjustment for everyone, and can bring up strong emotions.

That was especially true for Vivian. Her girls had anger and other emotional issues that needed to be addressed. Thankfully for Vivian she had learned, through her own therapy and drug treatment programs, how to listen and ride out the expression of difficult emotions. In the early days, she pressed for the family to do things together as much as possible. Throughout, she was able to stay steady and engaged, which helped deepen her children's trust in her as a parent.

For Brittney, it felt imperative that she secure her own apartment. Though she and the girls could live with her parents, she needed to prove to them, and herself, that she could fully step into her parenting role. It wasn't always easy. Once she found an apartment, and she and the girls were spending time together on their own, they had to learn how to relate to each other in new ways. Brittney was striving to be a protective, healthy mother, and the girls had to get accustomed to this sober mom and the new ways she was parenting them. At times it felt awkward and stressful as they were getting used to each other. As with many families, it is during the longer visits that some of the rougher edges start to show.

For Kyle, it was jarring to see how much his boys had grown during his time in prison. It made him realize how precious their time together was, which brought up painful feelings too. Returning the boys to their foster caregivers after their weekend visits, for example, was wrenching for Kyle. Though he had been a "tough guy" in prison, after dropping the boys off he would cry all the way home.

Restoring justice practitioner during this stage need to lend a listening ear and convey empathy for the parent's struggles. It's also important the practitioner convey that he/she/they have trust that the parent can handle the situation. They can do this by reminding the parent of all they've learned, and how far they have come. Brainstorming with the parent on what might be going on for their children, and inquiring what the children might be needing from them as a parent is also helpful. Practitioners can encourage parents to refine their parenting skills, while reminding them that it's normal to have challenges as the family is creating a new way of being together. The practitioners can also encourage the continued use of formal and informal supports, and remind the parents that they are not alone.

Finally, after their long trek, our travelers arrive at the sixth stage: **Home, Sweet Home.** This is the end of their reunification journey. The children are with them full-time, their parental rights are restored, and they have successfully completed a CWS supervised transitional period. At long last the moment has arrived: The Family Court Judge proudly announces that their CWS case is officially closed. For everyone it's time of celebration, joy, gratitude, and relief. They made it! What was once was a hope is now a reality and life is changed forever.

Now a new journey begins. It is one filled with possibilities, and one whose destination will be the family's to create. After years of struggle, Kyle wakes up every morning feeling like he's fully living again. Everything he does is for his boys. Vivian, with the addition of grandkids to her already large family of six children, feels clear and purposeful. Brittney finds deep satisfaction in caring for her girls and her new baby boy. She is proud to a responsible parent.

For restoring justice practitioners, though their work with the family has come to an end, there is one more thing they need to do. During this final stage, it's important for them to recognize and revel in their contribution to the family's success, and to give themselves that proverbial pat on the back. Even more than that, however, it's important that they take the time to really take in that they have helped reduce a family's trauma and the painful legacy that would have likely reverberated into the following generations. They have played a part in restoring a family back to pono, to righteousness and balance. That's no small feat, and it's a gift to the family, their future generations, and to the community at large.

Our three parents, with the support of their restoring justice practitioners, worked hard to make the changes needed so that their children could have a loving and safe home. Out of gratitude and a desire to help other families, Kyle, Vivian, and Brittney generously agreed to be featured in a film that EPIC helped produce entitled: *A Healing Journey: The Road to Reunification.*[3] In the film, they share the stories of their reunification process. They also give final words of encouragement to parents who are just starting on their journey. "Hang onto hope," they say, "Do what is needed to be done, and believe in the power of love and the preciousness of family." As they, and their children can attest, of all the excursions in life, the healing journey of reunification is the most important and worthwhile journey of them all.

---

3   The 25 minute film can be viewed on YouTube at: https://youtu.be/Eet2uUWZGGA

DISCUSSION QUESTIONS

Stage One: The Journey Begins. This is life before CWS involvement.

1. Imagine you are a parent who has had a child taken into foster care. Instead of someone talking to you about what you did wrong, imagine what it would feel if they asked you about times when you were doing things right as a parent.
   a) How might this impact how you think about yourself?
   b) How does it impact your trust in the person asking the questions?

Stage Two: Tripping, Falling, and Stepping Back. This is the stage when life takes a turn for the worse.

1. What are some of the strong emotions parents, and other family members, may feel during this stage?

2. As a restoring justice practitioner, what do parents need from you during this stage?

3. If strong emotions are directed at you, how might recognizing this stage help you stay balanced and respond more effectively?

Stage Three: Regaining Balance and Taking Steps Again. This is often a stage where there's a turning point, where the parent starts to engage in services, though there may be relapses and setbacks.

1. What do you think helps contribute to those turning points?

2. How might you respond to the parents' -- and maybe your own – disappointment after a relapse or setback?

3. What are some of the ways you can help parents regain their balance?

Stage Four: Finding Their Stride. During this stage parents are more fully engaged in services and are feeling more confident. Trust in the team is growing.

1. For the parents, what vulnerabilities might still be present during this stage?

2. As a restoring justice practitioner, how can you help to bolster a parent's growing confidence?

Stage Five: Almost Home. During this stage there is trust and collaboration between the parents, family, and service providers. Unsupervised visits are occurring. The parents are implementing the skills they've learned, and are becoming more confident in their ability to parent and live life differently.

1. What are some of the challenges the parents and children may have to deal with as the children reintegrate back into the home?

2. How might you support the parents and the children during this stage?

Stage Six: Home Sweet Home: Reunification happens. This is the stage where everything the parents have learned gets put into practice.

1. What can help you recognize and value your contribution to the family's healing?

2. How might you celebrate your hard work when a successful reunification occurs?

Healing Our Immigrant Children: Assessing Immigration Policy via Restorative Justice Lens

DANIELA VELEZ-CLUCAS[1]

Immigration is currently a hot topic at the forefront of the media and foreign and domestic policy. The following essay aims at exploring the state of immigration policy in the United States today, assessing how a restorative justice lens can guide the future of immigration policy, and evaluating how we can achieve restorative objectives for marginalized immigrants and vulnerable unaccompanied immigrant children.[2]

LEGAL PROTECTIONS FOR UNACCOMPANIED CHILDREN

The Trafficking Victims Protection Reauthorization Act of 2008 ("TVPRA") created procedures for processing the cases of unaccompanied immigrant children in recognition of the vulnerability of children traveling alone to human trafficking and other forms of exploitation. The procedures specified for unaccompanied children enhance the ability of our legal system to orderly and efficiently sort through the cases of children who are defending themselves against removal. *See* Trafficking Victims Protection Reauthorization Act of 2008. In some ways, the TVPRA utilizes some restorative justice principles, such as inclusion, and accessibility, in order to safeguard immigrant children's legal rights. Currently,

---

1   Daniela Clucas-Velez is an immigration attorney for a non-profit organization focusing on the representation of immigrant children. Prior to working as an immigration attorney, Daniela worked as a Restorative Justice Program coordinator and peacekeeper. Throughout her immigration law practice, she utilizes restorative principles to serve and advance her clients' legal interests.

2   Unaccompanied immigrant children are individuals younger than 18 years, who do not have legal status in the United States, and have no parent or legal guardian in the United States available to provide care and custody.

however, policy changes are debilitating the protections and opportunities for relief for immigrants and unaccompanied immigrant children.

The TVPRA filled a crucial gap in U.S. anti-human trafficking efforts by bringing unaccompanied migrant children within the scope of U.S. legal protections. Prior to the TVPRA, migrant children were not being adequately screened by the Department of Homeland Security to detect whether they were survivors of trafficking or at future risk of being trafficked or persecuted in the U.S. or in their home countries. These children, including children who were not Mexican nationals, were often summarily turned away at the U.S.-Mexico border, where they were left without any protection. In other cases, CBP was releasing children directly to adults who were not screened or confirmed to be related to the children. As a result, many of them ended up in the hands of smugglers and traffickers who came looking or were waiting for them. The TVPRA protects children from exploitation and trafficking The TVPRA requires Department of Homeland Security to screen all unaccompanied children arriving to the U.S. to more readily identify child survivors of trafficking.

The TVPRA provides protections for children eligible for the following types of legal relief: 1) Asylum: legal protection for refugee children who are unable or unwilling to return home because they fear serious harm or persecution; 2) Special immigrant juvenile status: children who have been abused, abandoned, and/or neglected by a parent; 3) T Visa: legal status that protects victims of human trafficking – either sex and labor trafficking; and 4) U-visa: for victims of certain crimes who have experienced mental or physical abuse and are helpful to law enforcement or government officials in the investigation or prosecution of criminal activity. The TVPRA adds safeguards for unaccompanied immigrant children who are victims of crime, human trafficking and Asylum and Special Immigrant Juvenile Status.

Asylum is a protection granted to foreign nationals already in the United States or arriving at the border who meet the international law definition of a "refugee." The United Nations 1951 Convention and 1967 Protocol define a refugee as a person who is unable or unwilling to return to his or her home country, and cannot obtain protection in that country, due to past persecution or a well-founded fear of being persecuted in the future "on account of race, religion, nationality, membership in a particular social group, or political opinion." Congress incorporated this definition into U.S. immigration law in the Refugee Act of 1980. As a signatory to the 1967 Protocol, and through U.S. immigration law, the United States has legal obligations to provide protection to those who qualify as refugees. Individuals are barred from asylum if they do not file for asylum within one year of entry into the United States.

The TVPRA aims at aiding unaccompanied children applying for asylum by recognizing that children are frequently transferred between various detention facilities during their first year in the U.S. and that filing applications is impracticable without a permanent location; the TVPRA eliminates the one-year asylum filing deadline for unaccompanied children. Accordingly, unaccompanied children have the opportunity to have their cases heard before United States Citizenship Immigration Services ("USCIS") in an interview process that is less antagonistic and more appropriate for children than applying for asylum in front of an Immigration Judge. USCIS Asylum Officers trained in trauma-informed interviewing techniques conduct these asylum interviews. The TVPRA reaffirms the transfer of responsibility for the care and custody of unaccompanied children to the Department of Health and Human Services (HHS), as provided for by the Homeland Security Act of 2002. Additionally, the TVPRA accounts for Special Immigrant Juvenile Status ("SIJS"). Mindful that many children applying for SIJS are fleeing an abusive parent in their home country and consistent with the TVPRA's intent to protect children from being returned to the hands of their abusers, the TVPRA adjusted the requirements for SIJS. Now, the law only requires that only one parents abused, neglected, or abandoned a child. [3]

Unaccompanied children comprise one of the world's most vulnerable groups. To prevent their unjust return, and in recognition of their unique vulnerabilities, Congress accorded unaccompanied children special legal protections under the TVPRA. This Act, which passed by unanimous consent, mandates that the U.S. government allow entry to, and screen these youth to determine whether they are at risk of trafficking or fear return to their home countries. Placement into ORR custody aims at providing children with the time, care, and access to

---

3 As of the date this article was written (12/2020), thousands of children have been summarily expelled from the United States and the protection the TVPRA offers, are being weakened. There are currently grave concerns over the Department of Homeland Security's expulsions of unaccompanied children at the U.S. southern border. From March 2020 to present time, The Department of Homeland Security has turned away unaccompanied immigrant children under the premise of COVID-19. These actions, which do nothing to protect public health and safety, violate the bipartisan TVPRA and run counter to domestic and international law ensuring the right to seek asylum, and place vulnerable unaccompanied children at immediate risk of human trafficking and other harm. The Department of Homeland Security appears to be summarily returning these children without proper screenings, placement into immigration court proceedings, or referrals to the Office of Refugee Resettlement. The Department of Homeland Security is betraying the TVPRA, bipartisan legislation that determines that unaccompanied children's pursuit of protection that is so essential as to warrant a unique array of due process safeguards.

legal services essential to processing trauma, obtaining counsel, and gathering evidence-all steps necessary to properly establish past harm, trafficking and susceptibility to trafficking in the future. However, these venues frequently do not carry out their mission due to a lack of resources and trauma-informed care. For instance, ORR shelter staff are required to write up children for even the smallest outburst. ORR staff are required to turn over all incidents and reports taken regarding the children to immigration officials. These reports could potentially affect a child's legal case negatively.

Restorative practices, which aim at understanding underlying behavior and importance of confidentiality in healing spaces, would be much better situated to ensure that the tenets and purpose of the TVPRA are met. Rather than punitive zero-tolerance policies within detention shelters, restorative policies would better help this vulnerable group and uphold congressional intent. Advocating via litigation, policy creation, campaigns and reaching out for congressional support may be able to bring these restorative principles to the forefront and improve the well-being of immigrant youth in detention shelters.

CRIMINALIZATION OF IMMIGRANT CHILDREN AND DUE PROCESS CONCERNS

On April 6, 2018, Attorney General Jeff Sessions directed federal prosecutors "to adopt immediately a zero-tolerance policy for all offenses" related to the misdemeanor of improper entry into the United States, and that this "zero-tolerance policy shall supersede any existing policies". The zero-tolerance immigration policy enacted in April 2018 has put a spotlight on the more than 5,400 immigrant children separated from their parents at the U.S-American border. This has caused the rise of detention of unaccompanied immigrant children entering the United States and family separation.

Immigration law labels unaccompanied immigrant children as "unaccompanied alien children." The term "alien" sheds light on the problem with current immigration policy. Immigration law and policy currently aims to criminalize the very act of immigrating and emigrating. Restorative justice principles such as inclusion and respect for all are essential in understanding why this term is offensive and why humans are not "aliens," nor are human beings "illegal." A restorative lens in analyzing the legal framework overview of immigration law is essential in drafting policies and protecting those that need protection, with the inclusion that one would expect from a nation built on immigrants.

Immigrant children are a vulnerable group, requiring special protections under U.S. and international law. Compared with nonimmigrant children, they face additional dangers to their physical and mental health because of the harmful immigration policies currently in place. The difficult hurdles set before them in order to receive protection from deportation (such as asylum protection), detention and deportation protocols, lack of regulation and access to physical and mental healthcare leave the children in a state of utter distress. This is apparent from conversations with unaccompanied children that arrive at ORR shelters. Before they even get a chance to delve into the reasons they fled their home countries to seek refuge in the United States, these children first talk of the conditions in which Customs and Border Patrol ("CBP") jailed them at the border. These kids, who have sacrificed their homes, families, and physical safety to arrive at the border, tell us that immigration officers place them in the "*hielera*," or "ice box" in English. Officers often do not provide protective clothing to kids, or sufficient food and water. In these situations, children often have no access to blankets, beds, clean water, personal hygiene products, or age-appropriate foods and conditions. Their stories disclose that these authorities place young kids in harsh environmental conditions. For example, they have to stay in cold temperature and continuous lights for 24 hours a day. When authorities finally remove these children from CBP detention and place them into ORR custody, the young kid's already deteriorating mental health is further aggravated. Doctors often diagnose these kids with PTSD, anxiety, and depression. Furthermore, there have been reports of children dying because of substandard conditions in immigration detention.

We must recognize the effects of political decisions on the wellbeing of immigrant children and further delve into how these policies are affecting immigrant children. Referrals to appropriate resources, including medical and psychological assistance, are crucial. In addition to these resources, restorative justice services ought to be used in their treatment. Restorative justice principles teach us that we cannot respond to an individual's needs without understanding trauma. Similarly, as a legal advocate for immigrant children, one cannot serve legal needs without addressing the immediate harms causing current distress. Without addressing these underlying harms, legal and other advocacy is difficult.

One cannot effectively provide legal advocacy without viewing these children through a holistic lens. In my experience of working with traumatized immigrant children living in ORR custody or in post-detention living facilities for immigrant children, if I do not respond to a child's mental and emotional heath, there is very little chance of having that child open up about his, her, or their past. If a child cannot participate in this and communicate effectively, I may not find that individual eligible for immigration relief. These children are very often suffering from post-traumatic stress disorder, depression, and debilitating trauma that impede their ability to advance or be helpful in their own legal case. These children often do not have access to spaces where they feel safe or heard. These circumstances create due process concerns because it harms an individual's ability to access immigration relief.

Capacity is another common issue that causes due process concerns and is at the heart of representing children. Capacity is an individual's ability to make decision or perform a task in given context. The law presumes a child in immigration proceedings has capacity and to be capable of expressing his point of view and wishes. This and mental competency issues, laid out in *Matter of MAM*, provide a framework for Immigration judges to consider due process issues and to develop a child-specific framework for considering children's capacities in the immigration system. The major issue that comes up with capacity with mental competency is due process. The presumption that a child in removal proceedings and immigration proceedings has capacity may ensure that a child's point of view and sense of autonomy are preserved. However, when a child suffers from intellectual and cognitive disabilities that may be result of serious physical traumas or suffers from mental health disorders, such as anxiety, depression, and PTSD that cannot be remedied with medical and psychological support, her due process rights may be affected as well.[1] Restorative spaces, like the use of circles in detention and post-detention, would allow these individuals to feel inclusion, community and be heard. These practices would advance due process as well as ethical standard for the care and wellbeing of immigrant and children.

A child's due process in immigration court proceedings is impaired if this individual cannot effectively communicate with clinicians, attorneys, or judges

---

1   *See* Matter of E-, 2003 WL 23269901 (BIA Dec. 4, 2003) (due process requirements satisfied where represented respondent offered no documentary or testimonial evidence of alleged incompetence); Matter of V-, 2006 WL 2008263 (BIA May 24, 2006) (no due process violation where respondent, who submitted detention medical records reflecting treatment for mental health issues for the first time on appeal, did not thereby prove inability to understand nature of proceedings or to participate in his defense).

because of mental health disorders caused by trauma. Restorative justice peace circles, and restorative justice check-ins and principles, could have a major effect on a child's ability to open up and as such, and ensure due process. For instance, I worked with a young man, a teenager from a Central American country. This child had previously been in the United States but was deported because a previous legal service provider, ORR shelter staff, and immigration judge (all of whom are trained in understanding the TVPRA, and in identifying the issues that the TVPRA protects against) failed to find the child eligible for any immigration relief. In fact, during his previous entry in the United States and previous stay in ORR custody, that child was written-up many times because of behavioral issues. Rather than investigating and building the trust necessary to understand these behavioral issues, people labeled him as a troublemaker. During that time, shelter staff understood that the child was deregulated, but rather than delving into the root cause of the conduct, they essentially labelled this child a "bad kid." Nobody advocated for him and a judge deported him from the United States. The child re-entered and officials placed him into ORR custody in the service area the organization I work for serves. About one year passed and the child did not open up about his past.

I began utilizing restorative principles and circles with him. Restorative Justice Circles provided an opportunity for he and I to come together to address his past in a process that explored how he was harmed and what his needs were. We used icebreakers, trust-building exercises, and established guidelines in which we operated when we were together. Once the child trusted me and understood confidentiality, we developed a relationship of real trust. He shared information he had never shared with anyone else. Thanks to the information he shared, I was able to pursue multiple forms of legal relief for him.

I now use these restorative techniques with all my clients. I understand that they are not just clients they are children. I provide legal counsel through this lens. I play games, engage in fun conversation, create grounding mindfulness exercises, draft my legal questions with compassion, empathy, patience, and tolerance and build-in safeguards for legal conversations. The child has autonomy and the power to stop the conversation at any point. I begin by asking the client whether she is okay and what she needs now. Instead of demanding my client meet my expectations, I adapt and meet my client's expectations. I uncover information, which is legally relevant, by getting to know the human, the scared child, sitting with me. In this capacity, I get to understand my clients' needs and often successfully advocate for the procurement of social workers, confidential psychiatrist or psychologist appointments and clinical treatment.

IMMIGRATION POLICY'S EFFECT ON IMMIGRANTS AND DEBILITATING RULE CHANGES

Children that make the decision to flee to the United States live in extreme desperation in their countries of origin. Recent immigration policy trends place kids, first and foremost, in confusing and complex court and detention system, rather than in places of safety. Deportation proceedings against children often begin in the jurisdiction where the child is in the custody of ORR. Once, or *if,* a child is released from an ORR shelter to a sponsor or to foster care, it is the child's responsibility – regardless of age or legal representation – to submit paperwork to inform the court that he or she has moved and to file a formal motion to change venue if the new address is under the jurisdiction of a different court. If a child does not properly update his or her address, he or she could be ordered deported *in absentia* for failing to appear in court.

Additionally, there is an absence of legally binding regulations to protect children in Department of Homeland Security custody. Unaccompanied children are held alone in Department of Homeland Security custody before they are transferred to an ORR shelter. Although there are standards to guide the treatment of unaccompanied children, Department of Homeland Security lacks appropriate legally binding regulations to protect children in their custody. Currently, little oversight exists to ensure that unaccompanied children are treated humanely and cared for according to child-appropriate protocols while in Department of Homeland Security custody. As discussed above, there are many reports of major human rights abuses in these jails.

Furthermore, recent immigration policy attempts to undercut protections for children in ORR detention. For instance, The Flores Settlement Agreement, a binding consent decree, has been actively ensuring the government's compliance with detention conditions and time limits on custody of children for over two decades. However, in 2018, the administration instigated a cruel campaign to strip away the few safeguards that are currently in place by publishing a proposed rule that would essentially eviscerate the Flores Settlement.

One of the most disturbing realities of immigration law and policies is the government's inability to quickly reunify children with family or sponsors. In an attempt to deter Central Americans from coming to the United States The Department of Homeland Security, and the Department of Health and Human Services (HHS) entered into an agreement in early 2018 requiring these agencies to share information about individuals attempting to reunify with an unaccompanied child. The information was then used by ICE to arrest and detain potential sponsors, typically family members. This ultimately created a domino effect of harmful consequences. Parents and loved ones of unaccompanied children now live under a cloud of fear that stepping forward to sponsor the child they love will trigger their own detention and deportation; this child has in effect dramatically prolonged lengths of stay for children in ORR custody.

Recently, the Department of Homeland Security has published two final rules on work authorization, engineered to keep asylum seekers impoverished. This will harm asylum seekers' ability to work while their cases are pending. One lifts a rule to process applications for work permits within 30 days of receipt--a measure previously tailored to the unique vulnerability of asylum seekers whose cases are frequently pending for years. A second rule erects even greater barriers. This rule prevents asylum seekers who have filed asylum more than one year after entry or entered without inspection from gaining work authorization. This rule also requires asylum seekers who are eligible to wait a full year before they can seek work authorization, all but ensuring irreparable harm while many fall prey to food and shelter insecurity.

Furthermore, the Department of Homeland Security and Department of Justice published a final rule making multiple changes to the regulations governing the procedures for Asylum, Withholding of Removal, and protection under the Convention Against Torture (CAT). The final rule adopts the notice of proposed rulemaking published at 85 FR 36264 on 6/15/20 with few substantive changes.[2] This new rule eviscerates few remaining asylum protections and goes against U.S. asylum and international law, and due process protections for asylum seekers. Among other things, the rule makes it extremely difficult for women, LGBTQ individuals, or gang violence survivors to obtain asylum protection. The law dramatically expands findings of fraud or frivolous applications, assaults due process, and rushes the process immigration officials go through to screen for torture and future fear. The Trump administration is essentially destroying United States asylum system by making it nearly impossible for most applicants to successfully gain protection in the United States by making pro-

---

2   The rule is effective 1/11/21. (85 FR 80274, 12/11/20).

tection from persecution impossible for almost everyone. It raises additional obstacles to passing a preliminary screening at the border, eliminates multiple long-established grounds for establishing merit for and granting of asylum, and allows immigration judges to deny people their day in court by rejecting applications without a hearing. The regulation denies protection to nearly all who pass through more than one country on their way to the United States.

These policy changes make an already hostile and complicated immigration system extremely difficult to navigate. These rules cement the message that immigrants are not wanted, and there is no place for them in our society and communities. With this mind, it is clear agencies and rulemaking entities would benefit from restorative principles and analyses. For those of us providing direct legal representation to immigrants and children, or anyone engaged in arduous advocacy for justice in any sector, it is vital we have restorative conversations within our own communities in order to avoid burnout and continue the fight. It is also important we bring compassion, understanding and hope to our legal representation. Finally, the most valuable gift restorative justice provides, is the realization that listening to immigrants' stories and their journeys provides the inspiration for perseverance required to continue trudging the road to equality and justice.

RESTORATIVE JUSTICE PRINCIPLES AND IMPLEMENTATION TO IMMIGRATION POLICIES AND IMMIGRANT COMMUNITIES

Restorative Justice utilizes a holistic continuum of services, providing for prevention, intervention, diversion, commitment, reentry, and aftercare for individuals that have experienced, or even perpetrated, a harm. This approach seeks to balance the needs of individuals, community, and consequences of harmful actions. In the world of U.S. immigration law labels such as "victim," "community," and "wrong-doer" are often inter-twined and ever-changing. From the author's perspective, all persons who wants to live in a peaceful world, and a peaceful country, where all people are valued and heard, are members of this community. As community members, we are responsible for holding spaces for storytelling and healing, and investing in marginalized communities. "Wrong-doer" and "victim" labels often change, as well, depending on your perspective. It is undeniable, however, that immigrants make an arduous journey based on faith for a better life, and arrive at borders that are closed to them. If immigrants make it across the borders, they find resistance. Policies and attitudes meant to marginalize, dehumanize, and deter them persevere.

Punitive trends and immigration policies meant to deter illegal immigration, in fact, weaken society as a whole from a practical (for instance, the cost of jailing individuals and children and administering an ineffective court system) and moral standpoint. Restorative justice provides a vision for true justice, in an often-unjust immigration system. Restorative justice rests on a set of principles designed to orient the response of a community to a wrongful occurrence. One of those principles is Empowering Community. This guiding principle transforms community by taking an active role, to be responsible, and to deal collectively with the impact, consequences, and reparation. Restorative Justice is a three-dimensional collaborative process that seeks to meet the needs of different stakeholders. In the case of immigrant-focused restorative justice responses, the objective of the community dimension is to offer a sense of security and safety to neighborhoods, to engage the community as a participant in healing processes, and to involve the community in offering a home to immigrants.

Transformation is another powerful restorative justice principle. All immigrants and allies, that stand up against injustice and support each other, through legal representation, policy work, or simply offering services, friendship or a place in their community, can cause fundamental changes in people, relationships and communities. Cooperative processes that lead to transformation of people, relationships and communities create restorative spaces. Inclusion and integration are guiding principles that allow communities to be whole, and enable vulnerable populations to tell their story and heal from their trauma.

CONCLUSION

It is vital that immigration policy the needs of these vulnerable populations holistically and with restorative principles. All human beings must be treated with dignity and worth, respectful of age, abilities, sexual orientation, family status, and diverse cultures and backgrounds — whether racial, ethnic, geographic, religious, economic, or other — and are all given equal protection and due process. The restorative justice principal of dignity, respect, and compassion ought to apply as soon as immigrants and immigrant children enter the United States. We ought to advocate eradicating policies that criminalize the act of immigration when done under emergency circumstances, or done by an individual without the means or ability to walk through the tedious and expensive process of migrating through mainstream avenues. Furthermore, we can advocate for restorative safeguards for individuals and children navigating the immigration system, including creating restorative justice hubs, with the intent of connecting individuals with legal services, confidential mental health counseling, and educational resources. Instead of demonizing immigrants and causing further isolation, the government and its policies should be supporting and investing in outreach programs, and community and family support services that help immigrant youth deal with trauma, family reunification and social stressors, among other issues, in order to ensure they feel connected to their new communities. Finally, individuals can lead or participate in healing peace circles designed to give space for immigrants to give voice to their experience, strength, and hope.

Why are immigrants an especially vulnerable population?

With these vulnerabilities in mind, why is a restorative justice philosophy an important tool for transformation?

What restorative principles are built into immigration law dealing with unaccompanied immigrant children? Specifically, what restorative principles can be found in the TVPRA?

What are some restorative justice principles that would protect immigrants and immigration law? What would a policy with this principle in mind look like?

In what ways do current immigration policies betray immigrant's international human rights and due process?

How can restorative justice improve immigration policy?

How can restorative justice-minded communities help immigrants?

THE VICTIMIZATION OF NATIVE AMERICAN WOMEN AND HOW RESTORATIVE JUSTICE CAN PROMOTE PEACE AND HEALING

ASHLEY SCHOENBORN

I. NATIVE AMERICAN WOMEN ARE THE MOST VICTIMIZED GROUP IN THE UNITED STATES AND RARELY RECEIVE PROPER HEALING.

The victimization of Native Americans in the United States is a serious problem. Native American women are victimized at much higher rates than white women. Native women are the most victimized group in the United States and the rates far exceed those of any other racial group.[1] More than 4 in 5 Native American women have experienced some sort of violence and 1 in 2 Native American women have experienced sexual violence.[2] Stated in another way, more than half of Native American women have been sexually assaulted, including over one third of them having been raped in their lifetime.[3] Compared to white women, this statistic is nearly 2.5 times higher, showing a prevalent problem in our country.[4] More specifically, 34 percent of American Indian women will be raped in their lifetime.[5] Whereas, 18 percent of white women will be

---

1   Sarah Deer, *Federal Indian Law and Violent Crime: Native Women and Children at the Mercy of the State*, 31 Social Justice 17, 19.

2   Ending Violence Against Native Women, https://indianlaw.org/issue/ending-violence-against-native-women.

3   Garet Bleir, *Murdered and Missing Native American Women Challenge Police and Courts* (2018), https://publicintegrity.org/politics/murdered-and-missing-native-american-women-challenge-police-and-courts/.

4   *Id.*

5   National Congress of American Indians, *Policy Insights Brief Statistics on Violence Against Native Women*, 3 (2013).

raped in their lifetime, showing how much higher of a risk Native American women have in this country of being raped.[6]

Statistics on the offenders of these crimes are also eye-opening. Around 67 percent of the offenders in rape or sexual assault cases against Native American women are non-Native offenders.[7] Also, about 46 percent of people living on reservations (in 2010) were non-Native.[8] This contributes to the lack of power within tribal government.

When it comes to justice, the victimization continues under the westernized criminal justice system. It is important to recognize some of the harm that the criminal justice system has caused tribal nations. This harm is shown when dealing with crimes that occur on tribal land, because the United States government has stripped power from tribal government over many years.[9] There has been 500 years of violence, maltreatment and neglect when it comes to the federal government's control over tribal nations.[10] After stripping the tribal nations of their power, the federal government has created the necessity of Native Americans to be dependent upon different federal agencies for basic human needs.[11] These programs are often found to be underfunded, understaffed, and all around unable to meet the need of the Native American people, creating more of a dependence.[12] This type of treatment by the United States sets up tribal governments to fail. If tribal governments are stripped of their power and put in a position to require federal help, the chances of success diminish greatly. In addition to the failing to support Native American people through programming, the United States is failing within the criminal justice system.

A vast majority of these victimized Native American women never see their abusers or offenders brought to justice in any way.[13] In 2010, when tribal law enforcement would send sexual-abuse cases to the FBI and the U.S. Attorney

---

6   *Id.*

7   *Id* at 4.

8   *Id* at 6.

9   Sarah Deer, *Federal Indian Law and Violent Crime: Native Women and Children at the Mercy of the State*, 31 Social Justice 17, 18.

10   *Id.*

11   *Id.*

12   *Id.*

13   Ending Violence Against Native Women, https://indianlaw.org/issue/ending-violence-against-native-women.

Offices, the federal prosecutors would deny prosecuting more than two-thirds of the cases.[14] Reiterating this statistic, between 2005 and 2009, federal prosecutors declined 67% of Indian country matters that involved sexual abuse, contributing to the further victimization created by such crimes because this provides no justice or healing process.[15] Not only is the failure of prosecution a huge problem, the diminished amount of law enforcement on tribal land makes investigating all of these crimes a long shot.[16] These failures are partly due to the flawed westernized criminal justice system that severely limits the ability of Native American nations to protect their women from violence.[17] This also makes it difficult to provide remedies.[18] These victimizations of the women enrolled in the tribes have a vast and profound impact on the future of Indigenous nations.[19] A system that supports proper resolution and healing, especially when it relates to the psychological trauma, is necessary on these tribal lands, or it will create a cycle of hurt in a continuation of the colonization process.[20] "Decision-making authority and control over violent crime should be restored to Indigenous nations to provide full accountability and justice to the victims."[21] Considering the current system, it is apparent that the focus is only on the typical theories of corrections; deterrence, retribution, or incapacitation. Some may argue rehabilitation is encouraged, but rarely is it proven to help. With the criminal justice system in place in the United States, there is not a focus on restoring the community and parties involved. Healing will not occur until this is the focus. Clearly, the westernized criminal justice system in the United States is not the ideal system when looking to the justice and healing of victimized Indigenous women.

---

14 Garet Bleir, *Murdered and Missing Native American Women Challenge Police and Courts* (2018), https://publicintegrity.org/politics/murdered-and-missing-native-american-women-challenge-police-and-courts/.

15 Ending Violence Against Native Women, https://indianlaw.org/issue/ending-violence-against-native-women.

16 *See Id.*

17 *Id.*

18 *Id.*

19 Sarah Deer, *Federal Indian Law and Violent Crime: Native Women and Children at the Mercy of the State*, 31 Social Justice 17, 25.

20 *Id.*

21 *Id* at 18.

II. THE HISTORY OF THE UNITED STATES' LIMITATION ON NATIVE AMERICAN LAND SHOWS THE CONTINUOUSLY STRIPPED RIGHTS OF TRIBAL NATIONS AND ATTEMPTS TO HELP RESTORE SOME OF THE POWER.

Historically, most Indigenous legal systems were victim-centered, focusing on providing a sense of spiritual and emotional recovery from violent crimes.[22] Evidence indicates that historical Indigenous practices within their legal system has led to strong deterrence in crimes against women.[23] Comparing to the Anglo-American system, Indigenous practices offer more protection and healing of victims.[24] This should always be the main focus when looking to remedy crimes, especially violent crimes that create a negative and difficult reaction from victims. However, over many years, the United States has weakened the Indigenous practices by stripping the power from tribal governments.[25]

a) The Major Crimes Act allows federal prosecution of Native American defendants in serious felony cases.

In a Supreme Court case in 1883, a Sioux Indian had murdered another Sioux Indian within Indian Country.[26] The defendant was convicted in federal court and sentenced to death.[27] The Supreme Court held that due to the treaty of 1863 and the agreement of 1877, upholding federal jurisdiction would be against the agreed upon restrictions and to do so, there must be a clear showing by Congress in which the Court was unable to find at the time.[28] Therefore, the Court held that there was no federal jurisdiction against the Native American man who committed a crime on a Native American victim on reservation land.[29]

---

22 *Id* at 19.

23 *Id.*

24 *See Id.*

25 *See Id.*

26 *Ex parte Kan-gi-shun-ca*, 109 U.S. 556, 572 (1883).

27 *Id.*

28 *Id.*

29 *Id.*

His imprisonment was deemed illegal.[30] This case inspired the creation of the Major Crimes Act.

The Major Crimes Act (MCA) follows the Supreme Court case of *Ex parte Kan-gi-shun-ca* (also known as *Ex parte Crow Dog*), because the federal government wanted to express the congressional view that tribal law is insufficient to punish the major crimes correctly and adequately.[31] The MCA mandates federal jurisdiction over 13 serious offenses that are committed by Native Americans on Indian Country.[32] Among these serious felony offenses is rape.[33] This governmental decision over the tribal government's power can be viewed as an intrusion upon the otherwise exclusive jursidiction that tribal government would have.[34] It also does not violate the Double Jeopardy Clause in most cases to have a defendant be prosecuted in tribal court and in federal court.[35] This creates further issues and divide between the federal government and tribal government. How is the federal government to recognize and understand the practices and culture of Native American victims and defendants when they cannot even work with tribal government to ensure a defendant is not charged for the same crime twice?

This not only creates more divide, but it also creates more uncertainty for every party in the criminal justice system. Different participants in the same or very similar crimes could be subject to prosecutions by different sovereigns under different laws with different results.[36]

b) Public Law 280 was passed, allowing jurisdiction over criminal matters in state governments.

Around 70 years after passing the MCA, Public Law 280 (PL280) was passed as part of a larger effort to ultimately eliminate tribal nations.[37] This law relin-

---

30 *Id.*

31 John Sands, *Indian Crimes and Federal Courts,* 11 Federal Sentencing Reporter 3, 154 (1998).

32 *Id* at 153.

33 18 U.S.C.A. § 1153 (West).

34 John Sands, *Indian Crimes and Federal Courts,* 11 Federal Sentencing Reporter 3, 154 (1998).

35 *Id.*

36 *Id.*

37 Sarah Deer, *Federal Indian Law and Violent Crime: Native Women and Children at the Mercy of the State,* 31 Social Justice 17, 20.

quished federal control over Native American territories in certain states, allow-ing state governments to take control.[38] "For tribal nations located within the boundaries of states affected by PL 280, criminal activity and violence fall under the authority of the state."[39] This jurisdiction transfer was required for the explic-itly stated six states and allowed other states to opt in to require jurisdiction.[40] Of course, Indian Nations had no choice in the matter, as they often did not in other government decisions on jurisdiction.[41] This law created a surplus of state authority and control of reservation activities without any consent from tribal government.[42] Sadly, this results in many states not having their own resources to effectively provide law enforcement on Native American land and has created more hostilities between tribes and the states.[43] As the federal government's relationship with tribal government diminished significantly after the MCA, so does the relationship between tribal government and state government after PL 280.

Since its enactment, Congress amended PL 280 to include a tribal consent requirement, but it only applied to future transfers of jurisdiction to the states; it did not apply to transfers of jurisdiction that had taken place prior to the amendment in 1968.[44] Clearly, PL 280 creates a significant divide between the state and the tribal government, furthering away from the autonomy of tribal governments to protect victims and prosecute offenders of crimes, especially violent ones.

---

38   *Id.*

39   *Id* at 21.

40   Ada Melton and Jerry Gardner, *Public Law 280: Issues and Concerns for Victims of Crime in Indian Country*, 1 (2007).

41   *Id.*

42   *Id.*

43   Sarah Deer, *Federal Indian Law and Violent Crime: Native Women and Children at the Mercy of the State*, 31 Social Justice 17, 21.

44   Ada Melton and Jerry Gardner, *Public Law 280: Issues and Concerns for Victims of Crime in Indian Country*, 1 (2007).

c) The Indian Civil Rights Act of 1968 was passed in an attempt to apply civil rights to tribal justice systems.

The Indian Civil Rights Act (ICRA) seems progressive on the face of it, by ensuring the people on tribal land have the civil rights protections on the reservation that all people have across the United States.[45] However, the ICRA actually minimizes racial discrimination suffered by Native American in order to impose Anglo-American conceptions of civil rights, completely ignoring the methods and practices that tribal jurisdictions had implemented long before colonization came to the United States.[46] ICRA focuses on honoring the language in the Bill of Rights.[47] It also imposes limitations that tribal courts have for incarcerating and fining criminal defendants.[48] This statute severely limits the tribal government's ability to respond to violence, since any conviction within tribal jursidiction must be under 1 year of imprisonment or under a fine of $5000.[49] By limiting the power that the tribal court has within their justice system, the results will only be negative in reacting to violent crime on tribal land. Combining MCA, PL 280, and ICRA, the United States has essentially taken any chance for tribal court to take care of crime on their own land, committed by their own people against their own people.

d) The Supreme Court decided in a 1978 case that the tribal justice systems will not have jurisdiction to prosecute any crimes committed by non-Indians.

The Supreme Court created a precedent that essentially strips the very little power tribal justice systems had left. In *Oliphant v. Suquamish Indian Tribe*, the court determined that tribal nations lack the power or authority to prosecute crimes that are committed by non-Native American people.[50] "This decision has created a vacuum of justice for crime victims who have the misfortune of being

---

45   Sarah Deer, *Federal Indian Law and Violent Crime: Native Women and Children at the Mercy of the State*, 31 Social Justice 17, 21.

46   *Id.*

47   *Id.*

48   *Id.*

49   25 U.S.C.A. § 1302 (West).

50   *Oliphant v. Suquamish Indian Tribe*, 435 U.S. 191, 192 (1978).

attacked by a non-Indian."[51] This makes the already vulnerable people of the reservations all the more vulnerable when it comes to violent crimes. When, in 2010, 46 percent of the people that live on reservations were non-Native, the Native American's home on the reservation becomes extremely susceptible to violent crimes against their women, without the threat of the criminal justice system.[52] It also creates this attitude surrounding crime committed on Indian country that, as a non-Native American, offenders can get away with committing crimes on Indian land because tribal government cannot prosecute them. This creates an unsafe arena for cases of domestic violence and child abuse where the suspect claims to be non-Indian and beyond the jurisdiction of tribal police who respond to those cases.[53] Even in cases where there may be effective law enforcement over non-Indians who commit crimes on Indian country, the results and procedures vary widely from one another and success itself is often rare.[54] Consistency is important for victims, offenders, and the community alike and by not creating a reliable and safe route to approach crimes on Indian country, the United States is severely hurting Indigenous people.

e) The Violence Against Women's Act gave reservations criminal jurisdiction over non-Indigenous people who commit domestic or dating violence against Native American women.

The Violence Against Women Act (VAWA) originated in 1994 and the goal was to change the attitudes towards domestic violence, grow awareness of domestic violence, improve the services for victims, and revise how the criminal justice system responds to such crimes.[55] This act included many facets and has been modified and reimplemented many times throughout the years. In the 2013 version of the act, it included provisions that grants authority to Indian tribes to have jurisdiction over all people who commit domestic violence, including

51 Sarah Deer, *Federal Indian Law and Violent Crime: Native Women and Children at the Mercy of the State*, 31 Social Justice 17, 22.

52 National Congress of American Indians, *Policy Insights Brief Statistics on Violence Against Native Women*, 3 (2013).

53 Troy A. Eid, *Beyond Oliphant: Strengthening Criminal Justice in Indian Country*, The Federal Lawyer, 5 (2007).

54 *Id* at 6.

55 Lisa Sacco, *The Violence Against Women Act: Overview, Legislation, and Federal Funding*, 1 (2015).

non-Native American offenders.[56] It also expanded the purpose of grants to tribal governments to include developing and promoting legislation to enhance best practices for responding to the violent crime against Native American women.[57] This act was a step in the right direction to allow tribal government the control to protect and advocate for their women who are victimized. However, this autonomy given to tribal government is not absolute in all sexual assault cases or other violent crimes. The crimes that qualify for tribal government to have jurisdiction over the offender must be one of the crimes defined in the VAWA, which basically only includes intimate partner violence or dating violence.

f) What needs to change to provide Native American victims with the perception of safety and justice?

There needs to be recognition of help to the Native American victims of violent crimes and accountability at the state and federal level.[58] This is the first step that needs to be explored. Understanding the rates at which Native American women are victimized, understanding their needs, and listening to the voices of the victims are imperative to the healing process.

Next, and most importantly, the power to respond and charge crimes must be reinstated to tribal governments, allowing them to help bring justice and healing to their Native American victims.[59] "Victims can ultimately find true justice within their local, Indigenous systems of justice."[60] Community focus is also a crucial piece in recovering from violent crimes and this type of focus is a main goal of restorative justice.[61]

To allow tribes more power back to prosecute crimes, it is important that tribal courts protect criminal defendants' civil rights on par with that of state court.[62] This is important because without ensuring this, every defendant would

---

56 *Id* at 14.

57 *Id.*

58 Sarah Deer, *Federal Indian Law and Violent Crime: Native Women and Children at the Mercy of the State*, 31 Social Justice 17, 25.

59 *Id* at 26.

60 *Id.*

61 *Id.*

62 Troy A. Eid, *Beyond Oliphant: Strengthening Criminal Justice in Indian Country*, The Federal Lawyer, 6 (2007).

expect to be retried in U.S. district court, wasting time, money, and undermining the decisions of the tribal government.[63]

These transitions would be just the tip of the iceberg and would not happen easily or overnight. Many changes would have to be made and there may have to be compromises on both ends for this to work. Any autonomy or control given back to the tribal government will be a benefit given the amount of control they have now. Ultimately, however, reverting the power back to the tribal government and allowing access to restorative justice practices which originate and rely heavily on Native American culture and ideals would be a great step towards the healing of harm created by these vicious crimes.

II. THE RESTORATIVE JUSTICE APPROACH CAN BRING PEACE AND HEALING TO NATIVE AMERICAN VICTIMS.

"In the Native worldview there is a deep connection between justice and spirituality: in both, it is essential to maintain or restore harmony and balance."[64]

a) There are different general types of restorative justice practices that can be implemented to resolve crime.

Restorative programs are designed to encourage offenders to express remorse, recognize their harm, and accept responsibility.[65] One approach that can achieve this is victim-offender mediation. This is when a facilitator assists between the victim and offender to provide an opportunity for the victim to meet the offender in a safe and structured setting outside of the courtroom.[66] Here, the parties would have the support of a trained mediator to guide them through the process.[67] In a study based in Texas and Ohio, the most common reasons stated by victims of sexual violence for wanting to participate in victim-offender

---

63   *Id.*

64   Sarah Deer, *Federal Indian Law and Violent Crime: Native Women and Children at the Mercy of the State*, 31 Social Justice 17, 1.

65   Mohamed Ismail Bin, *Restorative Model: the Alternative Justice Response to the Victims of Sexual Violence*, 11 Fiat Justisia 1, 78.

66   *Id* at 79.

67   *Id.*

mediation was to seek answers to questions that have been eating at them, to express the impact the crime had on them, to experience a human interaction with the offender and to advance their healing.[68] Often, the focus will lie in voicing impact from the crime and receiving validation, of which both the offender and the victim may seek.[69]

Similarly, another approach would be family or community group conferencing. This approach brings together the victim, offender, family, friends, and other key players of both of the parties in the aftermath of the crime.[70] The ultimate goal of this approach is to give the victim the opportunity to involve themselves directly, voice their side, and increase the offender's awareness.[71] A benefit to this approach is that the offender's support system is engaged to help the offender make amends and shape their future behavior.[72] This creates a stronger connection of both the offender and the victim to community support and raises the likelihood of the offender remaining an upstanding citizen afterwards.

One of the most important approaches tied to Native American culture is circles. This approach has origins from Native American practices and has maintained its relevance throughout time. Circles are designed to reach a workable consensus among the community, victims, offenders, victim's supporters, offender's supporters, judges, prosecutors, defense, police, and the court workers.[73] Circles are more extensive than mediations or conferences and are not likely to be the most cost-effective unless they divert cases that typically would result in a prison sentence, thus saving the cost of prison.[74] "Because crime signifies some breakdown of relationships that leaves people isolated, Circles focus on forging connections-reintegrating what has come apart."[75] When it comes to

---

68   Mary Koss and Mary Achilles, *Restorative Justice Responses to Sexual Assault*, National Online Resource Center on Violence Against Women, 6.

69   *Id.*

70   Mohamed Ismail Bin, *Restorative Model: the Alternative Justice Response to the Victims of Sexual Violence*, 11 Fiat Justisia 1, 79.

71   *Id.*

72   *Id.*

73   Mohamed Ismail Bin, *Restorative Model: the Alternative Justice Response to the Victims of Sexual Violence*, 11 Fiat Justisia 1, 79.

74   Paul McCold, *Handbook of Restorative Justice: A Global Perspective*, 29.

75   Kay Pranis *et al*, *Peacemaking Circles: From Crime to Community*, 33.

circles, it is important to identify specific values that will be referred to throughout the process. People that identify in different ways, from different cultures, from different walks of life all recognize the same core values that are necessary to fixing harm.[76] The ten core values that should be focused on are love, forgiveness, trust, empathy, inclusivity, courage, sharing, humility, honesty, and respect.[77] These are the core values that need to be the focus over the negative feelings that are bound to spill out.[78] Some of these negative feelings may be anger, confusion, hurt, or betrayal but focusing on the positive values below will create a higher chance of success.

There are two types of paths in the restorative circle practice model; a healing paradigm and a judging paradigm.[79] An example of the healing paradigm is the peacemaking circles. Peacemaking circles help communities come together when times get especially hard.[80] There is a justice brought from peace circles; the justice of being respected, heard, listening to others, and working things out in a way that honors everyone.[81]

Sentencing circles are an example of the judging paradigm and are community driven processes that work with the criminal justice system to find an agreed-upon sentencing plan.[82] Here, each member of the circle can speak from their point of view about the event and identify steps for healing the affected parties and how to prevent future occurrences.[83] Together, they will agree on an appropriate sentencing plan that addresses the concerns of all the parties.[84]

Within any type of circle in the restorative justice realm, it is often useful to include a talking piece, which signifies who is designated to speak and allows a broader expression of views and voices.[85] This talking piece creates an equal-

---

76   *Id.*

77   *Id* at 47.

78   *Id.*

79   Paul McCold, *Handbook of Restorative Justice: A Global Perspective*, 28.

80   *Id.*

81   *Id* at 3-4.

82   Paul McCold, *Handbook of Restorative Justice: A Global Perspective*, 29.

83   *Id.*

84   Mohamed Ismail Bin, *Restorative Model: the Alternative Justice Response to the Victims of Sexual Violence*, 11 Fiat Justisia 1, 79.

85   Mary Koss and Mary Achilles, *Restorative Justice Responses to Sexual Assault*, National Online Resource Center on Violence Against Women, 6-7.

ity that the victim has not gotten to feel through the crime committed against them. This talking piece also ensures that interruptions will not happen and that every person sitting there has a voice that will be listened to. The circular layout provides an attitude of mutual respect and community and cultural pride.[86] No matter who is in the circle and how different the levels of power may have been, once entered in the circle, everyone becomes equally as important and everyone matters. These circles in the context of Native American victims, offenders, or communities can also bring an added piece of spirituality of being connected to their culture, which can, in turn, encourage a positive outcome for everyone.

Community service is a form of restorative justice. This is beneficial because it can be used to help the community, it allows the offender to reflect, it addresses the harm caused, and it can even rehabilitate the offender.[87] This type of practice can help integrate the offender back into the community as well. It strengthens ties and connections to the community, gives the offender time to reflect on what happened, and can give the offender a confidence and pride back into themselves that will help cultivate positive actions moving forward.

b) The restorative practices that can be used for victimized Native American women focus on the Native American culture and traditional practices.

When it comes to approaching sexually violent crimes and considering restorative justice methods, there are many concerns that may create apprehension when reacting to such. "How does one move away from punitive reactions which – even when enforced – further brutalize perpetrators, without, by leniency of reaction, giving the impression that sexualized...violence is acceptable"?[88] This mindset will create a divide and cause pushback from the people who seek justice for these victimized women, and it is understandable. To consider restorative justice practices as a route to take with sexually violent crimes, we need to readjust our lens to understand the full range of success that it can bring. One of the ways to understand restorative justice better is to not view restorative

---

86   *Id* at 7.

87   Mohamed Ismail Bin, *Restorative Model: the Alternative Justice Response to the Victims of Sexual Violence*, 11 Fiat Justisia 1, 81.

88   Kathleen Daly, *Sexual Assault and Restorative Justice,* 1 (2001).

justice as the opposite of our criminal justice system.[89] Rather than being opposite of our current system, restorative justice takes the positive goals from our current system and combines them with more restorative goals that improve the lives of all involved. It would be incorrect to consider restorative practices as a lenient method intent on getting the offender an easy "punishment." These essential restorative practices bring healing to all involved and create a future full of potential.

When an offender commits a crime, especially a violent one, they create an inequality in which the offender is "above" the victim and can use them for whatever purpose they feel.[90] To respond to this, a punishment should fix this inequality created by the offender and create the victims' equal value.[91] This cannot be created by diminishing or degrading the offender, however.[92] We need to vindicate the value of the victim and not focus on destroying or tearing down the wrongdoer.[93] Being offender-oriented in our criminal justice system may be the wrong approach; turning the focus on the victim may create a better healing process for all, and that should be the ultimate goal of any justice system.

Native American communities have also recognized the positives of reintegrating restorative justice practices in response to sexually violent crimes. In order for offenders to eventually live peaceably in society again, we need to have the offender immersed in society, where their community will hold them accountable and everyone is involved in helping heal.[94] In turning to incarceration in these situations, an offender is essentially removed from the daily accountability where the likelihood of rehabilitation is higher, creating an "easier" out for the offender.[95] The problem with incarceration as the usual route for sexual/domestic violence, is that it creates a repression of communities of color without providing real safety for the survivors of such crimes.[96]

---

89 *Id* at 4.

90 *Id* at 11.

91 *Id.*

92 *Id.*

93 *Id.*

94 Andrea Smith, *Decolonizing Anti-Rape Law and Strategizing Accountability in Native American Communities*, 37 Social Justice 4, 39.

95 *Id* at 40.

96 *Id* at 41.

Within the current justice system, victims of sexual assault have voiced feeling overwhelmingly negative interactions with different players in the system; such as emergency personnel, police, prosecutors, and members within the civil suit realm.[97] Many feel that since it is the job of the prosecutor to prove beyond a reasonable doubt that the offender is guilty, often the victim feels as though they need to prove they were raped.[98] "Most survivor/victims who participated in trials before juries in the US believed rapists had more rights, the system was unfair, their statutory victims' rights were not implemented, and they weren't given enough information or control over handling their case."[99] This mindset about the current system is on par with the focus of prosecution; keying in on the offender and ensuring justice is brought against them. If we try to shift our focus more on the victim and what the victim needs to heal, we can create a united community in which all will benefit.

Intimate partner violence (IPV) is a category of the violent crimes that Native American women suffer which has high costs.[100] These costs mainly coincide with the extremely negative and serious health and social consequences that result from this type of violence.[101] This result of IPV is recognized as an issue generally, but within Native American communities, there are limitations to history and identification, signifying the seriously underreported and under detected nature of this particular crime.[102] This low reporting and lack of data creates huge problems on the tribal land. Current and accurate statistics are vital to be able to plan with public health prevention and other services.[103] This type of violence can create mental health issues such as anxiety, PTSD, substance abuse, and any other mood disorder. The current criminal justice system does not focus on the victim, so prevention or proactiveness about these issues are not prioritized. However, one of the goals in a restorative justice process is to focus on

---

97   Mary Koss and Mary Achilles, *Restorative Justice Responses to Sexual Assault*, National Online Resource Center on Violence Against Women, 3.

98   *Id.*

99   *Id.*

100   Bonnie Duran *et al, Intimate Partner Violence and Alcohol, Drug, and Mental Disorders Among American Indian Women from Southwest Tribes in Primary Care*, 16 2, 11.

101   *Id.*

102   *Id* at 12.

103   *Id.*

the needs of the victims and how to heal moving forward. This creates a safer, realistic, and higher chance of success for the victim to recover.

In Canada (like the United States), when the settlers brought colonization while arriving to the countries, they brought with them a legal system that was imposed upon the Indigenous people.[104] This created a very strained relationship between Canada (like the United States) and the Indigenous People which is still present to this day.[105] Why are Indigenous people that are in the system not given the opportunity to use Indigenous founded practices such as restorative justice? The Native American offenders and victims become subjected to a criminal justice system that is not theirs and the crimes committed are rectified not by the way of their people, but by westernized society who forced this system on them in the first place.

In the 1990's, Canada noticed the disproportionate numbers of Indigenous people appearing in courts.[106] It was recognized that these offenders should be dealt with in a more culturally appropriate and meaningful way.[107] This paved the way to recognize that there is a positive impact of Indigenous-based restorative justice initiatives that address the intimate victimization that disproportionately affects the Indigenous women.[108] Related to the positive outcome of victims, there was also proven to be lower recidivism rates.[109] These programs are not just quick changes, however. It takes time and a huge focus on healing to reach positive results.[110] Reiterating how most restorative programs succeed, the offender and the victims must consent to participate and if either are unwilling, then it is an unavailable approach.

Like any other approach to crime, seeking truth through perspective, experience, and reputation is the common ground that is found between restorative justice practices and the current United States legal system.[111] Also, with any approach, it is important to recognize the potential drawbacks or negatives.

---

104 Jeffery Hewitt, *Indigenous Restorative Justice: Approaches, Meaning & Possibility*, 67 UNBLJ, 324.

105 *Id.*

106 *Id* at 315.

107 *Id.*

108 *Id* at 317.

109 *Id.*

110 *Id* at 319.

111 *Id* at 321.

Here, when considering restorative justice initiatives with the complexity and seriousness of sexual victimizations, there is a potential of domination and power relations between the offender and the victim.[112] However, there are huge potential positives that the victim would not receive in the westernized criminal justice system like the ability to choose how to present herself, express her feelings, express her understanding of the events, and state her wishes and her demands for the future.[113]

Based on all the information out there, Native American victims, offenders, and community members alike would benefit immensely to get back to their roots and follow the original practices of their culture. Any of the restorative justice practices would be beneficial to use in these types of violent crimes. Peace circles have been adapted from certain Native American traditional practices.[114] They can be used to really include each key player in the crime and ensure the involvement of everyone so that all voices are heard. Other forms of restorative practices would be successful too, like victim-offender mediation and community service. With all the negative results coming out of the current criminal justice system and all the positive feedback flowing from studies on restorative practices, it would be the best route to try and approach some of these crimes with a new mindset. Relating the Native American parties involved back to their culture and practices creates a higher likelihood of success and since the current system is not working anyway, it does not hurt to change direction and bring the focus back on the people, rather than the crime.

---

112 Julie Stubs, *Restorative Justice, Gendered Violence, and Indigenous Women*, Restorative Justice and Violence Against Women, 106.

113 *Id.*

114 Mohamed Ismail Bin, *Restorative Model: the Alternative Justice Response to the Victims of Sexual Violence*, 11 Fiat Justisia 1, 80.

How will restoring jurisdiction over crimes committed on reservations improve justice for Native Americans?

Will the introduction of restorative practices on tribal lands make Native American women more or less vulnerable to sexual attack?

Is there any justification for not subjecting non-Native Americans to accountability for crimes committed on tribal lands?

Does the discussion of tribal jurisdiction over crimes committed on reservations have relevance to other communities?

What challenges do domestic violence crimes pose for restorative justice practitioners?

Restorative Justice — Lessons from Around the World

ELIZABETH CLARKE

INTRODUCTION

In the United States, the use of restorative justice is gaining popularity, with restorative justice practice in justice systems in most states. In some states, such as Delaware and Colorado, the restorative justice practices are embedded in statute and overseen by state agencies, courts and/or other system stakeholders. In other states, the restorative justice practices emerged organically from neighborhoods struggling to find new approaches to interrupt conflict. Some of the more innovative restorative justice organizations have developed organically and include Common Justice in New York, Impact Justice in Oakland and Washington DC, and the Restorative Justice Hubs in Chicago.

The challenge in the U.S. is that the lack of a national human rights framework leaves restorative justice programs without the protections of fundamental internationally recognized principles that are embedded in restorative justice practices in other developed nations based on their adherence to international human rights.

This article will explore the growth of restorative justice in the U.S., will examine developments in other developed nations, and will highlight the impact of human rights protections in restorative justice practices.

Restorative justice was embedded in the Illinois Juvenile Court Act rewrite of 1998. As an addition to the longstanding rehabilitative philosophy underlying the juvenile court, restorative justice was promoted as a conceptual framework to prevent and reduce juvenile delinquency. The framework was described as "balanced restorative justice", emphasizing accountability along with public safety and competency development. The statute did not contain any procedural or due process protections.

By 2013, a statewide survey identified 95 organizations across Illinois in an inventory of restorative justice practices:

> *Respondents reporting using restorative justice practices were found in 54 Illinois counties, and in many different types of organizations who respond to youth misconduct, including police departments, probation and court services, schools, community-based organizations, and other state and municipal departments. Restorative justice services were most commonly used with non-violent, first time offenders, and the most common practices used were peer juries, circles, family group conferencing, and victim-offender mediation.*[1]

Restorative justice was embraced by community leaders in Chicago, but with an emphasis on community leadership and on peace-building practices within the community. The resulting restorative justice hubs emphasized five pillars as principles for restorative justice practice:

1. A welcoming and hospitable place
2. The accompaniment of youth in their journey
3. Relationship building with youth and families
4. Relentless engagement of organizations and resources for the youth and families
5. Supporting collaboration and learning with other RJ Hubs[2]

---

1   http://www.icjia.state.il.us/assets/pdf/ResearchReports/JJSRFDIL2012_Annual_Report_082914.pdf

2   https://revistademediacion.com/en/articulos/restorative-justice-hubs-concept-paper/

These community restorative justice practices owed their vision to the original indigenous restorative justice practices of communities across the globe.[3] The goal was to heal communities as well as youth. One of the two "grandmothers" of the Chicago restorative justice movement, Ora Schub, described the community driven restorative justice practices:

> *The court system isn't about healing or relationships.* *There are three questions always asked in the criminal law system: Is there a crime that was committed? Who committed it? What can we do to punish the person? In restorative justice we instead ask: Was there a harm? Who caused the harm? Who was harmed? How can we hold the person accountable? What can we do to make the community safer again?*
>
> *When you look at a harm done, you need first to look at the four parts of a person: mental, physical, emotional and spiritual. In our court systems, you just bring the mental and physical. In restorative justice you bring your whole self.*
>
> *Courts take responsibility away from community, and that's part of the problem. We see a problem, and instead of taking care of it ourselves, we turn it over to the so-called professionals. The best thing is to keep young people from getting arrested, and entering the system at all.[4]*

The Adler School's Institute on Public Safety and Social Justice published a white paper titled "Restorative Justice: A Primer and Exploration of Practice Across Two North American Cities,[5]" examining the application of restorative justice in Chicago and Vancouver. The paper provides an overview of the history and philosophy behind restorative justice, takes a closer look at examples in Chicago and Vancouver and offers recommendations to practitioners and researchers.

In 2017, the first restorative justice community court opened in North Lawndale in Chicago. The court operated in an informal process around a conference table in a meeting room in a social service organization's building in the community. The community provided restorative justice circles to develop

---

3   https://kroc.nd.edu/news-events/news/restorative-justice-helps-rehabilitate-tough-chicago-neighborhoods/

4   https://chicagodefender.com/grandmothers-of-chicagos-restorative-justice-movement/

5   http://restorativejustice.org/rj-library/restorative-justice-a-primer-and-exploration-of-practice-across-two-north-american-cities/12286/#sthash.f7ugUE7m.dpbs

repair harm agreements which were brought to the court for review and over-sight in cases of young adults (age 18-26) charged with a nonviolent felony or misdemeanor.[6] Once the conditions of the agreement are completed, the young person can get the case dropped and record expunged. The court grew out of extensive collaboration between the court and community, and was modeled in part on the Red Hook Community Center in Brooklyn. The model proved successful, and in 2020 was expanded to Englewood and Avondale.[7]

GROWTH OF RESTORATIVE JUSTICE IN U.S.

This dichotomy between statutory/institutionally developed and operated restorative justice versus organic community-grown restorative justice practices continues in the U.S.

Delaware and Colorado developed vigorous restorative justice practices based on state legislation. In Delaware, statutory protections for restorative justice practices ("alternative case resolution") included a statutory confidentiality protection.[8] Restorative justice in Delaware has been embraced by the Joseph R. Biden School of Public Policy:

> *Restorative justice is an approach to resolving conflict that is built on the values of respect, responsibility, and relationship. Restorative justice is different than traditional approaches to justice. Instead of ignoring victims and isolating offenders it focuses on the needs of the victim, promotes accountability from the offender, and empowers both to grow from the experience.*
>
> *Restorative practices have deep roots in indigenous communities. Healing the harmed and rehabilitating the offender is the philosophy of indigenous peacemaking.[9]*

---

6   https://www.aboutrsi.org/court-adr-across-illinois/programs/restorative-justice-community-court-cook-county-north-lawndale

7   https://chicago.suntimes.com/2020/8/7/21357874/restorative-courts-expanding-chicago-tim-evans-cook-county-justice-system

8   https://legis.delaware.gov/json/BillDetail/GenerateHtmlDocument?legislationId=47304&legislationTypeId=1&docTypeId=2&legislationName=SB38

9   https://www.bidenschool.udel.edu/ipa/serving-delaware/crp/restorative-justice

By contrast, restorative justice grew out of community leadership in New York City (Common Justice)[10] and in Oakland, CA (Impact Justice)[11]. Both models focus on empowering communities to address conflict through practices that build upon and expand community relationships and resiliency.

While there are varying degrees of protections in these different states and cities, there is no national framework requiring the human rights protections (such as confidentiality) that are embraced in other developed nations.

GROWTH OF RESTORATIVE JUSTICE AROUND THE GLOBE

Restorative Justice following mass violence – Some of the most dramatic examples of restorative justice in recent years have occurred in nations seeking to address crimes against humanity. Argentina's 1983 Commission on the Disappearance of Persons, South Africa's Truth and Reconciliation Commission, and similar truth and reconciliation processes in nations as diverse as Rwanda, Cambodia and Northern Ireland all seek historical honesty as a basis for accountability, reconciliation and moving forward.[12]

New Zealand – Restorative justice worldwide is commonly attributed to indigenous Maori concepts of communal justice. The National Juvenile Justice Network in the U.S. documented the history and expansion of restorative justice practices in New Zealand, beginning with indigenous Maori protests against confiscation of their lands in the 1970's, which culminated in a transformative Children's Code:

> The Children's and Young People's Well-being Act 1989 (the Act), also called the Oranga Tamariki Act 1989,1 represented a seismic shift in youth justice in New Zealand. It dramatically downsized the entire youth justice system and established a restorative, rather than retributive, approach to youth justice. The Act's goals included reducing youth involvement with the courts, promoting diversion, empowering victims, strengthening families and communities, and utilizing culturally appropriate practices. **This Act is the first time that a**

---

10   https://www.commonjustice.org/

11   https://impactjustice.org/

12   Minow, Martha, When Should Law Forgive, New York, W.W. Norton & Company, 2019.

Western nation legislated the mandatory use of restorative practices throughout their youth justice system.[13]

A Ministry of Justice report from 2004 reviews protections that must be in place in restorative justice proceedings. The Ministry of Justice Principles of Best Practice include confidentiality:

> *The privacy and confidentiality of participants must be protected and respected to the extent possible.*[14]

Europe is developing a child rights approach to Restorative Justice that will include safeguards based on international and European child-rights standards.[15] Procedural protections that have long been in place in European restorative justice practice **include confidentiality**, with a practice guide from the European Forum on Restorative Justice noting that both the victim and the offender must enjoy the right to confidentiality.[16]

Northern Ireland embraced restorative practices in juvenile justice in 2002 as part of the peace building process following more than three decades of civil violence.[17] Restorative justice conferencing was mandated in the new Youth Justice Act to be considered upon a finding of guilt. The N.I. restorative justice statutory mandate included confidentiality as one of its core protections:

CONFIDENTIALITY – Restorative Justice Youth Conferences – NORTHERN IRELAND

b. Where a restorative justice practice is convened with respect to a child under the age of 18 and an offense, neither –

---

13 https://www.njjn.org/uploads/digital-library/New%20Zealand's%20Youth%20Justice%20Transformation%20Executive%20Summary__%204.26.18.pdf?phpMyAdmin=14730ab3483c51c94ca868bccffa06ef

14 http://restorativejustice.org/am-site/media/restorative-justice-best-practice-in-new-zealand.pdf

15 https://ec.europa.eu/info/law/better-regulation/have-your-say/initiatives/12454-EU-strategy-on-the-rights-of-the-child-2021-24-/F540877

16 https://www.euforumrj.org/sites/default/files/2019-11/practice-guide-with-cover-page-for-website.pdf

17 http://www.campaignforyouthjustice.org/across-the-country/item/northern-ireland-a-human-rights-approach-to-youth-crime

1. *The fact that it has been convened; nor*
2. *Anything said or done (or omitted to be said or done) in or in connection with any meeting constituting, or forming part of, the youth conference, is admissible in any juvenile or criminal proceedings as evidence that the child committed the offense.*[18]

A review launched in 2010 by the Northern Ireland Minister of Justice noted that one of the strengths of the juvenile justice system was the development of restorative justice youth conferencing.[19]

In 2011 the Youth Justice Agency in Northern Ireland reported the following outcomes:

- 7,608 youth conferences since the system was introduced.
- Over 44,000 people have participated
- 2 out of 3 (67%) had victim representation.
- Satisfaction rate among victims is 89%. 91% of victims prefer it for young people.
- 93% of conferences lead to a negotiated plan that is successfully completed. [20]

The establishment of restorative justice practices in Northern Ireland was no easy task. Northern Ireland was a deeply divided state, with a formidable wall dividing protestant from catholic populations in Belfast. The goal, as one of the early promoters noted in an informal talk in Chicago in 2015, was to establish peace building skills throughout its citizenry. As the restorative justice practices flourished, the youth justice system shifted its emphasis to prevention and diversion practices, according to Youth Justice Agency staff in a meeting with U.S. observers in 2019. This shift reflected both the diminishment of tension as peace became more established and greater acceptance of restorative practices as they moved into a more mainstream role in the justice system. A recent reviewer noted the role of restorative justice in transforming the justice system: *in a society going through a transition, it permeates all aspects of initiatives aimed at addressing crime, conflict and disorder. Importantly, in this context the values*

---

18   https://www.legislation.gov.uk/ukpga/2002/26/part/4/crossheading/youth-conferences

19   https://restorativejustice.org.uk/sites/default/files/resources/files/Report%20of%20the%20Youth%20 Justice%20System%20in%20Northern%20Ireland.pdf

20   file:///Users/elizabethclarke/Downloads/LI298_PAULA_JACK.pdf

of restorative justice reflect the aims of transitional justice more broadly, such as seeking accountability and truth, achieving reparation and restitution, and allowing for healing and reconciliation.[21]

The restorative justice practices in the juvenile system also contributed to a decrease in juvenile detention. The population in the Woodlands Juvenile Detention Center outside Belfast decreased by half from about two dozen youth in my first visit in 2014 to about a dozen in my second visit in 2019. Practitioners noted that when faced directly with the child involved in an offense, victims rarely wanted incarceration – rather they sought individualized sanctions and services to prevent reoccurrence. Yet, media reports a continuing issue with a disproportionate number of catholic youth incarcerated.[22]

Restorative Justice in North America – In 2015, academics gathered in Toronto with government officials and advocates from across North America. Organized by an ad hoc coalition of individuals from North America and Europe, including my organization, participants examined and compared restorative justice practices in Canada, Mexico and the United States. The participants also heard from international experts who presented a review of restorative justice practices across Europe and in Northern Ireland. In conclusion, participants drafted a **policy paper** that recommended ten points to improve the implementation of restorative justice in juvenile cases, including **a recommendation that fundamental restorative principles such as voluntary participation, confidentiality, proportionality, and neutrality of the mediator, should be guaranteed by law.**[23]

Calls for Confidentiality Protections in Restorative Justice Practices in Illinois. A wide range of organizations and individuals in Illinois have called for the creation of a legal privilege to ensure confidentiality protections are embedded in restorative justice practices. In the previous legislative session, the proposal was in House Bill 4295.[24] The proposal has broad-based support but met with some opposition from law enforcement during committee debate.

21 Eriksson, Anna; *Restorative Justice in the Northern Ireland Transition*, 1/2015, https://www.research-gate.net/publication/283620845_Restorative_Justice_in_the_Northern_Ireland_Transition

22 https://www.irishnews.com/news/northernirelandnews/2019/07/01/news/catholic-children-three-times-more-likely-to-be-locked-up-1652854/

23 https://jjustice.org/wp-content/uploads/nacjj_paper_on_restorative_justice-copy-2.pdf

24 https://ilga.gov/legislation/BillStatus.asp?DocNum=4295&GAID=15&DocTypeID=HB&LegID=123383&SessionID=108&GA=101

CONCLUSION –

Restorative justice is a promising and rapidly emerging practice that has the potential to transform our justice system by focusing both on individual and societal accountability. However, unless basic protections, such as **voluntary participation, confidentiality, proportionality, and neutrality of the mediator**, are guaranteed by law, it could easily be coopted and perpetuate racial disparities and other injustices. The U.S. should follow the lead of other developed nations and ensure full due process and human rights protections for restorative justice practices.

How can states and cities foster restorative justice practices to resolve disputes and social inequalities?

Why have restorative justice practices flourished in some parts of the world but not elsewhere?

How does the enactment of privilege rules foster the use of restorative justice practices?

Restorative Justice Abroad: A Case of the Czech Republic

LENKA KŘIČKOVÁ *&* TEREZIE BOKOVÁ

Things were usually rough with the 5th graders. We fought for their attention with diverging success, often leaving behind circle keeping guidelines and trying to anyhow navigate the tricky waters of our interaction. Sometimes, you could not hear a single word in the classroom. But then, six weeks into our peace circle weekly routine, the atmosphere suddenly changed. That day, someone shared that their relative had just been shot, one of the too many casualties of recent Chicago street violence. One after another, the children started to share stories of their relatives and friends who all were witnesses or victims of violence. They all have their wounds and were keen to learn about ours. It was quite an odd feeling, not knowing what to say because we haven't experienced anything like that. "In the country where I come from, there are not so many guns among people, so there is no gun violence." It felt important to tell them the world could be different from what they have experienced so far. "Wait," one boy said, "if you say there are no guns, how do people kill each other? With knives?"

CHICAGO EXPERIENCE

The opening story happened in 2016 when we, two law students from the Czech Republic, took a restorative justice course at The John Marshall Law School in Chicago. At that time, it would not be an overstatement to say that everything we knew about restorative justice, we learnt while studying in the USA. Before that, we had been barely aware of the concept and had found it difficult to even come up with an accurate translation of the term. During our Czech law studies, we were taught that criminal law serves the purposes of protection, prevention, repression and regulation. Restorative justice was mentioned only briefly and elective courses on this topic were not available. So the standard perspective of criminal law and criminal justice we were familiar with was predominantly retributive.

The restorative justice course consisted of a classroom component and a practical component. Even in American settings, the content of our weekly classes seemed extraordinary. We usually first had a chance to hear real-life restorative justice stories from interesting guests. Then we spent the rest of the class talking in a peace circle with our classmates and teachers. How often do law students share their personal experience and stories together or cry in a class? In our restorative justice class, that happened. In fact, it might sometimes have looked more like a therapy session than a law school class. For us, it was even more unusual because Czech students generally tend to assume a more passive role in classes than American students are used to.

However, the most intensive learning took place during the practical part of the course. We discovered restorative justice practices through many means, such as academic conferences, Alcoholics Anonymous meetings or study visits to courts and jail. Most importantly, we visited a Chicago public elementary school on a weekly basis to work with several groups of kids ranging from 3rd to 8th grade. We spent the time with them conducting peace circles, discussing various topics or playing games in order to help them with their truancy and disciplinary problems. Every kid we met was of course unique but what they had in common was the underprivileged community that they came from. And already at such a young age, they knew that life can be tough.

So we listened in disbelief to them sharing their experience of which the opening story above is just one example. We heard stories concerning gun violence, physical or sexual abuse, gang involvement or deaths among family and friends – stories that, in safety of our Czech homes, we would not have imagined happening, especially to kids in one of the richest countries in the world. For instance, when we were told the students can only wear black or white T-shirts, we at first understood it as a substitute for a school uniform, not as a rule aiming to prevent children from wearing colors of their local gangs. When a boy complained of not being able to watch TV in the evening, we thought it was because of his parents' bedtime rules. But the real reason was that he could not leave any lights on due to safety concerns.

Hopefully, the children benefited from our presence. The whole experience was definitely eye-opening for us. Above all, it convinced us how valuable restorative justice can be. The kids we got to know sometimes failed. But it is hard to blame them and only seek punishment when they are growing up in an environment that has been failing them for most of their lives. Therefore, it seems justified to demand that the society does its best to provide the kids with quality education instead of letting some schools become the proverbial "pipelines to prison".

Overall, the restorative justice course made us see law in its social context, rather than just as an academic discipline. We lawyers sometimes tend to live in our own world, far from the reality, even speaking our own language that nobody understands. It is, therefore, sometimes easy to forget what law actually stands for and how it impacts people. Maybe this particular experience was one of the reasons why we both started our legal careers at the ombudsman's office which is supposed to help the weak. Why we study constitutional law and human rights. Or why one of us launched a mediation course at our home university to teach future lawyers how to resolve conflicts more peacefully. Be it as it may, the course provided us with unforgettable experience (personally as well as professionally).

RESTORATIVE JUSTICE IN CZECH PERSPECTIVE

During our studies in Chicago, we sometimes wondered at how different the American and Czech legal systems are when it comes to restorative justice. Things which would be hard to imagine at home (both good and bad) were commonplace in the USA. Thus, we find it useful to give the reader a taste of these differences and present restorative features appearing in Czech law. In no way are we attempting to conduct an academic study in comparative law because that would require much more expertise in the field of restorative justice and related disciplines. We are merely offering a few observations, mostly based on our personal experience, that we believe could be of interest to the reader despite their rather sketchy and subjective nature.

1) Criminal law - the bedrock of restorative justice

In many ways, the American criminal justice system faces problems that do not occur under contemporary Czech law. For instance, capital punishment was abolished 30 years ago and is prohibited by Czech constitutional law[1] and also by international law binding the Czech Republic and the majority of European states.[2] According to the European Court of Human Rights,[3] even waiting on a death row can violate the prohibition of inhuman and degrading treatment and the risk of exposure to such treatment needs to be taken into consideration in extradition proceedings.[4] Notoriously long prison sentences (exceeding a lifetime), known in the USA, cannot be imposed in the Czech Republic either. The Czech Criminal Code allows for life imprisonment (always with a possibility of parole[5]) in extraordinary cases, but generally the prison sentence should not be longer than 20 years.[6] The age of criminal responsibility is 15 years old which prevents problems regarding children tried as adults and incarcerated in adult prisons.

Moreover, Czech and American criminal procedure is built on different foundations. Czech criminal law is an example of an inquisitorial system as opposed to the adversarial system used in the USA. Among other features, the adversarial process gives a lot of power to prosecutors and tends to emphasize the competitive nature of their relationship to defendants. Especially trials can turn into tough legal battles between two opposing parties, both doing their best to get the jury on their side. Defendants' fate then very much depends on their lawyers' performance. However, many cases do not reach the trial phase at all because the defendant pleads guilty instead.[7] While plea bargaining, so common in the USA, might be effective, power imbalance can also lead to heightened risk of deals very unfavorable for defendants or even to wrongful convictions. On the contrary, the basic principles of the Czech Criminal Procedure Code[8] place the responsibility of establishing the merits of the case on the state authori-

---

1   Art. 6(3) of the Charter of Fundamental Rights and Freedoms.

2   Protocol no. 13 to the European Convention on Human Rights.

3   An international court that interprets the European Convention on Human Rights which is binding for Council of Europe's members, including the Czech Republic.

4   See judgment of the European Court of Human Rights, *Soering v. The United Kingdom*, 7. 7. 1989, no. 14038/88. This case concerned extradition to the USA.

5   See also judgment of the European Court of Human Rights, *Vinter and Others v. The United Kingdom*, 9. 7. 2013, no. 66069/09, 130/10 and 3896/10.

6   Criminal Code no. 40/2009 Coll., § 54-55.

7   A plea bargain exists in Czech criminal law as well but it is a rather new and so far not very commonly used legal instrument.

8   Criminal Procedure Code no. 141/1961 Coll., § 2.

ties (police, prosecutors, courts). During the pre-trial proceeding, the authorities must actively and with equal care examine all the circumstances for as well as against the defendant. In addition, the authorities are obliged to examine all the relevant circumstances even if the accused person confesses to the crime. In the end, it is up to judges (there are no juries) to objectively evaluate all the evidence and decide whether the defendant's guilt was proven beyond reasonable doubt. Overall, the Czech criminal procedure seems in general to be less competitive and, although not always successfully, more focused on state authorities seeking the actual truth about the crime.

Last but not least, there are several issues that are rather U.S.-specific and do not occur elsewhere in quite the same magnitude, which makes the comparison with Czech law difficult. These issues involve for example mass imprisonment, tough-on-crime aspects of war on drugs (e.g. mandatory sentences, three-strikes laws) or racial disparities in the criminal justice system.[9]

For all these reasons, one can be sometimes tempted to question whether the U.S. criminal justice system could not be aptly called the criminal injustice system. Thus, it seems natural that the restorative justice movement arose and evolved in the USA since there has been a pressing need for alternative and more humane approaches. Nevertheless, that does not mean that the Czech criminal justice system does not need restorative justice. On the contrary – it could definitely use some improvements in this respect.

In the Czech Republic, restorative justice principles have not been implemented into the legal order in any systematic way so far. Therefore, only scarce examples of restorative approach can be traced within the criminal justice system. The next part of this chapter introduces the most significant of them.[10]

Regarding substantive criminal law, the Criminal Code includes some aspects that could be characterized as restorative – mainly when it comes to provisions on sentencing. For example, criminal penalties must be proportionate and individualized which requires (among others) that the legally protected interests

---

9   See more e.g. Stevenson, Bryan. 2014. *Just Mercy: A Story of Justice and Redemption*. New York: Spiegel & Grau.; or Alexander, Michelle. 2012. *The New Jim Crow: Mass Incarceration In The Age Of Colorblindness*. New York: New Press.

10 This part relies heavily on the work written by Petra Masopust Šachová - a Czech lawyer and academic who comprehensively described examples of restorative justice in Czech criminal law in her book Masopust Šachová, Petra. 2019. *Restorativní přístupy při řešení trestné činnosti*. Praha: C.H. Beck.

of the aggrieved party shall be taken into account.[11] The Criminal Code also contains many types of alternative sanctions such as house confinement, community service, pecuniary penalty, prohibition of activity, suspended sentence of imprisonment etc.[12] Courts should prefer these to the imprisonment sentence that is meant to be used as a means of last resort (ultima ratio).[13] Under certain circumstances, it is even possible to waive the punishment completely if the offender regrets committing the act and demonstrates genuine efforts of reformation.[14] Nevertheless, statistics show that the number of cases when imprisonment sentences are imposed still has not decreased very much.[15]

Things get slightly better when it comes to procedural law. In the Criminal Procedure Code, restorative justice ideas are present in regards to the so called diversions – legal instruments that serve as alternatives to trial.[16] They typically emphasize damage compensation to the aggrieved party as one of the conditions to avoid trial. For instance, the Criminal Procedure Code allows for settlement[17] (which terminates the criminal prosecution) in proceedings on a misdemeanor if the aggrieved person agrees with it. Among other conditions, the settlement requires that the offender compensates the aggrieved person for the damage or otherwise redeems the harm caused by the criminal offence, surrenders any unjust enrichment and pays a sum of money designated for helping crime victims. This might encourage communication between the offender and the victim and help them find restorative solutions to their situation. Unfortunately, these diversions have not been used very often in criminal proceedings according to the statistics.[18]

Another two statutes should be highlighted as significant from the restorative justice point of view – the Crime Victims Act[19] and Probation and Mediation

---

11 Criminal Code, § 38(3).

12 Criminal Code, § 52.

13 Criminal Code, § 38(2).

14 Criminal Code, § 46-48.

15 Masopust Šachová, 2019, supra, p. 38.

16 E.g. Criminal Procedure Code, § 307 (conditional discontinuation of criminal prosecution), § 309 (settlement), § 175c (plea bargain).

17 Criminal Procedure Code, § 309-314.

18 Masopust Šachová, 2019, supra, p. 46-47.

19 Crime Victims Act no. 45/2013 Coll.

Service Act.[20] The first one establishes a catalogue of rights belonging to natural persons who suffered harm through a crime. Thanks to this act, crime victims have a right to professional help, right to information, right to protection against danger, right to protection of privacy, right to protection against secondary victimization or right to financial aid.[21] Importantly, they are also guaranteed a right to make a statement during the criminal proceedings about the crime's impact on their lives.[22] Moreover, the act expressly mentions restorative programs.[23] However, not many of them are in fact offered in the Czech Republic.[24] The most wide-spread program would probably be mediation in criminal matters, offered by Probation and Mediation Service whose activities are governed by the second abovementioned act. The Probation and Mediation Service also runs various interesting activities, such as Restorative Justice Week or Yellow Ribbon Run (a charity race aiming to raise public awareness and acceptance of reintegrating ex-offenders into society).[25]

Restorative justice programs can also be organized by NGOs - a noteworthy example is called Building Bridges.[26] This project brings together crime victims and perpetrators for meetings in prisons. They then lead restorative dialogues together, supported by facilitators, covering topics like accepting responsibility for a crime, feelings of guilt or forgiveness. The goal is to help participants understand each other and the reasons why the crime was committed. It remains to be seen whether this will be an isolated project or whether more activities like this one will appear in the future.

To sum up, the Czech criminal justice system of course suffers from many shortcomings – a lack of restorative justice practices being one of them. Therefore, drawing inspiration from the USA in this particular area would be only right.

---

20   Probation and Mediation Service Act no. 257/2000 Coll.

21   Crime Victims Act, § 4-37.

22   Crime Victims Act, § 22.

23   Crime Victims Act, § 39.

24   Masopust Šachová, 2019, supra, p. 59.

25   See https://www.pmscr.cz/en/other-activities/yellow-ribbon-run/.

26   See http://mvs.cz/building-bridges/.

2) Restorative justice in civil law - a contradictory term?

We presented a number of examples of restorative justice in Czech criminal law system. However, is there any space for restorative justice outside criminal law?

As our personal experience showed us, restorative justice could be understood as a broader concept. Whereas the main goal is healing and restoring harmed relationships, such a goal could very well be achieved also outside the courtroom. (Arguably, the matters should preferably stay *out* of the courtroom.) Restorative practices find their place at courts, especially alternative or specialized ones, such as juvenile courts and problem-solving courts (drug courts, community courts, mental health courts). Moreover, their place is also at schools, community centres and in social services. In fact, the spirit of restorative justice could enter any area of human interaction, notwithstanding our day-to-day personal lives.

However, such a broader notion of restorative justice is missing in Czech legal and non-legal discourse. The very term "restorative justice" is mostly understood by both legal experts[27] and the general public as relating to the area of criminal law. At law school, students do not learn about broader notions of restorative practices nor how to apply them outside the criminal proceedings context. Czech Wikipedia site (admittedly non-expert source, but useful for illustrative purposes) defines restorative justice as "a criminal law concept".[28] In such an environment, one could not expect restorative justice to flourish outside criminal law.

Let's take a closer look at civil law[29] and whether it accommodates any features inspired by restorative justice. Despite a certain amount of flexibility in substantive civil law, procedural civil law contains a complex set of quite rigid rules concerning court proceedings. Parties find themselves facing a judge, an impartial and independent adjudicator, whose conduct of the proceedings is to considerable depth prescribed by codes of procedure.[30] These codes are not so detailed as to completely rule out personal input of judges sitting on a bench,

---

27 See, e. g. Karabec, Zdeněk. 2003. *Restorativní Justice: Sborník příspěvků a dokumentů*. Praha: Institut pro kriminologii a sociální prevenci.

28 See https://cs.wikipedia.org/wiki/Restorativn%C3%AD_justice.

29 To clarify, the term "civil law" is not used here as meaning the whole legal system based on codified law (Czech legal system is such an example), but it refers to the area of law that regulates a broad spectrum of issues including, inter alia, property, torts, family matters, contracts and labour.

30 Civil Procedure Code no. 99/1963 Coll.; Special Court Procedures Act no. 292/2013 Coll.

but detailed enough so as to prescribe particular steps of the judicial proceeding, aiming to secure that all parties enjoy their constitutional right to fair trial.[31] In order to fulfill this right, the judge must retain, above all, her impartiality. And a primary means to make an overall impression of impartiality is to stick to procedural rules, even if it could be at the expense of effective intervention into the dispute matter.

We do not intend to criticize the doctrine of impartiality nor the right to fair trial. On the contrary, we consider them to be essential elements necessary for the establishment of a judicial system aimed at finding justice. On the other hand, we are aware of the fact that a restorative approach at the courtroom usually requires much more active involvement of the judge. She does not lose her position as the "impartial third in between parties", but has to acquire specialized skills and be willing to step outside of the realm defined by traditional procedural conduct. As such, the restorative justice-centered approach requires judges to re-define their role in the proceedings. That is true especially for criminal law judges, but also for judges focusing on civil law matters.

That, of course, does not mean that "traditional" civil law courts do not support parties to the dispute in their efforts to reach an amicable settlement which could restore their relationship more successfully than an enforced court judgment. Yet, their role is according to the Civil Procedure Code limited to encouraging parties to enter court settlement and advising them about possibilities of mediation and counseling.[32]

Mediation, in particular, could be an attractive concept of alternative dispute resolution (ADR). Mediation aims at finding a settlement acceptable for all parties to the dispute who can focus more on their real needs than on their actual or alleged legal rights and duties. As such, it is an expert-supported process of communication. Due to its informality it could respond better to specific needs of the parties. Therefore, it is also highly recommended for example in family disputes concerning minor children.

In the Czech Republic, the process of mediation is partly regulated in a special Mediation Act,[33] stipulating, inter alia, qualification requirements for a

---

31   Art. 36 of the Charter of Fundamental Rights and Freedoms, Art. 6 of the European Convention on Human Rights, and extensive case law of the Czech Constitutional Court and the European Court of Human Rights.

32   Civil Procedure Code, § 100(1).

33   Mediation Act no. 202/2012 Coll. For unofficial English translation see http://www.amcr.cz/dokumenty/zakon-o-mediaci_aj.pdf

"registered mediator".[34] This step is aimed to raise trust of the public towards mediation, which is steadily gaining popularity as well as attention of scholars.[35] The strongest measure of a court for encouraging mediation is ordering parties to attend the first meeting with a mediator[36] (failing to participate would have detrimental consequences).[37] Whether the parties progress with mediation after the first meeting depends exclusively on their decision—there is no way of forcing them into the process when any party lacks interest.

Such an inducement to mediation could serve as a powerful tool to streamline disputes out of courts, into arrangements that would better serve parties' actual needs. However, the order to attend the first meeting with a mediator is used in a minimal number of cases,[38] albeit there are efforts to guide judges on an appropriate use of the tool.[39] Thus, we share a view expressed by some legal practitioners that mediation in the Czech Republic has not fulfilled its potential. It is, in our view, still not a major dispute resolution mechanism and does not offer a commonplace alternative to regular court proceedings.

But, as we have already seen with Czech criminal justice system, even a relatively rigid judicial system could be infected with restorative justice practices, the only limit being the level of acknowledgment of their usefulness and importance. In a way, the Czech judiciary finds itself at the same crossroads the U.S. judiciary was at a few decades earlier. Pioneer judges who explore the ground and find the way forward are true bearers of progress and innovation.[40]

These changes could occur even without express acknowledgment of restorative justice and other alternative judicial approaches (e. g. Therapeutic Jurisprudence) in the laws. The key to success is to find whatever space the procedural codes leave for judges' creativity. Such alternative approaches recently won notable praise in the field of family disputes, mainly disputes on child

---

34 Apart from registered mediators, mediation could be conducted by anyone. Hence the official registration should serve as a proof of minimal professional skills.

35 See explanatory memorandum to the Mediation Act.

36 Civil Procedure Code, § 100(2).

37 Either a fine or a ban on being awarded costs of the court proceedings.

38 Pjajčíková, Pavla. "Promarněná šance?" *Právní rozhledy* 2018, no. 23 (2018): 847.

39 Guidelines of the Ministry of Justice available at https://justice.cz/documents/12681/720931/ V%C3%BDkladov%C3%A9+stanovisko/d84c101a-28e7-407f-9f55-3bbfa1990568 (Czech only).

40 Traguetto, Jessica, and Tomas de Aquino Guimaraes. "Therapeutic Jurisprudence and Restorative Justice in the United States: The Process of Institutionalization and the Roles of Judges." *International Journal of Offender Therapy and Comparative Criminology* 63, no. 11 (2019): 1971–89.

custody after parents' divorce.[41] So called Cochem approach was brought to the Czech courtrooms by a handful of judges and activists who looked for inspiration abroad, namely to Germany.

Cochem approach[42] is an interdisciplinary approach towards parental disputes which places a strong focus on the child's best interest. Undoubtedly, divorce and custody proceedings are traumatizing for children. The Cochem approach is based on strong interdisciplinary cooperation between parents and judges, parents' attorneys, children protection authorities, therapists, counselors and others. The outcome of the effort in many cases is that parents are able to re-establish their communication in order to find a consensual solution for custody of their child themselves. In such a way, they prevent a situation of facing a court ruling on custody that would not suit any of the parents and possibly not even the child. By doing so, their voluntary agreement has better chances to succeed as a lasting solution, and hence lessen the burden of parents' separation on the child. That is a stark difference when compared with the "traditional" approach, in which parental dispute leads to authoritative and enforceable judgment on the matter that might not settle the dispute at all. As the Czech Constitutional Court once noted in its judgment, after all, courts could not follow King Solomon's "cut the child in half" judgment,[43] and so they usually leave one of the parents not satisfied.

CONCLUSION - THE CASE FOR RESTORATIVE JUSTICE

In this text, we aimed to familiarize the reader with our observations of the U.S. restorative justice practices and efforts to introduce some of them into Czech legal system. Even though the Czech examples might seem modest when compared to hundreds of specialized courts across the USA employing restorative justice and other alternative approaches, we believe they show that both countries can gain from each others' experience. Regarding the USA, we could conclude that despite significant success of restorative justice, some injustices at the

---

41 A series of articles devoted to the Cochem approach was, for instance, published in a mainstream journal Respekt in 2017.

42 The description is based on Rogalewiczová Romana. "Interdisciplinární spolupráce při řešení rodičovských konfliktů". *Bulletin advokacie* no. (12) 2017.

43 Judgment of the Czech Constitutional Court, 12. 2. 2014, III.ÚS 3965/13.

very heart of the criminal law system have to be remedied in a substantial way. On the other hand, the Czech Republic would need to embrace a more proactive role for the judges within the judicial system, or even establish new, specialized courts that would be adapted to a more far-reaching role of judges who intervene in a person's life beyond the very matter of the dispute.

However, we can conclude the Czech story in a rather positive way. It is no overstatement to say that restorative justice is coming to a spotlight of legal practitioners, who are best positioned to introduce restorative techniques in practice. There are bottom-up projects promoting restorative justice across a broad range of fields.[44] Moreover, the Judicial Academy, an official state-funded body that organizes expert-level education for future or appointed judges, has been working on several initiatives concerning restorative justice. Hopefully, all these efforts will keep their momentum and restorative justice will take root in the Czech Republic.

At the end of the peace circle, back in 2016 in Chicago when 5th graders shared their experience with gun violence, we did not feel down. We felt empowered. Despite sharing grieve and fear, the circle ended up with hope.

---

44   Such as the Institute for Restorative Justice, see https://restorativni-justice.cz/ (Czech only).

Why is it important to share stories and experience reality through the eyes of others? Consider the Chicago elementary student who wondered how Europeans kill each other if they do not have guns. Or, consider the Czech law student who assumed that a Chicago student was not allowed to watch TV in the evening because of family rules and not to reduce the risk of being shot in his own home.

What are the benefits of educating students through the sharing of personal stories about how people live their lives and survive as well as through facts and theories?

How is the approach to restorative justice different in the American and British adversarial system as compared to the European inquisitorial system? What are the merits and demerits of each system?

How have practices such as mediation and the Cochem approach in family disputes used to bring restorative practices into the civil system of Europe? What practices do we use to resolve disputes that are restorative in nature but that we do not label restorative?

Lessons from Native Americans and the Irish

IAN WOLFF

Restorative Justice is not a system for bureaucrats, sprawling cities or the impatient but for communities that want to restore and recover the interpersonal relationships that allow their community work. It is highly personal and listens to the needs and situations of all the participating parties with the intention to heal the wound rather than amputate the criminal limb. Restorative Justice prioritizes people and their relationships over property and punishments. This sort of system necessitates the cooperation of both the offended and the offender to sit for a peaceable and honest arbitration. Though a still developing theory, precursors of Restorative Justice have been found historically. One historical example of a similar, though not identical, system is the traditional justice systems of the Native Americans. Though each community handled their legal issues separately and differently, there is a sizable portion of tribes that did take on something that we would today recognize as Restorative Justice. Yet, the size of the tribes, their mindset regarding property and ownership of the land, as well as their introspective communities, all predisposed them to success with Restorative Justice. By looking at the similarities and differences this culture and its legal system has with western culture and its legal system, the benefits of Restorative Justice are highlighted. The remainder of this chapter will do just that, as well as catalogue the historical background that developed the current legal structure as it stands today[1].

In its foundation, America's legal system mirrors that of the British. America's Founding Fathers tore through the mess of laws they inherited from the United Kingdom. They kept what was deemed acceptable, and integrated those parts into the Constitution, but discarded the more tyrannically tinted

---

[1] Meyer, Jon'a F., and Gloria Bogdan. "Co-Habitation and Co-Operation: Some Intersections Between Native American and Euroamerican Legal Systems in the Nineteenth Century." *ATQ*, vol. 15, no. 4, Dec. 2001, p. 257. *EBSCOhost*, search.ebscohost.com/login.aspx?direct=true&db=lfh&AN=7552096& site=eds-live&scope=site.

aspects of the law. For example, the Eighth Amendment of the U.S. Constitution states: "Excessive bail shall not be required, nor excessive fines imposed, nor cruel and unusual punishments inflicted". This was likely adopted from the 1689 English Bill of Rights which contains a nearly identical statement. The document also contains direct precursors to Amendments Two and Three. Stating both that free citizens have the right to hold arms and that the burden of providing for soldiers could not be put upon the populace without their consent. Our Conscript Fathers all lived under British Law and thus, they would have been familiar with it intimately. The American Revolution was begun due to the American people's legal disenfranchisement and, famously, taxation without parliamentary representation. Furthermore, After living through the bloodiest and most heavy handed decades of English rule both at home and abroad, Washington, Hancock, Jefferson, Adams, Franklin and the rest argued their case and they would have read and reread English Law while they were forming the Constitution.

From about 1688 until 1823 England and its various holdings were subject to a vicious penal system known as the Bloody Code. This was not a single legal document but rather a collection of small decrees that gradually tightened the government's grip over their expanding imperial holdings. The number of capital crimes were increased four fold to a total of 220, these ranged from premeditated murder to petty theft. During this same period, the Industrial Revolution devalued and mechanised human labor which economically isolated an expanding lower class. Tedious record keeping maintained in the Old Bailey, England's central courts, testifies to the brutality of English law at the time. Between the years of 1780 and 1783 nearly 200 prisoners were tried and executed at Old Bailey alone. While some were killers or rapists just as many were small time "thieves" forced to steal for survival and to provide for their families. The Bloody Code did not discriminate by age or gender and if a child was old enough to steal they could be sentenced to death. Yet, this is half the story. Within the same time frame, 1780-83, the Old Bailey saw 460 people convicted of capital crimes.[2] Though some may have been pardoned, the vastity of these people were given the option to be deported to the colonies and work for a period of time (usually about a decade) as an indentured servant and upon completion of the sentence

---

2   Devereaux, Simon. "The Bloodiest Code: Counting Executions and Pardons at the Old Bailey, 1730-1837." *Law, Crime & History*, vol. 6, no. 1, Mar. 2016, pp. 1–36. *EBSCOhost*, search.ebscohost.com/login.aspx?direct=true&db=i3h&AN=117565433&site=eds-live&scope=site.

they would be awarded with land to work in the colony they were deported to.[3] The Bloody Code was eventually walked back by the 1823 Judgement of Death Act which reevaluated the possible punishments for a capital crime by allowing for death sentences to be commuted to prison time.

This system could not be further from our modern conception of Restorative Justice, it sees the smallest crimes wholly vilified and morphed into a capital offense, then those convicted were used to populate the colonies of the British Empire as it gradually expanded around the globe. From the modern perspective, the actions this government took look to be more similar to human trafficking than true justice. It is estimated that as many as 48% of the nearly 450,000 Europeans who came to North America willingly, before 1775, were indentured servants while another 48,000 were prisoners sent to penal colonies.[4] Meaning that over half of the European population that migrated to the Thirteen Colonies, and later Canada, were sent there by the British from their collection of islands. These people had families and friends that they were being torn from. But, to the Founding Fathers, their streets were being populated by a vulnerable population with little to lose who held a grudge against the heavy handed British rule. Despite the scope, the brutality and scale of these actions is not wholly unprecedented. The British were masters of both dividing a local population and playing it against itself. The British first colonized and attempted to assimilate Ireland even before they began to seriously colonize the Americas. Yet, the Irish had their own legal system.

The British legal system contrasts heavily with the Customary Law of Ireland and Native America both systems put people and their role in the community before penal justice. Instead of incarceration, which puts a direct burden to support the convicted on the community, a wrongdoer may instead be made to work for the aggrieved party until the debt is thought to be paid. Crimes relating to stealing or encroaching on land was seen as a crime against the community, be it clan or tribe, instead of an individual.[5] In these systems there is no one monarch who owns all the land, as it is in a feudal system, nor do individuals own small plots of land that are handed down hereditarily but instead the com-

3   Tomlins, Christopher. "Reconsidering Indentured Servitude: European Migration and the Early American Labor Force, 1600-1775." *Labor History*, vol. 42, no. 1, Feb. 2001, pp. 5–43. *EBSCOhost*, doi:10.1080/00236560123269.

4   Tomlins, pp. 9

5   Costello, John A. "The Leading Principles of the Brehon Laws." *Studies: An Irish Quarterly Review*, vol. 2, no. 8, 1913, pp. 415–440. *JSTOR*, www.jstor.org/stable/30082633. Accessed 4 Aug. 2020.

munity as a whole maintained the land. Furthermore, as a full and free member of the community you were owed use of the land on which to subsist and live and a child was expected to support their parents as they aged. Neither differentiated between Civil and Criminal Law as both disrupted the equilibrium of the community and it was the goal of the law to restore it. Yet, both of these systems have similar flaws A king or chieftain did not adhere to the same rules that kept the other men honest. Special provisions too were made for those who practised a trade or another specialized role in the community that granted them an aristocratic status and the luxuries that came along with it.

Irish Law, or Brehon Law as it is now called, is unique due to its isolation from other cultures and legal systems for such a long time. The Irish had no serious contact with the Roman's and their legal system and their insular location separated them from the neighboring British. Brehon Law was allowed to stew undisturbed as it evolved to suit the needs of Irish society throughout the generations. The Brehons, who lent their name to the system, were hereditary lawyers whose job it was to learn the laws and arbitrate cases. It was an evolving system of Customary Laws which were organized into three tiers. 1) Laws that held true no matter where you were in Ireland; 2) Laws that pertained to a specific clan held region; 3) Laws that dealt with interterritorial discrepancies between clan lands.[6] Their system before either the Christian missionaries or the imposition of English Law was wholly progressive. Though a patriarchal society, women were allowed many freedoms. They could hold property separate from their husbands and even while married their property remained theirs. Divorce could be arranged if a marriage was childless, something that either party could instigate, or if the man struck his wife hard enough to leave a mark. Women of this time were also allowed to be Brehons and learn and practice law. The progressive nature of early Ireland's legal system heavily contrasts with their neighbors during the same period of time. An Irish woman is more than just a wife, mother or object of beauty; they could be an intellectual as well as a property owner of equal or even greater status to their male counterparts. Even after the christianization of Ireland women still retained more freedom and independence than their mainland counterparts.[7] Yet, there are other aspects of Irish Law still unmentioned.

---

6 Costello, pp. 417

7 Costello, pp. 437

Brehon Law made no distinction between civil and criminal law, it was all the same as was the punishment for any violation of the law. From petty theft to murder and from assault to bribery, a fee, called an eric, of either coin or cattle would be required of the perpatrator, though serious crimes were met with serious punishments. It was the main job of the Brehons to hear the sides of both parties, gather any information that may pertain and then set the indemnity.[8] The system of Brehon Law is fully one of Retributive Justice. It sees the wrongdoer pay, literally, for their crimes but aims at not taking revenge on the individual. It is an impersonal justice that in its ideal form is impartial. The Brehons, in their schooling, are taught to imagine every possible situation and have the fee set already so that if and when the situation does arise everything has already been taken into account and the indemnity can be set as rapidly and impartially as possible.[9] In the event that one is not able to pay then they are taken on by the wronged party as an indentured servant for a period of time that fits the severity of their actions.

It was necessary for Brehons to know the laws of their clan as well as how those laws interacted with those of neighboring clans. Brehons held a position of authority in the clan itself because of their role as a legal advisor and arbiter. Yet, while the Brehons enjoyed the benefits of status, every person of the clan was cared for and assured land to farm and a voice in their assembly. These rights were granted with the understanding that each constituent would pay their taxes due to the clan. The money collected by this tax would then be put back into the community. This could be done by the chief taking on staff and paying them wages, settling disputes between clans, or even to pay for militaristic ventures. Individual clan members had other commitments and benefits in this clanic system as well.

Each clan member was expected to better and maintain the plot of land allotted to them through agriculture and raising cattle which was an indicator of wealth. The larger the cattle herds the more land they need to graze, therefore, large herds signified that you held a high position in one's clan. If a clan member had no cattle (something that could arise after paying an eric) they could be loaned cattle for a period of time from their overlord if they had none. This would allow them to gradually grow a herd, and therefore wealth, of their own. However, those who took this on were expected to return the same quantity of

8   Costello, pp. 431

9   Costello, pp. 417

cattle to their creditor. While using loaned cattle they would take on a lesser role in the clan until the debt was paid, thus, people were able to rebound from losses and regain wealth and status.[10]

The Brehon clanic system took care of its people and treated them justly, in a sharp contrast to the English system crimes were not met with violent reparations but with an indemnity levied against the wrongdoer. Such a system shows how the life of an individual is valued above the loss of property or injury to another. The punishments that this system handed out were reflective of the situation as well as the needs and mean of the offender and offended. It did so in such a way as to leave anger and vengeance out of the system. All of this was organized and maintained by the Brehons who acted not just as lawyers but as arbiters and judges. Their job mandated that they know and understand the relationships that acted as the frame for their clannish community. While this system of law is retributive and not restorative, there are evident restorative aspects contained within it. Brehon law was formed to preserve the status quo within the clan and it does this not with threats of violence but by offering incentives to those who cooperatively live within the system. The Brehon form of justice listens to both sides of the case and takes the context of both sides into consideration before passing judgment. But as the English turned to Protestantism they increasingly saw Catholic Ireland as an unlocked backdoor for an invasion and starting in the mid 16th century they began to colonize and to attempt to assimilate culturally Ireland. Naturally, a major stem in this process was to yoke the Irish with their foreign laws.[11]

The plight of the Irish and the Native Americans have a number of similarities. Both developed a system that prioritizes the individual as an aspect of the community over heavy handed punishments which would only ostracize the individual. The justice system of the America's First Peoples, much like maize or potatoes, is wholly indigenous to America. Their system is the closest thing to Restorative Justice that can be found among all the various legal systems globally and it starkly contrasts with the punitive system that much of the world adheres to today.

---

10 Costello, pp. 429

11 Patterson, Nerys. âGaelic Law and the Tudor Conquest of Ireland: The Social Background of the Sixteenth-Century Recensions of the Pseudo-Historical Prologue to the Senchas MÃ¡r.â *Irish Historical Studies*, vol. 27, no. 107, 1991, pp. 193â215. *JSTOR*, www.jstor.org/stable/30006537. Accessed 21 Aug. 2020.

While little is known about the legal systems of the Americas before the arrival of Columbas, the biased reports of adventurers and colonists of the Age of Discovery help to paint a picture. It is accepted that some of the more northern tribes, removed from the Empires of Central and Southern America, sought to restore the internal harmony of their communities with peace circles and arbitration rather than pain and penalties. To the settlers just coming into these lands from abroad, this system appeared weak and ineffective compared to their "stronger" European legal model. Crimes like assault or theft were not handled with incarceration or another punishment deemed fit for the crime but by public shaming and group conversations. To the onlooking Europeans this was seen as inferior and gave the encroaching white man a reason to forcibly assimilate the native peoples in an attempt to provide them with law, order and civilization.[12] This encroaching assimilation was only made worse when the colonists were the victims of crime committed by natives, which under the European system would have punished the perpetrator, yet, instead the accused was walking around unpunished. This situation was again made worse by the disadvantages of the natives, inferior technology and weapons, a lack of horses to provide rapid transportation of people of goods, no resistance to diseases that were coming over from the Old World. All of this must have seemed apocalyptic to those who lived through it. Yet, the diseases and technological disadvantages only served to provide the Europeans with a foothold in the Americas. While the United Kingdom carved out the Thirteen Colonies on the East coast of North America, things only got worse for the natives after the formation of the United States of America.

The invading colonizers regularly incited tribe on tribe violence to keep the natives disorganized and fractured politically. This proved to weaken the natives and make it easier for the well trained and well provisioned armies of the English to sweep in and conquer the natives.[13] Yet, nowhere is this history of genocide better codified than in the laws and court cases of the United States of America. Specifically, those laws that directly dealt with and concerned the Native American population within their borders. A population who were treated more as an inconvenience than as people worthy of human rights. 1823,

---

12 Meyers, pp. 258

13 Minges, Patrick. "Beneath the Underdog: Race, Religion, and the Trail of Tears." *American Indian Quarterly*, vol. 25, no. 3, Sum 2001, pp. 453–479. *EBSCOhost*, search.ebscohost.com/login.aspx?direct=true&db=lsdar&AN=ATLA0001284276&site=eds-live&scope=site.

saw the first U.S Supreme Court case involving a Native American. Johnson vs. M'Intosh. The outcome of which concluded that only the federal government could purchase land from the Native Americans and that land could then be resold by the government. This outcome prevents individual citizens from competing with one another to purchase the land. Such competition would have raised the price of the land and given more money to the native population. Instead, one buyer with a massive purchasing power was able to buy the land at the lowest cost possible without any competitors. Cheap land purchases allowed the United States to expand rapidly across the continent. However, in doing this the First Nations were twisted out of a great deal of profit that could have been derived from the competitive sale of their ancestral lands.[14] Not even a decade later, the passage of the Indian Removal Act of 1830 saw the forced migration of the Native Tribes who resided East of the Mississippi. This Act initiated what is now known as the Trail of Tears, a grueling path across a continent in destitute conditions that saw the dead line the path as hunger, exposure, and disease ravaged the itinerant population. The American Natives continued to fall victim to Manifest Destiny and so too did their culture and traditional system of justice.

The civilizations living in the Americas declined rapidly after the arrival of Columbas. As Europeans came into closer and closer contact with the native populations over generations they pushed more aggressively to assimilate and white wash the differing native culture. What started small with the small land grabs developed into mass relocation and concluded with usurpation of the traditional justice system by the justice of the colonizers. Much like the English, the American Government wanted to make all people accountable to their laws. After being put on reservations the natives were then policed and directly held accountable to American Law, despite the promise that they would be allowed to govern and manage themselves on their reservations. The 1881 trial of Crow Dog, who killed one of his tribesmen, was first held the traditional way and the conclusion of that trial was that he was set to make reparations to the family. Yet, after the police understood what went on Crow Dog was seized. He was tried and sentenced to death by the American system. All of this was done at the behest of the caucasian towns people, who felt that the Native American's system was insufficient. This process was abetted by the Major Crimes Act of 1883 which allowed for tribespeople to be tried for what the government deemed

---

14   Meyer, pp. 259

to be heinous crimes.[15] The system of Restorative Justice, which had developed undisturbed for thousands of years before European colonists sucked the life out of it over four centuries, went dormant for over a century.

It is only in these past three decades that Restorative Justice has seen a renaissance. This has taken place specifically in American schools as a reaction against the Zero Tolerance Policy which began in the 1990's and instituted the harshest possible penalties for students in possession of weapons or drugs on campus. After the 1999 Columbine Colorado school shooting these policies were even more tightly enforced across the nation.[16] This resulted in an increase of suspensions, expulsions and juvenile detention for all students but targeted students of color at far higher rates. No evidence implies that this kept schools safer and the students who missed instruction time due to these punishments were twice as likely to drop out and three times as likely to serve in a juvenile detention facility.[17] The Zero Tolerance Policy established in America over the past three decades served only to fuel the school to prison pipeline and favored for-profit privatized prisons which placed property before either people or community. The resurgence of Restorative Justice in the United States can be seen as a direct rejection of these policies. The school system of Oakland California implemented restorative practices that take a more holistic approach to justice and the role of the individual within their community.

Restorative Justice for Oakland Youth, or RJOY, is a group that advocates for rRestorative Justice across America and in 2006 they were asked to pilot an in school Restorative Justice based system in Oakland. The priority on community and the inherent social connections in engenders saw an 87 % decline in suspension as well as improved academic performance across the board[18]. It was a resounding success and by 2010 all of Oakland's schools had not just adopted Restorative Justice but provided the funding to ensure the program would be appropriately supported. All together suspensions dropped from 7.4% to 3.3% this included a decline in the suspensions of people of color, though they still had higher rates than those of their white peers.[19] Nevertheless, the implementa-

---

15 Meyer, pp. 261

16 Davis, Fania. E. "The Little Book of Race and restorative Justice: Black Lives, Healing, and US Social Transformation." New York: *Good Books*, ch.4. pp. 46 (2019)

17 Davis, pp. 47

18 Davis, pp. 50

19 Davis, pp. 51

tion of such a system proved to be a solid step in the right direction and allowed for each individual to have their voices heard as equals hoping to move forward together.

Where there are people gathering and living together there is crime and justice. However, the various groups of people around the globe developed different kinds of justice to meet the needs of their community and its constituents. These systems vary, just as the people do, in their effect and appearance. The system of the Irish, before they were colonized by their British neighbors, saw a payment for every crime committed and it was the role of the Brehons, Ireland's lawyer class, to levy the indemnity on the guilty party. Theirs was a retributive system that contained clear aspects of restorative justice within it and provided equal rights to both male and female community members. In the Brehon system, the individual's obligation to the community was clearly stated as was the community's obligation to the individual. Both aspects were together to create a functioning clan. The restorative system of justice formed in the Americas is the system that most closely mirrors our modern conception of Restorative Justice. Though not all tribes adhered to a restorative system those who did took part in a system focused on the restoration of the community and the maintenance of peace and civility within it in lieu of punishing criminals the community would sit down, listen and come to a consensus respectful of the personhood of all the members. Conversely, the English Bloody Code kept the population in check and either sent criminals to death or penal colonies. Without the fear of corporal punishments, fines, incarceration, or deportation the guilty were able to assimilate into their community rather than being labeled as criminals and ostracized.

Costello, John A. "The Leading Principles of the Brehon Laws." *Studies: An Irish Quarterly Review*, vol. 2, no. 8, 1913, pp. 415–440. *JSTOR*, www.jstor.org/stable/30082633. Accessed 4 Aug. 2020.

Davis, Fania. E. "The Little Book of Race and restorative Justice: Black Lives, Healing, and US Social Transformation." New York: *Good Books,* ch.4. Pp. 42-58 (2019)

Devereaux, Simon. "The Bloodiest Code: Counting Executions and Pardons at the Old Bailey, 1730-1837." *Law, Crime & History*, vol. 6, no. 1, Mar. 2016, pp. 1–36. *EBSCOhost*, search.ebscohost.com/login.aspx?direct=true&db=i3h&AN=1175654 33&site=eds-live&scope=site.

Meyer, Jon'a F., and Gloria Bogdan. "Co-Habitation and Co-Operation: Some Intersections Between Native American and Euroamerican Legal Systems in the Nineteenth Century." *ATQ*, vol. 15, no. 4, Dec. 2001, p. 257. *EBSCOhost*, search.ebscohost.com/login.aspx?direct=true&db=lfh&AN=7552096&site= eds-live&scope=site.

Patterson, Nerys. âGaelic Law and the Tudor Conquest of Ireland: The Social Background of the Sixteenth-Century Recensions of the Pseudo-Historical Prologue to the Senchas MÃ¡r.â *Irish Historical Studies*, vol. 27, no. 107, 1991, pp. 193â215. *JSTOR*, www.jstor.org/stable/30006537. Accessed 21 Aug. 2020.

Minges, Patrick. "Beneath the Underdog: Race, Religion, and the Trail of Tears." *American Indian Quarterly*, vol. 25, no. 3, Sum 2001, pp. 453–479. *EBSCOhost*, search.ebscohost.com/login.aspx?direct=true&db=lsdar&AN=ATLA000128427 6&site=eds-live&scope=site.

Parliament of England. (2008). English Bill of Rights 1689. Retrieved August 21, 2020, from https://avalon.law.yale.edu/17th_century/england.asp

Tomlins, Christopher. "Reconsidering Indentured Servitude: European Migration and the Early American Labor Force, 1600-1775." *Labor History*, vol. 42, no. 1, Feb. 2001, pp. 5–43. *EBSCOhost*, doi:10.1080/00236560123269.

There is a vigorous debate in the United States about whether judges should look to the legal standards of other countries in applying the law. What are the advantages and disadvantages of looking to other justice systems?

What factors should we consider when analyzing the efficacy of a legal system?

If you were asked to design a legal system, what would you want it to look like?

In addition to the Irish and Native American traditions, are there other traditions we can look to in grounding restorative justice practices?

PART VIII
HEALING AND RESTORATIVE JUSTICE

The Intersection of Crime, Mental Health and Trauma

The role of the court system, including the Judiciary and members of the legal profession, has been a complex and ever evolving process when managing individuals who are court involved and have extensive mental health needs. The system was never designed to handle the large influx of mentally ill clients and litigants. Much of the problem lies in the fact that Judges and lawyers do not receive extensive training on how to manage mentally ill individuals, and when they are court involved, what strategies to use in trying to minimize the negative impact on both the court system and on the mentally ill individuals. As such, it has created some complex problems in both the criminal and civil divisions of the Court system.

Historically, it has been assumed that mental health problems were likely correlated with higher levels of criminality, violence and aggression. However, ongoing and current research shows this assumption has often been conflated and the ways in which mentally ill people are portrayed in the various forms of the media, increases this inherent hypothesis and bias. The reality, based on research, actually supports the alternative hypothesis; that people with mental health problems are less likely to commit crimes and are more likely to be victims of aggression and violent crimes.

According to a 2014 study published by the American Psychological Association, in a study of crimes committed by people with serious mental health disorders, only 7.5 percent were directly related to symptoms of mental illness. In fact, this study analyzed 429 crimes committed by 143 offenders involved with a mental health court in Minnesota, with three major types of illness and found that 3 percent of their crimes were directly related to symptoms of major depression, four percent to symptoms of schizophrenia disorders, and 10 percent to symptoms of bipolar disorder. This study confirms an increasing

PART VIII HEALING AND RESTORATIVE JUSTICE   233

body of data supporting that most people who have mental health disorders are not predisposed to being violent, aggressive or predestined to committing crimes in their communities.

In Cook County, Illinois, where I spent my entire career as an Assistant Public Defender, a third of the population detained at the Cook County jail suffer from some form of a psychological disorder. According to the National Alliance on Mental Illness (NAMI), around 400,000 inmates currently behind bars suffer from some form of mental illness. Additionally, the statistic related to incarceration from NAMI is that between 25 to 40 percent of all mentally ill Americans will be detained, jailed or incarcerated at some point in their lives.

The criminal justice system has unfortunately borne the brunt of exposure to mentally ill defendants and victims as well. Everyone involved in the criminal court setting is involved in an intricate, complex system that is interrelated with many overlaps between systems. Often times these systems must choose from a limited list of choices when confronting the mentally ill, and in the end is a system that funnels the mentally ill into the jail system and detention. When a police officer first encounters someone who might have symptoms of untreated mental health problems, they must decide whether to arrest the person, bring them to a hospital setting, or determine if they have a family support system to whom they can turn, to help them manage the person's mental health problems. In a system that is understaffed, overwhelmed and where time is of the essence, oftentimes arresting a person is the easiest and quickest solution, instead of finding a hospital that will take them despite no insurance, or identifying a family member willing to take them and find them appropriate care.

Once these individuals get to a detention facility, the prosecutor must decide whether to proceed with charges, the Judge must determine appropriate bail or bond if any, and if a bond is set, the mentally ill person most likely is unable to post it, and then eventually becomes detained and "housed" at the jail. The jail must now make accommodations to house the person, who is vulnerable to being victimized by detainees in the general population. The mentally ill individual also might be hostile to any form of medication and mental health treatment options the jail is offering, due to higher levels of paranoia, fear, and re-traumatization.

Representation of the mentally ill defendant then becomes especially troublesome and problematic. A defendant must have capacity to assist in their own defense and due to having untreated mental health problems, this might not be the case. Usually the mentally ill person, has no money to hire a private attorney and often becomes a client of the Public Defender's office. The lawyer representing the mentally ill person must first determine if the person even has the capacity to understand the charges against them and then determine if they have the capability to assist in their own defense, understand the court process and in their representation of the client. If not, they often are sent away for extensive periods of time to make the mentally ill client either fit or determined unfit for trial. This slows down the high-speed pace of the court system, and often places people in difficult moral situations related to the prosecution, representation and sentencing of a person who was deemed unfit during the initial stages of the court process, and who when fit, may have little memory of the actual charges against them while in the throes of untreated mental illness.

I recall the heartache of defending the most vulnerable members of society, and oftentimes the lack of common-sense protocols that could have prevented these individuals from becoming part of a complex court system that has its own complicated standards of rules and standards that it must follow. I remember knowing that even if a mentally ill client pled guilty, the likelihood of them returning to court was extremely high, since access to quality healthcare, treatment and medication in many communities is limited. Once a mentally ill client is released from custody, the likelihood of them maintaining a medication regiment, being able to meet with their Probation Officer, and paying restitution through the Court System is slim to none. The barriers are too great, the system is too complex, and the investment in the human being is too little.

I often look back on my life as an Assistant Public Defender as part lawyer and part Social Worker. I was often tasked with figuring out how to navigate the complicated worlds of the law, substance use treatment, and mental health care, with clients who came from lower socio-economic backgrounds, often were unemployed, often had no health insurance, and had limited family and financial resources to get the help they needed. The neighborhoods in which my clients lived had limited community resources and access to care was difficult and challenging. Once the court imposed any condition of bond or any condition on a sentencing order, it added one more burden to the lives of those already marginalized and challenged. For many, even having bus money is often taken for granted. For many, even asking them to go into a new unfamiliar neighborhood can be emotionally taxing and physically dangerous. And the assumption that they have support networks to help them manage their worlds is the biggest mistake the court system often makes. Finally, restitution orders on those with mental illness, most of whom are unemployed, is often a means to violate their sentencing orders and then bring them back to Court, creating a system, in which it is hard to break free from and can hold people captive for many years.

The goal of writing this chapter is to highlight the complexities of the intersection between criminal law and behaviors and the role mental health plays in it. As a former criminal defense attorney and now a Clinical and Forensic Psychologist, I have been a witness and bystander to some of the heightened complexities that play a role in juvenile and adult behaviors, whether they be healthy or maladaptive. To underscore how complex these concepts are, I will walk you through my careers and what I observed while engaging in my work to help highlight what I learned as I navigated this complex network of legal and mental health providers.

I do want to first say that I have often been blessed to have been surrounded by some of the finest human beings in both of my careers, including the Judiciary, lawyers, law enforcement, probation officers, mental health professionals. Many of these people have dedicated their lives to improving the systems they work in and have been compassionate in their approach to the marginalized people with whom we work. While I have encountered people in my career, who did not inspire me and often dehumanized these individuals, for the most part, it is a dedicated group of individuals who are doing the best they can with the limited resources they have available and limited "rulebook" they were given to manage these types of cases and people.

As an Assistant Public Defender in Cook County, I started off my career young, naïve and unaware of the impact of nature versus nurture, as well as the roles parenting, intergenerational dysfunction, poverty, and past trauma played in the outcome of people's lives. I wanted to be a voice for the voiceless, and an advocate for people who lacked the resources to be able to hire private counsel. In my role as a lawyer, I was first placed in the Domestic Violence Courts in the early 1990's when this was a newer court system designed to help those who were abused by their partners. The Judges with whom I worked, the lawyers who worked beside me both on the prosecution and defense side, were all committed to increasing safety for those involved in these courtrooms. Orders of Protections were a new concept, and we were all trying to create a system of justice that protected the most vulnerable amongst us. However, what we all learned quickly, was that the system often failed, not due to our lack of effort and due diligence, but because of the lack of recognition of how much a person's historical data related to their own upbringing and expectations played a bigger role in outcomes than we anticipated. We discovered that substance use, trauma, and intergenerational poverty and family dysfunction often played a bigger part in the outcomes of many of the cases that we faced. It was an imperfect system fraught with a lack of insight related to the complexities of the criminal court system and the people who often got involved in the system.

Along the way, I found myself inspired by individuals in the criminal justice system who were innovators, and who viewed the system differently than many of us toiling away doing the same thing without change or forethought. One of the first Judges that left a lasting imprint in my mind, was a female Judge in the Domestic Violence Courtrooms. Although many viewed her as controversial, she believed that creating support groups for perpetrators of domestic violence was necessary to find the commonality amongst them and to hold members of the group accountable. My guess is she received a lot of critical feedback for thinking outside of the box, and the program was disbanded after the group leader was rearrested for another Domestic Battery. I do remember that many of my clients who participated in these groups found it helpful to discuss their anger and aggression with peers who experienced the same feelings and exhibited the same type of maladaptive coping mechanisms. In my mind, this was a precursor to Domestic Violence Groups for perpetrators that exist today.

Another innovative male Judge I worked in front of at an outlying Branch court that was housed in a police station at the time, created alternative sentencing for women who were charged with prostitution cases. He referred them to an agency that helped women who were part of the sex trades, to get them off the streets by creating programming dedicated to reducing their substance use, completing their education and developing self esteem and self-worth concepts that allowed them to leave the streets behind. He would encourage the prosecution to drop their criminal cases and sentenced them to attending a social service agency to provide them the opportunity to get the help and support they needed. He also created a program for young gang members to attend meetings with police officers who were trained in gang tactics to minimize future risk. While it was not always successful, it did create a belief that we might be able to view individuals in the criminal justice system differently and provide a new lens in which we could potentially redirect them to move in. I found it inspiring and hopeful that we could create a level of restorative justice long before the phrase became popular.

When one of my colleagues represented a person who later murdered his victim by shoving the victim into the path of an oncoming train, the entire courtroom grieved. Nothing about the case indicated from a retrospective standpoint, that this defendant was capable of this level of atrocity after the crime that was initially charged and then dismissed for an active Order of Protection. How could all of us dedicated to our clients, have failed so miserably on this case, leaving a person dead in the most horrific way? We grieved as a group, including the Judges, the State's Attorneys, the Assistant Public Defenders, the Victim Advocates, and the pain of the loss was remarkable and the ripple effect was long-lasting. At the time, none of us had the ability to dissect what went wrong, other than to vigilantly prosecute the next set of cases without dismissing the underlying criminal charges, sometimes negatively impacting defendants wrongly charged, but with the intent to prevent another human tragedy from unfolding around us.

As I navigated through the various Cook County branch courtrooms, prior to arriving at 26th and California, it became clear to me that high levels of substance use, poverty, broken families, absentee fathers, domestic violence, sexual, physical and emotional abuse, neglect and other problematic behaviors walked hand in hand with the clients that I represented daily. I advocated fervently for my clients, fueled by my belief that color, ethnicity, socioeconomic level, educational background should all not be held against a person and that they were entitled to the same rights and benefits that any other person was. However, I began to recognize that a history of trauma, abuse and neglect in childhood played a significant role in the criminal justice system.

When I worked in Night Narcotics court at 26th and California, it was a time when prosecution of drug offenses was at an all time high. Cook County created a separate court system to handle the increasing numbers of arrests for drug crimes, and the court hours began at 4 pm and ran until ten or eleven at night. There was never a shortage of cases, and I quickly learned that drugs were rampant, particularly in certain areas of the city, and men and women were getting arrested in record numbers, and more men served extensive prison sentences, leaving a huge generation of families without male role models in family systems. At the time, I wondered, what type of impact this would have on the children, since I recognized that my own father had provided me with a completely different skillset than my mother had. I often met mothers who sold drugs to support their children, to purchase diapers and formula, to pay rent and the majority of them never completed high school and had very little family support. The phrase with biblical origins "There but for the grace of God go I," often would repeat in my head while representing some of my clients. Who would I be without my parents, without encouragement, without social supports, without opportunities to get educated, and without a community and school system that encouraged my growth and learning mindset?

In creating Night Narcotics Court to manage the increased load of drug arrests mostly in marginalized communities, looking back, I can see we created more harm than good. Children were left fatherless, motherless, and family systems were shattered, without addressing why drug use and drug sales were so high in impoverished communities. What would happen to the children of these individuals? Working with gang members throughout my career, the research shows that children without strong parental support and supervision are more at risk of becoming gang involved. We also know that a healthy family system, a strong supportive community, an excellent school system and stable housing can counter the effects of children becoming gang involved. However, based on the number of cases that came through these courtrooms, and the number of young adults and parents who were incarcerated for small amounts of drugs, I feel heartbreak and despair thinking of the long term results of a short term plan for harsh sentencing laws related to drug charges.

In conducting investigations for many of my cases, it became clear that the opportunities I had growing up, were different from the ones my clients had access to. In many neighborhoods, there were no places to work, to engage in positive social activities, or to safely spend time hanging out in a park or in their own community. Instead, there were only neighborhood stores that sold very little fresh food, but where you could easily purchase alcohol and cigarettes. The neighborhoods were filled with abandoned buildings where high drug activity took place, billboards hung everywhere referring to alcohol or cigarettes, and urban blight was all you could see. The thought of something better out in the world or even in Chicago would be hard to imagine or fathom. The local drug dealers or gang members with their fancy cars, jewelry and clothes were the only people to emulate, since very rarely, were there other models or mentors in the community outside of church or neighborhood community agencies.

When I worked in the Sex and Violence Preliminary hearing courtrooms, I remember being astounded by some of the circumstances surrounding high profile murder cases. I remember one case with clarity, in which an older married man murdered his wife, while under the influence of PCP and marijuana. When he woke up, he found her dead body beside him, and all I can remember is the regret, shame, and tears related to how his untreated substance use problem destroyed the very thing that meant the most to him. Another time, I represented a Vietnam Veteran who prior to his service had an unremarkable and normal life, and then after coming back from Vietnam, began a life of substance use and criminality. He ended up being charged with several Felony charges by the time I met him and when I asked him what happened, and how his life had taken such a drastic turn including his spouse and children being estranged from him, he responded "Ma'am, I lost everything because I fell in love with heroin when I wanted to forget what happened to me in 'Nam and my love for heroin destroyed everything else I cared about." His words still haunt me to this day.

By the time I ended up working in the Felony courtrooms at 26th and California, my understanding about the deficiencies of the criminal justice system were more realistic. I recognized that the concept of justice is elusive, and by the time I represented a client on a Felony case, layers and layers of loss were already woven into the fabric of the case. I had to make the best of a lifetime of lost opportunities: Failed interventions; neglect from the community; neglect from the school system; neglect from the family system; physical, sexual and emotional abuse; poverty; lack of access to quality health care, mental health care, and school systems; and dehumanization and re-traumatization by the very system intended to help them. With keen awareness, when I requested discovery in cases that were being set for trial, I often would see this legacy of loss, and as the years passed and clients returned from sentences served, only to be charged with a new crime, I wondered how things could change if we did not do something different. Albert Einstein's phrase often reverberated in my thoughts: "Insanity is doing the same thing over and over again and expecting different results."

One case stands in my mind, as the impetus which drove me into the mental health field. Although I think of this process as years in the making, with me being unaware most times that my disillusionment and dissatisfaction with the system was related to being reactive rather than proactive in our approach to crime. I was asked to co-chair a high-profile murder case in which a seven-year-old had been murdered by his 19-year-old half-brother. The victim's mother was also the defendant's mother. As a mother myself, this case was particularly difficult for me, and I could not even imagine the grief that the mother must have been experiencing. I felt a level of compassion for her related to the loss of both children, one permanently and the other indefinitely to the criminal justice system. This case was not about guilt or innocence, but about life versus death, as the death penalty still existed in Illinois at the time of his trial.

When I went to interview the defendant in this case, I was met with a very disturbed young man, and I could not comprehend how such a young person could be so damaged. When we received the discovery in this case, all I could comprehend was a multitude of missed opportunities to intervene and change the trajectory of this person's life. There was a legacy of a broken family system, of abuse and neglect, of poverty, of intergenerational family dysfunction, of a lack of interventions by the school system during his school years, by a lack of long-term care for his mental health needs, and by a lack of caring overall by the entire community and systems this child had been involved with. A legacy of missed opportunities and loss. That is what I saw. I could not understand how someone could be cast aside, discarded, not made important, not recognized for the extensive needs he had, and then by the age of 19 was an outcast from society, charged with a heinous murder of a young innocent child. How could we allow and become complicit in this type of outcome?

The case was very life altering for me and I began to see the profound nexus between the intersection of trauma, untreated mental health problems, and poverty. Here was a 19-year-old, who had been told throughout his lifespan that he did not matter in big and small ways, who murdered his 7-year-old half-brother, whose life was still filled with hope, love, shininess and opportunities. The psychological undertones of this crime did not evade me, and I lost much sleep over the facts of the murder, the way in which the child died, the horrors of the aftermath of the crime, and the photos that bared witness to the horrors that had happened. For years, I thought about this case. I never forgot about the mother. She has remained in my thoughts and with me even decades later. I wonder, how did she ever get past this? What happened to her? What I do know is that trauma upon trauma begets higher levels of substance use, suicides, violent endings to lives, and a perpetual legacy of loss and hopelessness.

After the trial ended, the thought kept ruminating in my head that maybe I could be more effective in working with people before they were "at the end of the railroad track." I kept thinking about if outreach and interventions occurred earlier in a person's life, than could we perhaps change the trajectory of a person's life and prevent them from going in and out of the criminal justice setting. I had no plan about changing professions, but the thought never left my mind. With every client, I continued to see lost opportunities and a sense of hopelessness that permeated the clients, the professionals who worked there, and that hung in the atmosphere all around me. I continued to work in the Felony courts, and never lost the belief that the work I was doing was important, and that by listening and advocating I was making a small difference for the people I represented. I felt great pride in my work and in what I did. I still feel that way.

However, the constant influx of new, young, and repeat offenders was disheartening to me. There were no specialty courtrooms at the time to deal with chronic mental health issues, chronic substance use issues, or military veterans. If there had been, most likely I would have stayed, because of my firm belief that we can effectively create positive changes in the human experience by offering short- and long-term help and opportunities earlier in the lifespan.

Instead, the system still used punishment as the solution to complex and systemic social problems with no end in sight. When I had to deal with clients who were severely mentally ill, and had no memory of the crimes they committed, and were often sent away for fitness restoration. They would then return to the criminal courts and ask to go home by taking a plea on a case they did not even remember, often making me feel discouraged and disheartened. People who work in the criminal justice system in any capacity are aware of the deficiencies that exist within the system and the lack of funding opportunities for those most desperately in need of these services. It often feels like a gerbil wheel spinning around and around with no end in sight and no progress made. However, the tenacity and hard work to achieve some level of change can be inspiring despite the inequities that are faced.

As I transitioned into the world of mental health, I avoided the criminal courts and settings at all costs in any internship or externship I did when completing my master's in clinical psychology. I wanted to leave that world behind and do something different. I wanted to be a changemaker and wanted to find opportunities in which I could affect a level of hope and optimism for people who were disadvantaged. I was surrounded by compassionate teachers and professors who were willing to help me in my new career and who helped me learn the skills that were necessary to become capable as a mental health professional. As time went on, the pull to return to an overwhelmed criminal justice system where I might be able to effect change as a mental health professional became stronger and I was committed to creating positive systemic change.

When I went to get my doctorate due to my increasing quest for more in-depth understanding and knowledge related to mental health, substance use, and the impact of trauma on a person's life trajectory, I got pulled back into the criminal justice field. I did a therapy externship at a Juvenile medium security prison, and it was at this point, that I began to put the pieces together related to what often transpires in the life of a person, which leads young adolescents to commit egregious crimes despite their age. One of the tasks that we had to perform while working at the prison, was to review the historical data that followed an adult adolescent offender after sentencing and at the onset of their juvenile prison term. We had a one-page sheet that had to be filled out listing among other things relevant data related to their incarceration, including a history of trauma, abuse, neglect, and other adverse childhood experiences. What I learned quickly was to transform my writing into the smallest yet legible writing I could, to input all the data into this section. Every adolescent had such a significant history that it boggled the mind that so many bad things could happen in such a small amount of lifespan. What became clear was the more trauma and negative experiences an adolescent had in their lifetime, the more likely they were to have entered the criminal justice field at a young age, and the more likely they were to have anger, behavioral disorders, school related problems including truancy, drop-outs and school refusals, gang involvement, and emotional and psychiatric problems.

The legacy of loss and the understanding of the loss became significant to me by then. Violent anger outbursts were the norm at this facility, and oftentimes, adolescents had to be placed on suicide watch to prevent harm to themselves and others. Building trust and rapport required effort and time, as these "children" had learned to not have faith in the system, or the people involved in these systems. They used to refer to many people as "posers," people they identified as doing the job for the money and not because they cared. They were able to detect inauthenticity and became more difficult to work with if they believed you were not really invested in them. It was really a learning ground for me, that systems fail children long before they end up in jail and prisons and we must invest in young people before they lose trust and belief that there is more out there for them to aspire and attain, other than selling drugs or being gang involved.

When I finally did my clinical internship for my doctorate degree, I looked for a place where I could really understand psychological testing to further create understanding about the factors that contribute to delinquency in youth, and the factors that lead to criminality in adults. I worked at a county diagnostic center where for a full year I did Risk Assessments related to perpetrators of Domestic Violence, along with a variety of psychological assessments including but not limited to sex offender, sanity, and fitness to parent. Again, what I discovered along the way, was astounding to me. It became clear that where we come from, what we have available to us, and how much support and guidance we have plays a huge factor in our development as human beings. Nature versus nurture, the age-old debate, and the influence each play became even more fascinating to me. Clearly genetic predispositions play a huge role in what maladaptive coping skills a person might have the predisposition to develop, but so did the environment in which they were raised. Repeatedly, due to family dysfunction, neglect, sexual, physical and emotional abuse, children began to develop problems at school, an increase in use of substances beginning usually in middle school, leading to more risk factors the older they got. Negative peer groups became a greater influence the more difficulties they were experiencing at home. Although some factors might change, it seemed the recipe leading to delinquency and criminality involved a host of adverse childhood experiences. The more negative experiences a person experienced, the more it seemed to be correlated to higher levels of substance use, more negative involvement with peers, less empathy, more psychological and emotional problems, behavioral problems in school, a likelihood of criminal justice involvement, and a higher likelihood that they did not graduate high school.

Once I completed my doctorate degree, I continued to be involved in the Criminal Justice system in various ways including as a Juvenile Drug Court Coordinator in a Specialty court. I continued to do psychological evaluations on at risk youth offenders and continued to see similar patterns leading to criminal justice involvement. When working in the specialty courts, it was a relief to see the amount of effort placed into making people whole again through intensive interventions and support. The method in which we achieved the most amount of success involved not just the delinquent adolescent, but also providing family therapy, parenting classes for the parents, and creating scaffolding and support around the whole family system, which often was fractured and broken, in order to give the adolescent, the opportunity to succeed. Much emphasis was placed on school, maintaining grades and creating prosocial activities and behaviors.

These programs tend to be very intensive, very expensive, with many spurts of growth and failures. However, the data that should be looked at most closely is keeping the adolescent sober and free of the use of illegal substances and alcohol as much as possible, especially during formative brain development. What we know from addiction treatment is the earlier a person begins using substances inappropriately, the more entrenched this behavior will become over time, and the less likely they are to overcome their addiction patterns as adults, leading to higher levels of criminality, incarceration, unemployment and reliance on social services throughout their lifespan costing local governments more money in the long run. Sadly, this program was disbanded years later due to the belief that the program was not making enough of a positive impact and was too costly to run. In my opinion, money invested in the youth, is money well spent and the lens in which to determine positive outcomes should not always be markers like long term sobriety and abstinence, and no other delinquency charges. Instead, the goal should be much more realistic including reducing the number of arrests, increasing the length of time remaining sober and abstinent, and to get the adolescent more school involved with prosocial activities and outlets. This then can change the negative trajectory for these adolescents leading to more positive long-term behaviors.

At one point in my career, I worked for a county jail as the mental health team leader for adolescents charged with adult crimes such as sexual assaults, armed robberies, and murder cases. They were held in juvenile detention while awaiting trial at 26th and California. They faced long prison sentences for oftentimes horrific crimes and remained in juvenile detention for long periods of time. While there, intensive services and support were provided including evaluations for psychotropic medications, psychiatric care, mental health services, group and peer support, and trying to further their education until they either went to trial or were sentenced. They presented with significant behavioral disorders and frequently became involved in aggressive behaviors with staff and other detainees. They often engaged in higher levels of self-harm and self-injury, and oftentimes these adolescents would have to be put on suicide watch after a court date or bad news from their family systems. The significance of their deficits became apparent the longer they were detained. The legacy of loss for all of them was significant. Broken families, murdered family members, family gang involvement, born with substances in their systems, chaotic home lives, homelessness, and a history of many more traumas in their short lives. The more loss, the more disruption and the more problematic their detainment became.

The answer to the broken system and legacy is already too late by the time they are detained. Interventions that should have been started at a young age, and perhaps even before the child was born. Head start programs, while good, are still too late. We know that children need to be nurtured during their first year of life with "good enough parenting" and if they do not get that, then brain development changes, and these children have more problems the older they get. So why if we know this, do we not do anything about it? Why not create programs where young mothers learn to parent before they have the baby, so they understand the differences in crying when an infant is born and learn how to respond to their needs, so the baby's life trajectory and opportunity for a healthy life is increased. Why not create programs for mothers and their children, where they are nurtured while the mothers finish school, find a job, and can climb out of the hole of poverty so more opportunities are available to her and her children? Why is childcare such a problem, when we know that minimum wage jobs cannot provide housing, food, and childcare for the neediest family systems? Why do we invest all of our money in detainment and incarceration, when if we placed more money, into children, and families, it would cost us less in the long run? The many whys of working in a system that is broken, that is slow to change, and always relies on the most expensive outcomes, jail and prison, to manage problematic behaviors like delinquency and criminality.

I am no genius, but I see what has always been in front of me, as both a criminal defense attorney and a mental health professional. Adverse Childhood Experiences (ACE) includes emotional abuse, physical abuse, emotional neglect, physical neglect, domestic violence, substance abuse, parents living apart, mental illness, and/or a family member incarcerated. Per the Compassion Prison Project, 97% of the prison population has at least one ACE. When looking at children and adolescents exposed to ACEs, 60 percent have been exposed to crime, violence, and abuse either directly and indirectly, 50% of youth have been assaulted at least once, and 39% of youth between the ages of 12 and 17 have witnessed violence. The more traumatic experiences a child or adolescent has, the more extensive the problems become. According to the Compassion Prison Project, if a youth experiences six or more ACES without intervention they are more likely to become an opiate addict and more likely to have severe mental illness with hallucinations; if a youth experiences five or more ACEs without intervention they are more likely to have delays in language, and problems with emotional and brain development; if a youth experiences four or more ACEs without intervention they are more likely to struggle with anxiety, engage in illicit drug use, have problematic alcohol use, go to prison, attempt suicide, struggle with opiate abuse, and are more likely to experience violent victimization; and if a youth experiences one to two ACEs without intervention they are more likely to smoke, have serious job problems, have serious health problems, and use antidepressants.

The data is clear. There is no disputing what is in front of us. The nineteen-year-old young adult I represented in the criminal court system decades ago, had experienced so many adverse childhood experiences, without intervention, that created a cataclysmic event resulting in the murder of his 7-year-old brother. He had experienced more than six ACEs in his short lifespan and although I did not understand it at the time, the system failed him long before he entered the criminal court system. What I know now is that we create life templates that we can follow and observe, and the less we do, the more we pay in the long run. Restorative justice is about challenging the old ways of doing things and seeing how to intervene from a different lens, in which we expend money in more proactive ways. We must invest in our youth to prevent long term criminality, long term substance use issues, and long-term mental health problems. We must invest in human beings and if we do, we create a community in which hope and change is possible.

What are some of the problems with how the criminal justice system has traditionally handled defendants suffering from mental illness or trauma?

How can the criminal justice system be more effective in addressing the intersection of trauma, untreated mental health problems and poverty in the criminal justice system?

How can we sell the need to implement change in our current justice system?

BRIAN'S STORY

RELATED BY THOMAS R. MURRAY

"Life is what I make it, and I have been very fortunate with mine."

Brian was raised in a middle class household, accompanied by the typical dysfunctions which reside under today's modern-American 'nuclear family'—a stagnant standard of living perceived as restricting any guarantee to organically succeed. He is entering high school when his parents divorce, and the parameters that give way to his struggle of youthful purpose begin to formulate.

A young aspirer of music, Brian is floating through his initial years at high school when he is introduced to alcohol for the first time, while attending a family gathering. He takes his first sip at age fifteen (15). He enjoyed the flavor and the feeling of social prosperity that accompanied. However, what started as something enjoyed socially, rapidly progressed towards him nurturing a burdensome addiction.

In the short span of four (4) years, from age sixteen to twenty, Brian is drinking and smoking as a means to find purpose amongst his peers. A product of inclusivity that amassed two DUI (Driving Under the Influence of Alcohol) offenses, a drug charge, and him being removed from two high schools. With the first DUI offense, he is given probation, but without the necessary support to commit to recovery. It is during the end of his initial probation that he receives his second DUI. This leads to his confinement to house arrest, curfew, and periodic home visitations by his parole officer as Brian awaits sentencing. It was at this time, at the age of twenty (20) that he is faced with change, self-described as divine intervention.

While confined to his mother's home awaiting sentencing on his second DUI, Brian experiences a moment of clarity when his mother—whom he believed to be out for the day—opens the garage door to him attempting to take his own life. As he described it, "that is the moment where it all clicked". He began sobriety, and freely adopted the changes that accompanied it.

At age twenty-five (25), Brian is presented a second chance at purpose. He commits to a 12-step program and picks up work to make ends meet, as he rebuilds himself and attends college for the first time. Unsure what to pursue, and in hopes that it would get him out of the library, Brian registers to take a class on fire-science. He completes the course ranked top of the class. There, he meets a paramedic employed with the City of Chicago, who suggests that Brian pursue an EMT (Emergency Medical Technician) position with the Chicago Fire Department. He considers the prospective and attends the paramedic course. Again, he completes the course ranked top of the class. As someone who had previously attained mediocre grades, this new pattern of success influenced an advantageous beatitude that grew to become a daily reality. Brian continued this ascension of purpose to become employed with the City of Chicago Fire Department as an EMT.

As Brian explained his story to me, it became one of unimaginable success which arose out of the struggles many young individuals find themselves similarly faced; but his story suggests that the preservation of hope in oneself can motivate purposeful pursuits that expose the joys of life's progression. As Brian would summarize: his story is one filled with lessons where one moment of change allowed an avenue to "the good life" he now enjoys.

What does Brian teach us about the power to focus one's life in a new direction?

How might Brian's life have proceeded if he had not taken control, entered the 12-step program, and proceeded to change the course of his activities?

What has enabled Brian to succeed where so many in like circumstances fail?

Technical Violations on Probation, Mass Incarceration, and Restorative Justice – Finding a Better Way

CHARLES R. PYLE[1]

PART I

AVOIDING PRISON SANCTIONS FOR TECHNICAL VIOLATIONS:
REDUCING CONTROL TO INCREASE OFFENDER SUCCESS ON
SUPERVISON

On November 6, 2017, 30-year-old rapper Robert Williams, known professionally as Meek Mill, was sentenced to 2-4 years in prison for violating his probation conditions.[2] Mr. Williams was arrested in 2007 when he was 19 years old, and was ultimately convicted of seven charges related to guns and drugs.[3] In 2009, Mr. Williams was sentenced to 1-2 years in prison and 7 years-probation.[4] He was released from custody after seven months.[5]

Over the nine years of probation supervision there were many small violations. Most were related to his often music-related travel, as well as drug use problems related to a probable opioid use disorder.[6] At one point, the judge ordered Mr. Williams to take an etiquette class to correct his use of crude language in the courtroom.[7] Following his fourth revocation petition for technical

---

1   United States Magistrate Judge, District of Arizona.

2   Marc Hogan, *Why Did Meek Mill Go to Prison?*, Pitchfork (Nov. 17, 2017), https://pitchfork.com/thepitch/why-did-meek-mill-go-to-prison/.

3   *Id.*

4   *Id.*

5   *Id.*

6   *Id.*

7   *Id.*

violations of supervision conditions, on December 10, 2015, Mr. Williams was sentenced to 6-12 months of house arrest and 6 years of probation.[8]

The revocation petition that led to Mr. Williams being sentenced to 2-4 years in prison alleged the following violations:

1. In 2016, Mr. Williams violated his travel restrictions by leaving Philadelphia and traveling to New York City to attend a benefit concert and visit his then-girlfriend Nicki Minaj;

2. In March of 2017, Mr. Williams was involved in a physical altercation at the St. Louis Airport with an airport employee who was trying to get a picture with the famous rap artist; and

3. Later in 2017, after appearing on The Tonight Show Starring Jimmy Fallon, Mr. Williams was cited for reckless driving for "popping wheelies on a dirt bike" in New York City traffic and while not wearing a helmet.[9]

Many in the entertainment industry, including Jay-Z and Kevin Hart, quickly began advocating on Mr. Williams behalf.[10] On April 24, 2018, after 138 days in custody, the Pennsylvania Supreme Court ordered Mr. Williams be released on bail. On July 24, 2019, Mr. Williams' original conviction was vacated due to problems with the credibility of the arresting officer.

In May of 2020, a 15-year-old Michigan girl known by the pseudonym Grace had her juvenile probation revoked, resulting in immediate incarceration in the juvenile detention facility in Pontiac, Michigan. The Family Court judge ruled that Grace was "guilty on the failure to submit any schoolwork and getting up for school."[11] Grace's school at the time was completely online due to COVID-19 restrictions.

Like the Meek Mill case, Grace being incarcerated for not doing her homework became a national news story. Like Mr. Williams, Grace is Black, and her

---

8 *Id.*

9 *Meek Mill: Probation Violation Case Study*, Law Offices of Douglas Herring (Dec. 11, 2017), https://herringdefense.com/meek-mill-probation-violation-case-study/.

10 *Celebrities react to Meek Mill's 'unjust' prison sentence*, Associated Press (Nov. 6, 2017), www.usatoday.com/story/life/music/2017/11/06/meek-mill-gets-prison-sentence-probation-violation-earlier-gun-and-drug-case/838448001/.

11 Beth LeBlanc & Mike Martindale, *Oakland Co. girl jailed for not doing homework gets released*, The Detroit News (Jul. 31, 2020), https://www.detroitnews.com/story/news/local/oakland-county/2020/07/31/oakland-co-girl-jailed-not-doing-homework-ordered-release/5557997002/.

story unfolded during a summer of protests regarding ongoing racial injustices within the justice system. That Grace was confined during the COVID-19 pandemic for missing schoolwork made the situation even more outrageous. After Grace was in custody for two-and-a-half months, the Michigan Court of Appeals ordered Grace immediately released from confinement on July 31, 2020.[12]

These two cases brought the nation's attention to the little known, but commonly utilized practice of sending people to prison, frequently for substantial periods of time, not for a new offense, but rather for not following the rules of supervision. From 2001 to 2018, I was a United States Magistrate Judge in the District of Arizona. During that time, I oversaw hundreds of cases about people being returned to prison for violating conditions of supervision. Now in retirement, I am working with the National Acupuncture Detoxification Association to improve treatment options for people with substance use disorders, and with Second Chance Tucson to help people returning from prison overcome the barriers that a criminal conviction creates. And I am working to put an end to the all too frequent judicially imposed outcome of sending people to prison, when options for treatment and understanding were called for instead. The impact and causes of sending people to prison will be explained below, along with suggestions for alternative responses that would avoid this expensive and socially debilitating practice.

In June 2019, the Council on State Governments Justice Center (CSG) released its report, The CSG study concluded that 45% of all state prison admissions nationwide were for violations of probation or parole for either new offenses or technical violations.[13] Nationwide, technical violations accounted for one-fourth of all state prison admissions at an annual cost of 2.8 billion dollars.[14] That figure does "not account for the substantial local costs of keeping people in jail for supervision violations."[15]

Reliance on punishment and incarceration in response to technical violations is expensive, counterproductive, and has a multi-generational impact on individuals, families and communities. A focus on the possibility of redemption, creating restorative justice responses instead of punitive ones, and developing

---

12   *Id.*

13   *Id.*

14   *Id.*

15   *Id.*

more integrative, client-centered responses to substance use disorder and trauma will prevent prisons being filled with rule breakers rather than criminals.

INDIVIDUAL AND INSTITUTIONAL IMPACT OF REVOCATION AND RETURN TO PRISON

Revocation and returning to custody has severe impacts on individuals. Any success the person had finding stable housing, employment, treatment, and restoring family connections, is lost by incarceration. The traumatic impact of incarceration on the children of those in custody is exacerbated when the parent is recycled back to prison. To lose either a source of financial support or a caregiver, or both, has a dramatic negative impact on the stability of the whole family. The entire family moves farther from cycling out of poverty and closer to cycling into prison.

The evidence of the impact on children of incarcerated parents when they enter adulthood is dramatic and troubling. A Duke University study found that people who as children had a parent or parents removed from the home by incarceration were:

Six times more likely to suffer from substance use disorder;

Two times more likely to be diagnosed with an anxiety disorder;

Three times more likely to be charged with a felony;

Five times more likely to be a teenage parent; and

Two and a half times more likely to feel socially isolated.[16]

These tragic and socially costly outcomes are undoubtedly exacerbated by repeated, unpredictable incarcerations for technical violations of release conditions. The family is briefly reunited only to have the court pull the rug out from under them.

---

16 Gifford, et. al., "Association of Parental Incarceration with Psychiatric and Functional Outcomes of Young Adults," JAMA Network Open, 2019; 2(8): e191005.DOI:10.1001/jamanetworkopen.2019.10005.

Receiving technical violators has negative impacts on prison administration as well. Many sentences for technical violations are less than a year in custody. Such short sentences do not allow the prisoner to program or get well settled. One prison administrator told me that people returning from the community with short sentences, after balancing their physical safety and the duration of their confinement, were more prone to ask for protective segregation. This has a resource implication for the prison and a negative mental health implication for the prisoner. The impact on the local jail is negative as well, because the supervisee must ordinarily be held in custody while the court processes the revocation petition. These short stays are costly and disruptive. They involve transfer of the person's personal property, including identification, as well as transferring responsibility for physical and mental health treatment to the local jurisdiction. If a new charge is being processed as well, such jail stays can last many months.

For the probation or parole officer (PO), the revocation and return to prison increases the likelihood that the supervision will ultimately be closed unsuccessfully. The level of trust with the PO and the Probation Office is greatly diminished, leading to less cooperation and honesty in the relationship. It does not appear to me that PO's are evaluated on how many unsuccessful case closures they have in their caseload. This speaks to our understanding of their role. The emphasis is on surveillance and return to prison, not support and successful integration with the community. If it was the latter, the rate of successful and unsuccessful case closures would be closely watched.

When a person finishes their revocation custody and returns to the community, they do not start from where they were before. Rather, they start with a much more problematic housing and employment history and more discouraged family and community support. They also now have a more distrustful and surveillance focused relationship with their PO and reinforced doubts and despair of their own. Now, they have to decide whether to try to climb out of this deep hole to return to where they were, or whether to just "kill their number." A tough job has become much tougher. All of which was completely unnecessary – an unforced error. And the revolving door continues to spin.

WHAT ARE TECHNICAL VIOLATIONS?

While the range of possible technical violations is as broad as the number of conditions imposed, certain characteristics of the population being supervised have the greatest impact. About 65% of criminal justice-involved people are dealing with a substance use disorder (SUD), most of whom also have a co-occurring mental health condition.[17] Among justice-involved individuals, 15-20% have been diagnosed as severely mentally ill.[18] For people who are in or have been in prison, 100% have been exposed to a traumatic event, with a majority having unresolved issues in responding to those experiences.[19] Almost 100% of justice-involved women with an SUD have a need for trauma-related treatment.[20]

The two biggest causes of a revocation petition being filed are substance use relapse and absconding; giving up on supervision. This is interrelated. Does the stress of compliance encourage relapse? Does relapse encourage giving up and waiting for the inevitable return to prison? Does this repeated cycle of failure and incarceration encourage the ultimate surrender; the decision to accept more punishment to "kill my number," with the negative public safety implications of that outcome?

The system experiences repeated technical violations because it principally enforces compliance with supervision conditions using two tools: the threat of incarceration and incarceration. The threats are ineffective and the term of incarceration is always grossly disproportionate to the behavior it is responding to. The focus on surveillance and distrust of the person under supervision, and perhaps a subconscious expectation of failure, predictably lead to this revocation experience. A system that encourages people to give up and accept prison and immorally incarcerates people for disease relapse needs dramatic change.

THE KEY CRIMINAL JUSTICE DICHOTOMIES

There are two key criminal justice dichotomies. First, are criminal justice-involved people inherently bad people or people who made a bad decision? Secondly, are criminal justice-involved people with a behavioral health condition suffering from a disease or a moral failing? The fundamental premise to the four decades long development of the mass incarceration crisis is that society was dealing with bad people with a chronic moral failing.

---

17 *National Center on Addiction and Substance Abuse*, Columbia University (2010).

18 *Serious Mental Illness (SMI) Prevalence in Jails and Prison*, Office of Research & Public Affairs (Sep. 2016), https://www.treatmentadvocacycenter.org/storage/documents/backgrounders/smi-in-jails-and-prisons.pdf.

19 *2017 Annual Report*, Illinois Criminal Justice Information Authority (published on April 2, 2018), www.icjia.state.il.us.

20 *Id.*

Today, many people in the criminal justice system would understand that the system, for the most part, deals with people who made bad choices. Frequently made as a result of an underlying behavioral health condition; an underlying disease condition. That dramatic change in understanding is important, but has minimal impact on a system whose policies and culture were established during decades of the "bad people with a moral failing" understanding. Zero tolerance policies, felon association prohibitions, and travel and residency restrictions are based on a bad people with moral failing premise. The horrific conditions and disdain for rehabilitation efforts in our prisons confirms the bad person perception, while incarceration for relapse emphasizes the moral failing understanding.

We have known for decades that addiction is a disease requiring a medical response. For many, the use of chemical substances can lead to an organic insult to portions of the brain. And now we know that childhood trauma can have a similar negative impact and detract from normal brain activity.[21] We must incorporate the medical understanding of the physical and emotional implications of addiction and trauma into our criminal justice system. A determined system-wide effort, supported by important public and private institutions will be required to implement policies and change the culture to align with our new understanding of seeking redemption and recovery for people who made bad decisions and have a behavioral health disease.

BURDENSOME CONDITIONS LEAD TO FAILURE

The premise to community supervision is to prevent future criminal conduct while supporting the person's efforts to successfully reintegrate into the community. The system approaches this mission relying on the fallacy of control instead of developing trust. Control is established, and trust diminished, through 15 or so standard conditions coupled with a half dozen special conditions. A violation of any condition could lead a person to prison. Not only are there too many conditions, many of them are ill-advised.[22]

---

21 Van Der Kolk, Bessel; The Body Keeps the Score: Brain, Mind and Body in the Healing of Trauma, (2014)

22 In this section we will discuss the following restrictions that people on probation face: (1) felon association prohibition; (2) employment condition; (3) housing restrictions; (4) travel restrictions; (5) answering truthfully to the PO and following all rules from the PO; and (6) not violating any local, state, or federal laws.

The prime example of this is the felon association prohibition. The premise that associating with people engaged in bad conduct can lead a person into the same conduct is valid. But the felon association prohibition is both unrealistic and demoralizing. Much of the supervision population can be prohibited from seeing family members, neighbors, and relatives that have a criminal history. Meanwhile, we order people to drug testing, halfway houses, residential and outpatient drug treatment, and even probation office waiting rooms where the bulk of the people present have a criminal history.

Beyond being unrealistic, the felon association prohibition is harmful. To tell a person with a felony history that they cannot associate with a "known felon" sends the explicit message that they too are beyond redemption and a bad influence on others. For people who have throughout life had emphasis placed on their failings, this message seriously compromises any capacity for success. The gold standard in supervision is when a person in custody or under supervision has their "Aha Moment." The most unlikely source of inspiration for the Aha Moment is something a judge or PO would say. The inspiration is more likely to come from someone with shared experience; a "credible messenger." Someone who has experienced SUD, an alcohol use disorder (AUD), trauma, and prison. The felon association prohibition discourages those associations from occurring.

Mentors and sponsors are important to success, particularly for those facing significant challenges. A frequent supervision condition is participation in 12-Step Treatment Groups. A core concept of 12-Step Principles is for the group member to have a sponsor they can turn to in difficult times. I would frequently ask defendants who had a 12-Step Program requirement if they had a "sponsor", but rarely would a defendant confirm they had one. We should encourage that connection, not inhibit it with our felon association prohibition. Our understanding of the defendant's treatment should go beyond collecting a written log reflecting meeting attendance, to a trusting and supportive interaction seeking successful treatment responses while recognizing how difficult the road will be.

The employment condition logically presumes that employment provides both a prosocial activity in a prosocial environment as well as income to negate the need to make money illegally. While logical, should employment be encouraged or ordered? People should be free to decide, like free members of the community, that education, childcare, adult care, returning to a traditional homeland, or even attending to physical or behavioral health needs is a better choice than employment. Why would the PO be in a better position to make that decision? Why do we need job search sheets, copies of pay stubs, or job change/

loss notifications? The supervisee should be encouraged to pursue education or employment, or both, and be supported by the PO in those efforts. But neither should be court-ordered as a condition of freedom.

Residency restrictions can be important. Preventing a child sex offender from living near an elementary school is clearly a vital restriction. Assigning someone to a halfway house, residential SUD treatment or a sober living environment can also be important and may need a court order to support court-ordered payment for that residency. But requiring that a person live at an approved residence with people approved by the PO is problematic. Most people on supervision will find housing options severely limited by financial considerations and background checks. The PO's focus should be on helping people find safe, affordable housing, not restricting their options. Restricting who someone can live with frequently has romantic implications. While concern for a troubled romantic liaison may be well-founded, prohibiting the connection ends not the relationship, but rather the trust and exchange of truthful information between the person supervised and the PO. This both increases the danger of the relationship and decreases the likelihood of success on supervision.

The restriction on not leaving the state has nothing to do with lawful behavior, but instead relates to the court's jurisdiction – its power to return you to prison efficiently. If you live near a state border, this requirement is particularly inane. The requirement does not physically restrict travel, it just provides a basis for returning you to prison regardless of what occurred across state lines.

The catch-all requirement that a person answer the PO truthfully and follow all PO instructions opens a very wide gate for finding a violation. Will the court send a person to prison for lying to an officer, withholding information from an officer, or not following a written or verbal instruction? We are trying to teach that dishonesty and unreliability impede the chances for law-abiding behavior and a comfortable lifestyle. The old grade school saying, "if you cheat you're only cheating yourself," applies. Threats of imprisonment and actual incarceration do not inspire honesty and cooperation. This catch-all requirement should not be in the court ordered conditions.

No doubt the most controversial of my criticisms is suggesting that the condition ordering the defendant to obey all local, state, and federal criminal laws be removed. Preventing new criminal conduct is a fundamental aspect of the supervision mission, but as a basis for revocation, this condition creates unnecessary procedural problems and gives unfair leverage to probation and prosecution to expeditiously return a person to prison. The fundamental unstated premise to a person seeking to successfully integrate with a community is to obey all laws – whether or not you are on supervision. The requirement to obey criminal laws continues after supervision ends.

If a new criminal charge is pursued separate from a revocation petition, a dual prosecution track is created that can cause delays and logistical problems, particularly if different jurisdictions are involved. A probation or parole warrant can lead to a person being held in custody even if pretrial release is ordered on the new charge. The new charge can be used as leverage to get someone to admit to a long ago disregarded technical violation in exchange for dismissal of the new charge. How fair does that appear to the defendant? If revocation sentence is perceived as adequate for the new charge, how serious was that new conduct? Was the conduct greedy and violent or was it behavioral health related? What was the likely sentence on the new charge, or even the actual sentence if charges weren't dismissed, compared to the revocation sentence? The two-track prosecution of new charge and revocation should be avoided because too many problems, delays and unfairness accumulates as a result. We need to trust the system to get a fair result on the new charge. The best way to avoid these complications is to not list the obvious requirement of every citizen that they obey all criminal laws as a court-ordered condition of supervision.

My query about whether the defendant will perceive that he was treated fairly may elicit dismissive responses of "who cares." We should always care that our criminal process is perceived as fair. The landmark study and book by Tom R. Tyler concluded that it was not potential punishment that encouraged compliance, but the belief that the law and the process was legitimate.[23] To reduce recidivism, we must convince those we supervise that the law and the process is legitimate, not merely efficient for the prosecution. When we catch ourselves forgetting the importance of the perception of fairness, it is another sign of the importance of a significant culture change in our criminal justice system. The goal of supervision is to help a person live successfully and lawfully in the community. Too many conditions foster an "I'm the boss of you" relationship between the PO and supervised person. Too many conditions encourages us to accept failure when success was readily achievable.

---

23 Tom R. Tyler, *Why People Obey the Law*, Princeton University Press (2006).

DON'T GIVE UP!

Transitioning from prison to community is intimidating enough, but the burden of supervision conditions makes it much worse. Fewer conditions and a more supportive, less suspicious attitude from PO and judge is needed. And we need to instill a fervent, "Don't Give Up" attitude in judges, officers, and those on supervision.

Mandatory, standard and special conditions of release could be combined into 8 conditions:

1. Report to your PO within 72 hours of release and as directed thereafter;
2. Allow home visits and reasonable searches of home and person;
3. Report police contacts within 72 hours;
4. Not possess firearms, explosive devices or other dangerous weapons;
5. Not act as a confidential informant without prior PO knowledge and approval;
6. Participate in treatment programs recommended by your PO;
7. Abide by court-ordered or statutory movement restrictions and residency placements, including curfew, home detention, sober living housing, halfway house, residential treatment facilities, restraining orders and sex offender restrictions;
8. Maintain your PO issued cell phone with you at all times, sign the user agreement allowing PO access to data on the phone, and charge the phone daily.

Instead of stating in the conditions that a violation will return you to prison, the explicit message prominently and repeatedly stated in the conditions should be <u>"Don't give up on supervision – we do not want to send you to prison."</u> We want to encourage communication and follow through as opposed to avoidance and surrender.

Except for the movement restrictions, these conditions are not particularly detailed. The purpose of the conditions is guidance instead of setting someone up for revocation and confinement. Putting responsibility for reference to treatment programs within the authority of the PO allows more flexibility for establishing and changing treatment plans, as well as more opportunity to collaborate with the defendant/patient concerning needed changes to encourage success.

Restrictions on location are in some instances very important and in all instances a significant limitation on a person's liberty interest. For both reasons, such restrictions need to be court-ordered as opposed to a directive from the PO. Nevertheless, it should be remembered that prison is usually a poor response to an unsuccessful residential placement.

Finally, I suggest that supervised people in the higher risk classifications be provided a cell phone, and that the person being supervised be required to keep the phone charged and with them at all times. If we want to maintain communication, a cell phone is the most versatile and effective device. The most frequently used form of communication should be text message. The phone should be provided free with an agreement that we can access any data on the phone. We can have our own obnoxious "I agree" box. Cell phones create an effective communication and surveillance tool, for a modest cost. Fewer conditions should be imposed, and those conditions should not be focused on sending someone back to prison.

I recommend an additional procedure to be utilized but not as a condition. Both the PO and the person being supervised should be responsible for keeping a contact sheet up to date. The contact sheet should include the address and cell phone number for the defendant and require the defendant to designate a person to be notified, supplying their name, relationship, address, and phone numbers. The PO needs to keep his name, office address, and cell phone number up to date and also provide the name, office address, and cell phone number of the PO'S supervisor. Putting this responsibility on both the PO and the supervisee is both fair and pragmatic. If we had shorter supervision terms, changes in the PO assigned to the case would occur less frequently, but today it is a frequent occurrence we should anticipate. Making this a mutual responsibility instead of a one directional order emphasizes the importance of both communication and cooperation.

It is important to recognize that the probationary system in place is focused on finding failure. It offers only two forms of enforcement – threatening imprisonment and sending people back to prison. Clearly, neither of those options are helping people successfully complete their time on probation. This system is also not keeping people safer because even if the offender is sent to prison, they will eventually be released with even less of a chance of success and community restoration. It is imperative that the system change in a positive way; and as a society we must decide how to achieve success in the probationary system. Part II will ruminate further on this issue and provide some restorative justice based ideas for change.

PART II
APPLYING RESTORATIVE JUSTICE AND INTEGRATIVE TREATMENT CONCEPTS TO AVOID IMPRISONMENT FOR TECHNICAL VIOLATIONS

As explained in Part I, sending people back to prison or threatening to do so has not fostered a successful probation and reintegration system. Rather than continue with this unrealistic system, we need to focus on realistic strategies that may lead to success on supervision. A new approach should focus on rewards rather than trying to find failure. A new approach should also be more individualized and address the underlying issues such as drug and alcohol addictions. If we can change the ideals and goals of supervision, we will find more success. With success will come a more restorative experience for all participants and a more peaceful society.

EXPANDING REWARDS AND SANCTIONS TO DEVELOP RESTORATIVE JUSTICE RESPONSES TO NON-COMPLIANT BEHAVIOR

The most frequent scenario I used to see in revocation of supervision cases was a series of positive or missed urinalyses (UA), understandably leading to the exasperation of the PO and ultimately a petition and a return to prison. In this common situation, the judge and the PO feel justified in this harsh outcome because they have showed patience but there are still repeated violations. The frustration of the judge, PO, and prosecutor with the defendant's non-compliance will be quite evident at the disposition hearing. The system will be shaming the defendant for failing to "stay clean." But the more accurate statement would be that the defendant is being returned to prison for not successfully recovering from the disease they are dealing with. Shaming, incarcerating, and ramping up conditions will not facilitate recovery.

One of the most important tools in effecting behavioral change is the application of rewards and sanctions. Currently the criminal justice system almost never utilizes rewards even though evidence shows that rewards are more impactful than sanctions.[24] To be effective, rewards and sanctions need to be applied promptly, predictably, and proportionately. When imposing sanctions, we fail on all three considerations.

The time-consuming nature of court proceedings and the overwhelming caseloads PO's are burdened with means that sanctions are rarely imposed promptly. The use of only threats and admonishments for non-compliance, before finally imposing a prison term for the same conduct that was excused earlier, means that sanctions are not predictable. And both responses, doing nothing and months in prison, are not proportionate to the conduct being sanctioned. Probation administrators and PO's understand from a policy standpoint that sanctions need to be applied in a graduated fashion, but because there are so few sanctions available, applying that policy becomes impractical. The two principal sanctions are threatening imprisonment ("I admonished the defendant...") and imprisonment. Other graduated sanctions could be home confinement, which is another form of custody, increased reporting requirements, and increased drug testing. As we tighten the conditions, we get the defendant closer to returning to prison and further from the defendant believing he can succeed.

Rewards and sanctions do not need to be significant to be effective. A commendation letter, a $5 gift certificate, and even recognition in a group setting can be an effective reward. Small and promptly imposed sanctions can also be effective. A written assignment, a craft or art project, 3 hours of community service, a reading assignment, and even a weekend in jail can be an effective sanction if ordered and complied with within a few weeks of the violation.

We must become much more imaginative in developing a range of rewards and sanctions that are directed at helping a person succeed instead of setting them up for failure. No response, or a mere admonishment, is a bad response. Remember, imprisonment is acceptance of failure when success can be had.

"SOFTER" BUT SMARTER SUPERVISION STRATEGIES

Our nation's prisons have a poor track record when it comes to rehabilitation. So supervision that presupposes imprisonment for non-compliance is inherently damaging to a person's capacity for reintegration with family and community,

---

24   Paul L. Cary, M.S., et. al., *The Drug Court Judicial Benchbook*, 139-55, National Drug Court Institute (Feb. 2011), https://www.ndci.org/sites/default/files/nadcp/14146_NDCI_Benchbook_v6.pdf.

success in multiple endeavors and relationships, and redemption in whatever form the person chooses. Supervision needs a new and smarter approach that responds to non-compliance, but insists on focusing on success instead of the ultimate failure, a return to prison.

The response does not need to be onerous or even particularly punitive to be effective. Possible responses could be: instructing the defendant to write (but not send) a letter to the victim of his property crime; listen to a Brene Brown Ted Talk on shame and send the probation officer three text messages about what was learned; stack wood or haul water for an elderly couple's house on your reservation; wash and interior clean your father's work truck; or attend warrant resolution court this week and resolve all local warrants. In other words, almost anything is a better response than nothing. The response should be agreed upon between the officer and the probationer, which will improve compliance, motivation, and perhaps even problem-solving skills. I would suggest the following guidelines for these "agreed responses:"

1. Must be accomplished within 10 days;
2. Must not require more than three hours to accomplish;
3. Is either agreed upon by defendant or chosen by defendant from multiple options;
4. Ideally the response is more constructive than punitive.
5. Should be a restorative activity that gives back or builds supportive relationships.

That the response is agreed upon is important both legally and in terms of the relationship between officer and client. Legally there is no particular authorization for these responses, but I do not suggest any legislative change. If it is agreed upon there is no legal challenge and it diminishes the inherent adversarial nature of the officer-client relationship. People on criminal justice supervision are distrustful of probation officers, incorrectly believing the officers want to send them to jail or prison. Gaining agreement is possible if the requests are quickly accomplished and not demeaning. A possible encouragement to agreement would be to instruct the client that the non-compliant behavior needs to be reported to the judge and prosecutor, but won't be reported for ten days so that the client's response can be included with the report, thus putting them in a better light.

Additionally, these small tasks could be used to create opportunities for rewards. Rewarding positive behavior is a fundamental aspect of specialty courts, but in standard supervision there appear to be fewer opportunities to use positive feedback effectively. These small tasks could be part of the monthly reporting discussion with a short term view of agreeing on the next task and a long-term view of working towards an appropriate reward. The most important reward to someone on supervision is ending supervision early. This is frequently a desired goal of the officer as well. This exercise changes the focus of the monthly interaction from compliance to personal growth and future plans in a subtle but constructive way.

"Softer" strategies will often be more effective than a more directive and threatening approach. But these strategies are inconsistent with the inherent focus on punishment, deprivation, and force that the criminal justice system relies on despite decades of disappointing and damaging outcomes. It would take exceptional leadership to move towards these more patient, accepting, and interactive strategies that focus on voluntary rather than compelled action. While extraordinarily difficult, I believe that change in attitude and culture is critical to successful criminal justice reform.

TESTING

For decades the criminal justice system has relied on urinalysis (UA) and breathalyzer (BA) testing to determine if a defendant has been using illegal drugs or drinking alcoholic beverages. Positive or missed UA's are no doubt the most significant factors leading to revocation for technical violations and returning a person to prison. We do not want people breaking the law or using illicit substances, so testing seems to be a logical requirement. But putting UA testing as a direct supervision requirement causes unnecessary problems.

UA and BA testing is an evidence-based practice for SUD/AUD treatment programs. When a person has a positive or missed UA in a treatment context, there will be a therapeutic response. But when testing is done in a criminal justice context, a punitive response occurs. Sober living houses and halfway houses frequently use BA testing on site. While the response to a positive test can be punitive, on site testing is much less difficult for the supervisee to comply with. Testing that is not treatment or residency related creates an additional hurdle for the supervisee to manage and fit in their schedules.

I am not opposed to two or three UA's in the first 60 days to determine if there is a need for treatment. Otherwise, UA testing should usually occur within the context of a treatment or residency requirement. Testing should be a part of recovery, not an excuse for a return to prison. Today the testing focus is surveillance – meant to catch you doing something wrong. But the focus of testing should be therapeutic, and the goal of supervision should be responding to the behavioral health problem with a plan for recovery.

As presently used, the consequence of a failed UA is punishment, with the ultimate punishment being incarceration. Contingency management is an alternative approach that focuses on incentives not sanctions. An example of contingency management would be a cognitive behavioral therapy (CBT) based SUD treatment program that calls for on-site UA testing twice a week. If the test result is negative, the test subject gets to reach into the "Prize Box" and pull out a prize, usually a small gift coupon. If the test is positive, that person does not get the reward.

Contingency management has been used and studied as a behavioral health treatment technique for decades and has consistently been found to outperform a punitive approach.[25] Despite the long-standing evidence of the efficacy of contingency management, it is almost never used in the criminal justice system. In fact, almost no one in the criminal justice system has heard of contingency management as our institutional inertia directs us to continue pursuing the same inadequate protocols.

Having testing occur at treatment sites and using rewards based treatment modalities like contingency management removes the punishment focus from SUD treatment. Our reliance on punishment and then yet harsher punishments has pushed us into the mass incarceration crisis. It is time to change to a more therapeutic course of supervision.

ESTABLISHING INTEGRATIVE, CLIENT-CENTERED TREATMENT
OPTIONS FOR SUD AND TRAUMA

Because most people under supervision suffer from SUD, improving treatment and widening treatment options is key to having greater success on supervision. In the commonplace event of relapse, therapeutic adjustments to treatment need to be pursued instead of custody. Patients are individuals, but our treatment options are somewhat regimented, relying primarily on 12-Step programs and

---

25 Sterling M. McPherson, et. al., *A review of contingency management for the treatment of substance-use disorders: adaption for underserved populations, use of experimental technologies, and personalized optimization strategies*, Substance Abuse and Rehabilitation 2018:9 43-57 (published online on Aug. 13, 2018), https://www.ncbi.nlm.nih.gov/pmc/articles/PMC6095117/.

CBT. These treatments need to be supplemented with other therapies and the defendant/patient must be involved in designing the pathway to recovery.

Medication-assisted treatment (MAT) is grossly underutilized in the criminal justice system because of a moralistic "Just Say No" approach to addiction instead of a therapeutic approach to dealing with cravings and triggers. MAT is clearly appropriate for opiate use disorder (OUD) and AUD and has been an evidence- based practice for decades. MAT should be available in medically appropriate cases for individuals who want to try it. MAT should not be denied because someone is criminal justice involved, but the extraordinarily low penetration of the utilization of MAT for treating criminal defendants indicates that is exactly what is going on.

Ear acupuncture, sometimes referred to as acudetox, has been utilized in this country for almost fifty years to treat addiction and trauma. The procedure calls for 5 needles to be placed in 5 specific "points" in each ear after which the person sits and meditates, usually in a group setting, for about 30 minutes. Ear acupuncture is not a stand-alone cure, but what is? MAT is supposed to be accompanied by talk therapy. CBT and 12-Step should be coming to the realization that their programs could benefit from supplemental therapies and activities. The cost of 10 needles and an alcohol wipe is about 70 cents and the procedure has close to zero risk.

I often talk about the ten advantages of acudetox. The first five I described as logistical: inexpensive, extremely low risk, low barrier to training, direct supervision unnecessary, and portability facilitating treatment in remote areas. The second five I described as procedural or philosophical: specific diagnosis unnecessary, not judgmental, group dynamic, family member and custodian treatment available, and trust creating – community members putting healing hands on other community members.

These second five acudetox considerations definitely emphasize providing disease treatment for good people, putting us on the right side of the criminal justice dichotomy referred to earlier. Conditions related to addiction, stress, and trauma are stigmatizing. No diagnosis necessary means no stigmatizing inquiries, even ones not intended to be so. Routine acudetox inquiries like, "would you like to try acudetox," or "are you ready for the first needle," are non-threatening and reassuring, not stigmatizing. The group dynamic emphasizes good people facing a shared problem. It would take extraordinary callousness to label the entire group as consisting of bad people with moral failings. That family members or officers might choose to receive treatment shows stress to be a normal human reaction, not a moral failing.

The two most impactful considerations are that acudetox is non-judgmental and that "community" Acudetox Specialists create trust through administering treatment. To conclude that someone is a bad person or beyond redemption, is the pinnacle of being judgmental. Acudetox shows the strength and effectiveness of rejecting such damaging conclusions and focusing on reenergizing a person's inherent goodness. As we in the criminal justice community pursue behavior change, hoping for that "Aha Moment," building trust is the critical skill to be effective. Judgments, orders and directives do not build trust. However, it is difficult to imagine a more effective way to build trust than to provide a simple, calming, effective treatment in a completely voluntary, non-threatening setting.

Traditional indigenous therapies and ceremonies would be helpful and more culturally appropriate for American Indian defendants. This could include sweat lodge, smudging, talking circles, labyrinth walking, and other traditional practices. The importance of recognizing the impact of trauma on the behavioral health of justice-involved people is a relatively recent initiative. The impact of historical trauma is a concept that was developed only a few decades ago by Dr. Maria Yellow Horse Brave Heart. Centuries of subjugation with genocide, family separation, relocation and loss of land, Indian schools, and repression of Indian culture has an understandable intergenerational impact on the behavioral health of many American Indians. Incorporating cultural practices to respond to that trauma has proven effective.[26]

Acupuncture and traditional therapies are little understood and largely not accepted by the criminal justice community. Both practices are several thousand years old. Both are extremely low cost and low to almost no risk. Both are non-directive and non-judgmental, which comes as quite a relief for people being pushed through the stress and judgment of a criminal justice process. And in both modalities, the humility and caring of the treatment providers is extraordinary.

These and other supplemental therapies need to be explored if we are to obtain better outcomes on our addiction treatment referrals and reduce warehousing people with SUD in prison. Expanding the range of voluntary and optional supplementary treatment protocols available necessarily requires

---

26 Gone, Joseph P., 2019, "A Community Based Treatment for Native American Historical Trauma: Prospects for an Evidence-Based Practice," Journal of Counseling and Clinical Psychology, DOI 10.1037/a0015390.

the defendant to make choices and be involved in creating the recovery plan. Intuitively, a person will be more committed and willing to stay on a path they choose than a path they were told to take.

ZERO TO SEVEN DAYS

Even if you reduce the number of conditions, there will be violations. If more progressive, non-custodial sanctions can be implemented, hopefully the need for a custodial sentence can be averted. If a potential custodial sentence for a new violation is left to the new case, then a custodial response in the supervision case is not required. There may still be times when a short custodial term may be the most appropriate response.

What is the appropriate custodial sentence for missing an appointment, not reporting a change in employment status, or a positive UA? Today we respond to that question in terms of months. However, none of those transgressions for an unsupervised citizen would merit even a day of custody. The months long term is a reflection of our frustration with non-compliance, not the direct danger posed by that behavior.

The people who have suffered through the frustration of dealing with chronic non-compliance, judges and PO's, are comfortable with sentencing people to months in custody for technical violations. To change that practice and culture, a stringent objective standard is needed. In my view, the appropriate sentencing range for a technical violation is zero to seven days' confinement. That range would apply for all outstanding technical violations; in other words, no consecutive 7-day sentences for multiple violations. The consecutive sentence prohibition should encourage responding to technical violations close in time to when they occur instead of letting them accumulate. After this short confinement term is served, the defendant starts with a clean slate, which is where all concerned should want to be starting from.

I have heard these very short term periods of confinement referred to as "flash incarceration." Ideally, the term would be served within a few weeks of the objected to conduct. These short term custodial sanctions can be imposed without a defendant losing all the hard-earned gains they have achieved earlier in the supervision term; and the chance for the PO and supervisee to have a successful supervision can remain high.

REDIRECT FOCUS AND FUNDING

In the summer of 2020, racial injustice protests developed a slogan, "Defund the Police," which called for funds to be redirected from law enforcement to social service agencies. We need to step back and reflect on what we have been doing for decades. Is imprisoning someone for relapse, even repeated relapses, moral? Is reliance on punishment and deprivation instead of incentives effective? Is our approach to supervision threatening and moralistic or supportive and therapeutic? Is the goal of supervision to have people live like we do even though their circumstances are completely different?

We should not be spending $2.3 billion sending people to prison largely for failing to recover from one or more behavioral health conditions. We need to redirect that money away from enforcement and towards therapy. We need to change our focus from being resigned to accepting failure, to insisting on finding success in collaboration with the client. The current system puts the blame of incarceration on the person with the serious behavioral health problem and gives the judge and PO few alternatives to incarceration. The statistics show that returning people to prison for technical violations is a major problem in our nation. And the outrageous injustices faced by Meek Mill and Grace dictate a moral imperative for us all to correct this problem now.

What are some of the technical violations that can get someone sent back to prison? Out of these technical violations, which one is most ripe for re-evaluation or elimination?

Why is it important that people who have just been released from incarceration be treated like all other individuals?

If you were a Parole Officer, how would you balance surveillance with support for the person you were assigned to monitor? Which is more important and why? Are the two in conflict?

Why does sending someone who is suffering with an addiction back to prison not help with their recovery?

Which of the restorative justice techniques mentioned in Part II do you believe would be the best to implement in the current justice system? Should we prescribe a restorative techniques that works best for everybody or should we individually tailored our responses?

Can you list any other restorative justice techniques that might help end the cycle of incarceration in your community?

How do you answer the fears expressed by the community when offenders are released back into society?

What NADA Means to Me: Vindication, Solace, & Neuroscience in the Work of Restorative Justice

DR. KENNETH O. CARTER[1]

PREFACE

Huffington Post, December 10, 2020: "The Trump administration executed 40-year-old Brandon Bernard....The government went through with the killing despite high-profile opposition from 5 of 9 surviving jurors[,]...the prosecutor who defended his death sentence on appeal, several members of Congress, 23 current and former

---

1   Student editor and President of the UIC John Marshall Law School's Restorative Justice Initiative, Deijha Monét Swanson, both directly and indirectly made my writing of this chapter so much better. Although I began considering ideas for this chapter in summer 2020, it was not until some months later when Deijha offered her editorial assistance that the project took on its current form, and the writing began to go well. I wish to express my deepest appreciation to her. I want to thank her for so graciously, on so many occasions, sharing her sense of the text and going over troubling passages with me.

Deijha's clear and direct critique, content curiosity, and superb editorial suggestions are inseparable from any success I may have had in struggling with the intertwining of professional and intensely personal themes herein. If this chapter ultimately lacks sufficient relevance or proves ill-received, the responsibility is only mine. However, if there is anything praiseworthy to be found here, I give full credit to the Divine and to Deijha for helping me along the way.

Currently, I serve our country's veterans as a lead psychiatric physician in Primary Care-Mental Health Integration in the Veterans Administration Health Care System. In June 2020, I was elected for the second time as president of the National Acupuncture Detoxification Association (NADA) – a not-for-profit healthcare organization with national and international reach.

Forty years ago, as a curious college graduate, I travelled to the South Bronx's Lincoln Hospital Recovery Center (aka The People's Clinic) for a two-week apprenticeship to study what would become NADA's signature protocol – a unique style of ear acupressure and ear acupuncture. Since my Lincoln days, I have achieved other academic and career accomplishments including a fellowship in psychiatric epidemiology, a master's in public health, a medical school professorship, and board certifications in both psychiatry and full body acupuncture.

NADA is just as good as pharmaceuticals and psychotherapy for most issues in mental health and substance misuse treatment. It is an excellent complement to mainstream treatment modalities and with components easily adapted to personal self-care. It is the best tool I have ever encountered for safely and efficiently helping most patients and personnel in most settings – and one of those settings is Restorative Justice.

prosecutors, reality television star and criminal justice reform advocate Kim Kardashian West, and The Washington Post's editorial board. Hours before the execution, controversial lawyers Alan Dershowitz and Ken Starr... joined Bernard's defense team."

This makes me mad as hell.

Why aren't there alternatives to scenes like this? Why only this kind of fossilized "Justice" that feels most often like "Just Us?" What can I do with this kind of pain felt for this Black man? What can his defenders do, his family, the BIPOC, and White communities that have even a hint of a heart?

It makes me want to scream. And it is deeply personal.

"THERE BUT FOR THE GRACE OF GOD GO I"

My father escaped the apartheid of 1958 South Central Virginia. He was the first in his family to ever go to college, majoring in agriculture. He said, "The only job for me there was share-cropping." So, he left me and my mother in search of a foundation for a better life. He left right after I was born. For years I thought he hitched the ride North with $10 in his pocket, but he recently corrected me, "It was actually $13." He now has a terrible diagnosis of mesothelioma lung cancer thought in large part due to taking the first job he could find—one in an asbestosis based brake factory "where the dust was so thick sometimes you could barely see in front of your face, and we had no ventilation, no mask, no nothing." Dad came back to get us when I was one year old and that is how I came to grow up in rural Southern New Jersey. Dad eventually made a proud 40-year career as a Soil Conservationist for the U.S. Department of Agriculture.

Sometimes the only 1 of 3 Black students in the classes of my mostly White high school, in 1976 I became the first Black Valedictorian in its 50-year-old history—also its first Presidential Scholar and its first Johns Hopkins Achievement Scholar. My graduation speech was not the Bi-Centennial praise speech the school officials wanted. I spoke of my closest Black friend's father who was lynched by the Klan in Georgia. I embraced my inherited dark trauma cloud from a "routine" traffic stop that happened several years before I was born. During that "routine" stop, one my father's four brothers was murdered by the police; another was shot nearly to death; later that day another brother was smuggled away to escape the Klan; and another soon escaped to urban New Jersey to later join the Nation of Islam under the auspices of El Hajj Malik Shabazz (aka

Malcom X). Along with my father, these are my real-life heroes. In the undeclared war against America's Black, Brown, Indigenous, poor, and unconnected, we are all sufferers of intergenerational trauma, institutionalized racism, and structural inequity...just like Brandon Bernard.

I entered medical school in 1980, and two weeks after classes began, I went to a workshop that proved to be transformative. The workshop was led by my soon-to-be-mentor AfricanAmerindianShamanGriot, Brother Isma'el Jamal (aka BJ). Before medical school, I had graduated from Johns Hopkins profoundly disillusioned and very nearly radicalized by a combination of the suffocating Eurocentric "liberal" education I'd received; the daily witnessed injustices on Baltimore's Eastside; and immersion in out-of-class Afrocentric history from the pre-dynastic Black Egypt/Khemet to the pre-Black Holocaust of the European/Arab slave trade. After completing undergrad at Hopkins, I was still left praying with all my heart that God would reveal a professional pathway that recognized and honored the ageless wisdom and gifts that my Black (Khemetic) African Ancestors had given to the world. I saw the answer to my prayers in Brother Jamal's sophisticated style of AfroSynergy—a masterful blending of Ancestral and contemporary medicine; complementary and alternative medicine; and integrative medicine and healing. During the workshop's intermission, I told him there and then that I wanted to leave medical school and apprentice with him. He told me to stay in medical school. He said his path was a difficult one and that if I really wanted to join the struggle for real, I should use my privilege AND stay true to my yearnings.

In 1982, I took a year's leave from medical school to study at the Lincoln Recovery Center (aka The People's Clinic or simply, Lincoln) in the South Bronx under the advice of Brother Jamal. But when I heard that my supervising director would be a White man, I resisted strongly. I still wanted a practical, Black based, clinically reliable, and effective technique that I could call my own that also synergized with my contemporary western medical training. At first, BJ patiently schooled me on the Black African origins of all civilizations and medical systems including Chinese civilization and Traditional East Asian Medicine. He continued to school me on Lincoln's history of being a multi-ethnic, multicultural epicenter that sincerely appreciated the Black African origins of civilization and medicine. He impressed me with his admiration for Lincoln's creative and practical operationalization of this reality in meeting the community's pressing healthcare needs. But despite all this, my resistance was still strong. I didn't think a White man could teach me about my history and the practical applications of Black African ancestral wisdom healing techniques. Finally, he came back just as strong with "Get your head out of the way! Just go, and you'll see what I mean!"

The White man I tried so hard to avoid was psychiatrist Dr. Michael "Mike" Smith, who was Lincoln's supervising director for most of its existence. Although not the originator, he was a central link in the chain of transmission of Lincoln's profound treatment style and technique known variously as "Lincoln detox," "Acudetox," "NADA style treatment," "NADA protocol," or just "NADA." Its originators were community organizers and activists—the Young Lords and The Black Panthers—inspired in their work by the egregious health inequities and callous official indifference of NYC's medical elite to the overwhelming needs of the South Bronx's BIPOC community. Mike eventually became the other great mentor of my personal and professional life.

My experience at Lincoln was my initiation into the United States' earliest model of integrated wholistic health care. It is a model that brings into reality the elusive "bio-psycho-social-cultural paradigm" that is taught as a gold standard in mental health and substance use treatment.

NADA STYLE TREATMENT ENHANCES CAPACITY TO CARE FOR ALL

The infamous War on Drugs has largely been a war on Black and Brown. The NADA style treatment initiated in South Bronx was born in response to a raging heroin epidemic that relied on official indifference at best and active complicity at its worst. NADA followed the rejection of widespread indiscriminate promotion of opiate replacement therapy (methadone) as yet another means of individual and social control. I came along to begin learning NADA when the crack epidemic was in full stride and when concern about long term effects on babies born of crack addicted mothers was a major public health concern. While other drugs continue to ply our communities in a seemingly endless stream, alcohol endures as the most pervasive and destructive to overall population health. From endemic fetal alcohol concerns to today's amphetamine and fentanyl crises devastating rural America, NADA helps make things better.

As a tool that is transdiagnostic and pansymptomatic, NADA is effective regardless of substance or situation; diagnosis or setting; or chronicity or acuity. Over the past 40 years, the medico-legal community has gradually come to appreciate its universally health enhancing properties—including mitigation of work-day stress, professional burnout, compassion fatigue, induction of calm, and sense of wellbeing. Barriers to broad NADA implementation are extremely low. It is easy to learn with minimal training requirements, and it can be performed in groups making it efficiently as well as effectively administered. NADA acupuncture materials are 10x more costly than those for acupressure; however, costs for both are minuscule. NADA acupuncture costs less than one dollar, and NADA acupressure costs less than one dime for materials per treatment episode. Both have evidence of effectiveness across the lifespan, and NADA acupressure has even proven to be effective in neonatal abstinence syndrome for babies in opiate withdrawal who are born to opiate dependent mothers.

Restorative Justice processes are necessarily grounded in the belief that positive transformation is possible. Offenders can transform and be rehabilitated. Victims can transform and be reconciled. Institutions can transform by learning to prioritize rehabilitation and reconciliation over harsh retribution and punishment. NADA has a long-standing and rich record of use as a healing-centered physical intervention that is psychologically informed and behaviorally transformative.

The NADA related neuroscience is compelling and well established. Distressed emotions and dysfunctional cognitions fuel undesirable individual and social responses underlying criminal behaviors; socially learned fears and behaviors; inclinations to punishment over restoration; inclinations to self-destructive guilt; and inclination to self-medication with intoxicants rather than redemption and recovery. But persons of influence charged with responsibility for maintaining law and order will achieve better outcomes by factoring practical neuroscience considerations into their decision-making.

Limitations of time, budget, personnel, and other resources are also practical considerations that are minimized through NADA implementation. NADA style and technique are easily learned, taught, and enacted. It is safe and easily adapted to existing program structures in the hands of existing program personnel. Robust in rapidly balancing neurophysiology, it is a gold standard in integrated mental health, behavior health, trauma, and substance misuse treatments.

NADA acupuncture and acupressure have the unique potential to provide all of these benefits to all consumers, personnel, and systems involved in Restorative Justice processes. It is uniquely well-suited to the purposes and pursuit of Restorative Justice for all.

The work of rehabilitation and reconciliation is the foundation of Restorative Justice, and this work is emotionally demanding. When emotions are distressed, thinking and behavior are not optimal. NADA is a technical method and style of intervention that calms this emotional distress. In doing this, it improves cognition, behavior, decision-making, and potential for relationships that heal rather than punish and kill. This is critical to the success of Restorative Justice work.

WHAT IS NADA AND THE NADA PROTOCOL? WHO ARE NADA PRACTITIONERS?

The National Acupuncture Detoxification Association (NADA) provides education, training, and consultation in the integration and implementation of its standardized ear acupressure and acupuncture protocol.

Restorative Justice personnel at all levels can learn to practice the NADA protocol in a short period of time, usually a matter of days. NADA is an easily integrated adjuvant to usual and customary care in established work settings. Treatment takes about an hour and is best provided in groups of any size. A single NADA practitioner can treat many customers in an hour.

In addition to medical personnel, NADA supports the training of all professionals including law enforcement officers, parole officers, peer support specialists, counselors, social service workers, lawyers, and judges. It helps them perform the work they already do with greater ease, flexibility, and less likelihood of burnout. When personnel treat the consumers they serve, the work goes better for everyone.

NADA acupressure techniques use magnetic beads and seeds that adhere to the ear with hypoallergenic surgical tape. They can be used as a self-care modality for both professional personnel and programs' consumers.

NADA is a nonverbal style of treatment. It does not depend on a "verbal passport" – this means that potential barriers of culture, language, etc., are minimized. There are no special administrative requirements. No clinical diagnosis, assessment, or evaluation is necessary before NADA is initiated.

Like Cognitive Behavioral Therapy (CBT), Mindfulness Based Therapy (MBT), and psychopharmaceutical interventions, NADA causes neurophysiological change that is reflected in emotions and behavior. NADA rapidly detoxifies emotions that can cause behavioral impairment (e.g., anger, anxiety, irritability, posttraumatic dissociation, etc.) with extremely low risk of any significant side effects. It differs from psycho-pharmaceutical medications in that there is no potential development of tolerance or withdrawal. For psychotherapy to work a minimum requirement is the motivation and the time to acquire a new skill, whereas, NADA effects reliably induced even in guarded and suspicious consumers with little apparent motivation at all. Psychological preparedness to interact with and benefit from other core aspects of Restorative Justice programming is improved.

NADA ENDORSEMENTS AND ACKNOWLEDGEMENTS

In 2006, the Treatment Improvement Protocol #45 (TIP 45) for Detoxification and Substance Abuse Treatment established NADA as the first complementary and alternative medicine (CAM) modality to be officially recognized as a best practice in the United States. This early recognition focused on NADA's benefit to consumer engagement and retention in substance misuse treatment. Substance misuse and related matters are major considerations in Restorative Justice settings as well.

Since 2006, both the Veterans Administration Health Care System and the Department of Defense have incorporated NADA in clinical settings and have formally recognized acupuncture as having good evidence to support its use in relieving anxiety including the anxiety associated with post-traumatic stress disorder (PTSD). The Veterans Administration Health Care System's Center for Integrative Health currently identifies acupuncture as a first-tier integrative medicine modality and recently required that it be made an accessible treatment at all Veteran Administration Medical Centers.

Most NADA clinical research has focused on its integrated use as an adjunct to usual and customary practices, but some researchers have also studied NADA as a stand-alone intervention. The evidence is now clear – although NADA is not a panacea, it can be an extremely valuable part of comprehensive integrated care programming.

NADA's national office website www.acudetox.com is a rich source of related information and materials. Links to peer-reviewed articles provide access to the latest NADA research and scholarly critique. *Guidepoints* is the quarterly NADA newsletter providing stories and images of NADA know-how, cultural acceptance, and relief of suffering around the world.

In more than 30 years, there has never been a lawsuit brought against the NADA governing board, its cadre of Registered Trainers, its more than 25,000 ear Acupuncture Detoxification Specialists (ADSes), or its organization partners providing NADA treatment and/or training. All ADSes are required to have earned a competency-based NADA Certificate of Training Completion. Trainings are manual guided and standardized using the organization's extensive *NADA Training Resource Manual.*

Registered Trainer trainings are flexible; tailored to program needs; personalized to trainee experience and aptitude; and are a mix of didactic instruction, clinically supervised client interaction, and technical skills training. ADS candidates with prior healthcare experience are typically able to demonstrate all requisite competencies within a 30-hour training period. ADS candidates without prior healthcare experience overwhelmingly are able to demonstrate all requisite competencies within a 70-hour training period.

Personally, I have used NADA as a foundational treatment over the course of my entire career as a NADA registered trainer, full body acupuncturist, psychiatric physician, and public health advocate. When addressing physical complaints in my role as a full body acupuncturist, I always lead with NADA and find that it reliably works to relieve most somatic discomfort and aids in the discernment of what more may need to be done.

The clinical complexity of addressing both mental illness (MI) and co-occurring substance use disorder (SUD) is especially challenging. My most telling experience with the utility of NADA for MI/SUD co-occurring disorders came in 1982 while I was still a medical student. After completing the first two years of medical school didactics and before beginning the next 2 years of clinical instruction, I took a year off for travel and personal exploration to "see if this alternative medicine stuff could really help really sick people." I ended up spending most of that time at Lincoln. Following an initial week of observation and training at Lincoln, the first person I was directed to apply NADA to on my own is one I remember vividly even now. He was a thin Black man, diagnosed with chronic paranoid schizophrenia and crack cocaine dependence. He had been out smoking crack all night, and upon voluntary arrival at the clinic, he declared that he was feeling suicidal and that he was hearing hallucinated commands telling him to kill himself and others. At the beginning of the treatment hour he was wide eyed; hyperverbal and rambling; hyperkinetic externally and internally restless; as well as anxious and fearful. I recall thinking to myself, "Wow. He's already talking about killing himself and other people. What's he gonna do to me when I stick a stainless-steel pin in his ear?" My anxiety must have shown on my face because he reassured me that he was familiar with the process and that all would go well. He told me, "no," he was not ready for formal substance use disorder treatment or regular mental health care. And, "yeah," he did drop in regularly to Lincoln's only large group treatment room (where it was not uncommon for the daily client census to exceed 200 or more) when things went "too far." And, "no," he was not yet ready to commit to more comprehensive SUD or mental/behavioral support services, "but I'm starting to think about it." While I sat near him, hovering silently and watching intently during the course of his treatment hour, HE fell asleep! When he awoke after about 30 minutes, there was a different person sitting in front of me. The wide-eyed wild look was gone, and he looked and felt much calmer. The hallucinated commands to kill others was gone. The commands to kill himself had greatly diminished and were no longer compelling. His speech and thought processes were normalized to the extent that a productive reciprocal conversation was possible. He requested the placement of the acupressure beads (a round seed or magnetic pellet on hypoallergenic surgical tape) and affirmed that this simple ear acupressure device prolonged the "peace" associated with the use of ear acupuncture pins. He felt that the ear acupoint beads and pins worked together in facilitating harm reduction by decreasing drug craving, drug use, and other dysfunctional, impulsive, and sometimes dangerous behaviors.

I was sold.

In the 1990's, the Washington D.C. Superior Court instituted a Drug Court Diversion Program. The country was well into "Three Strikes and You're Out," and the outrageously inequitable sentencing for cocaine in crack form (mostly urban Black and Brown) versus powdered form (mostly suburban/rural and White) had taken hold. I was hired by the D.C. Superior Court as Director of Acupuncture Treatment and Training. The program itself was federally funded as a field demonstration project to provide data on NADA implementation and efficacy to the Center for Substance Abuse Treatment (CSAT). It further confirmed NADA's adjuvant value as an important aspect of comprehensive substance use disorder treatment programming. Consumers liked it and wanted to come back for more. Consumer engagement and retention are well established as parameters that correlate best with treatment outcome.

I have since treated and trained in virtually every imaginable setting including churches with ministers; Employee Assistance Programs in factories; in emergency rooms; in general medicine inpatient units; in general psychiatric inpatient units; in community mental health centers; in primary care and specialty private practices; at community health fairs; at employee wellness fairs; for families in their homes; and in situations of post-traumatic stress for soldiers, veterans, civilians, and communities.

The are no absolute contraindications to the use of NADA. It is extremely unlikely that an allergic reaction will occur with the seeds, gold-plated beads, hypo-allergenic tape, or stainless-steel pins that are used in NADA acupressure and acupuncture. The recognition of NADA's safety as well as utility across the healthcare spectrum is well established from its effectiveness in acute crisis, stabilization, maintenance, and promotion of well-being. It is safely applied without regard to diagnosis or symptom profile.

"Who helps the helpers?" is a crucial question that is often overlooked. Frontline workers, managers, administrators, personnel in criminal justice settings, etc., confront behavioral health, MI, SUD, and co-occurring MI/SUD issues as much as the speciality treatment setting charged with addressing these issues, and they are in need of the suitable tools to properly help with these problems. NADA can be one such tool. England is a notable example where NADA is now present in most prisons. Administered by prison guards to prisoners and to each other, rates of violence have been cut in half. Following the 2001 NYC World Trade Center Twin Towers attack, NADA ADSes responded in strength. They underscored the fact that many victims cannot or do not want to talk in the immediate aftermath of great tragedy and are often made worse when driven to "debrief" before resiliency is bolstered, but they can benefit greatly from the NADA style of treatment and therapeutic engagement.

Practitioners in Juarez, Mexico, which has been described as the murder capital of the world, have currently established "NADA safe zones" in churches in cooperation with local faith leaders. In African and East Asian conflict zones, NADA providers alleviate the sufferings of war, displacement, and loss of life. During the COVID 19 pandemic, NADA publications have increasingly emphasized the effectiveness of acupressure in self-care and in decreasing burnout and compassion fatigue in healthcare providers.

There are many reasons why NADA is a good fit for Restorative Justice set-tings, processes, and goals. It is easily learned by any and all personnel, and so training can be made widely available to all. Improved balance of brain and emotions can occur rapidly, consistently, inexpensively, and safely in this setting where mental and emotional stress abound. More specifically, NADA has proven effective for improving anger, anxiety, depression, concentration, body aches, headaches, decreased energy, and in decreasing professional burnout. These are conditions that interfere with the psychological availability of consumers and staff to participate optimally in Restorative Justice processes and goals. The ben-efits that NADA provides produce a strong foundation that increases the likeli-hood for successfully achieving rehabilitation and reconciliation.

NADA is extremely unlikely to produce any significant adverse reactions or consequences. It is best for programs to use existing staff to provide in-house NADA treatment and training, thereby keeping cost for providing NADA low. Evidence supports its use in the short term and in producing benefits that are sustained over time – even after discharge or program completion and in the absence of active ongoing NADA intervention.

Challenges exist in making psychotherapy universally available to all those who might benefit. Sufficient numbers of psychotherapists are unlikely to be available over long and indeterminate periods of time, and they are a relatively expensive resource. With psychotherapy there is limited expectation of imme-diate response to a psychotherapy episode. Psychotherapy engagement can be difficult for consumers and personnel who are influenced by stigma; lacking in trust; reluctant to provide full and honest disclosure of issues; too fragile or otherwise unable to expose vulnerabilities; and for those without any prior psychotherapy encounters.

Fast acting psychopharmaceutical agents are not a good fit for widespread use in Restorative Justice settings. Licit and illicit psychopharmaceuticals/drugs can certainly bring about reliable neurophysiologic change, but they often bring other baggage that is undesirable and can be difficult to manage.

Sedative-hypnotics like Valium and Xanax; opiate analgesics like Oxycontin and Fentanyl; psychostimulants like Methamphetamine and Adderall; antide-pressants like Elavil and Remeron; and antipsychotics like Seroquel and Zyprexa are certainly effective drivers of emotion and behavior. Unfortunately, they also can cause significant side effects that are not trivial or uncommon. Costs for the management and oversight necessary for the medically prescribed use of licit agents can be high. Diversion and other secondary gain can be ulterior motives for medication-seeking consumers. Sedative-hypnotics dull cognitive and emotional responses. Opiate analgesic "painkillers" decrease emotional distress and physical pain but also decrease brain function and emotional resiliency. Problems of tolerance and withdrawal associated with fast acting psychopharmaceuticals/drugs are proof that they are not essentially homeostatic or balancing in nature.

When consideration of psychotherapy and psychopharmaceutical intervention is appropriate, NADA is of use in clarifying the clinical picture. The calming and balancing effects of NADA help to eliminate the "noise" created by the various sources of emotional distress that can worsen the course of a co-occurring mental illness. Where a co-occurring diagnosis may be indicated, NADA can assist in making the process of determining diagnosis easier and more likely to be accurate. Clarification of this sort is critical to the accurate selection and implementation of specific psychotherapy and targeted psychopharmaceutical treatment interventions.

Psychotherapy and psychopharmaceuticals simply cannot compare to NADA where universal population-based accessibility and ease of utility is concerned. It is uniquely suited to helping, managing, and assisting in the triage of the various mental and emotional challenges encountered in Restorative Justice settings.

EMBRYOLOGIC ORIGINS OF NADA NEUROPHYSIOLOGY

NADA balances emotions and behavior through its effects on the sympathetic, parasympathetic, and central nervous systems. The hypothalamic-pituitary-adrenal (HPA) axis is the chief mediator of stress response in the brain, mind, and body.

HPA axis dysfunction and overactivation is involved in most emotional, mental, and behavioral disorders (e.g., disorders of mood, cognition, personality, sleep, and substance use); a broad array of physical diseases (e.g., chronic pain, chronic fatigue, immune dysfunction, cardiovascular disease, and gastrointestinal illness); and even to measurable atrophy of those brain anatomical areas associated with emotion, memory, and decision making (e.g., hippocampus, amygdala, and medial prefrontal cortex).

The homeostatic and universal impact of NADA treatment on brain chemistry and HPA axis hormonal physiology promotes improved balance, resiliency, and recovery from the effects of pathologic stress. Sources of pathological stress and distress can be many. Sources may be endemic, enduring, situational, and transient; they can also occur due to toxic substances, licit or illicit substance use, and social interactions – all of which can be encountered in Restorative Justice settings.

In humans, the physical and physiologic capacities underlying the broad NADA effects begin with formation of the gill slits at five weeks of embryonic life. The gill slits are a collection of cells that establish and maintain feedback loops of mutual influence by way of nerve impulses, neurotransmitters and hormones during the process of embryonic development. The gill slits precede the development of more complicated "downstream" structures such as the HPA axis; the brain and other body organs; the nervous system; the cardiovascular system; and the myofascial system. As the gill slits assume the structure and function of the external ear, they maintain the interconnectedness with those "downstream" structures through mutual feedback loops.

Notably, the vagus nerve innervates the entire lower half of the external ear and is responsible for regulation of blood pressure, pulse rate, and respiratory rate; it helps with regulating the function of all the internal organs. The vagus nerve both transmits impulses from the brain to the organs and from the organs back to the brain. Similarly, other nerves innervating the external ear communicate directly with the brain and spinal cord. It is these interconnections and feed-loops that facilitate and support our inborn capacities for maintaining whole body/mind balance and homeostasis.

The embryonic gill slits can be further characterized as having three distinct germ layers. They are the ectoderm that develops into the brain, nervous system, skin, and bones; the endoderm that develops into arteries and veins; and the mesoderm that develops into our system of internal organs, including heart, liver, kidneys, and lungs. When gestation is complete, the external ear is the only location in the entire body where the three germ layers continue to co-exist in one anatomical structure. They are readily accessible for NADA acupuncture and acupressure manipulation. As with the motor cortex of the brain, their correspondence to body parts and functions can be mapped in detail.

The five ear acupoints utilized in NADA acupuncture and acupressure are pictured below.

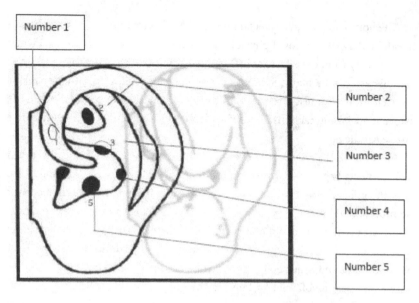

NADA protocol ear points map and description. Number 1, Sympathetic; Number 2, Shen Men; Number 3, Kidney; Number 4, Liver; Number 5, Lung.

NADA BUILDS ON NATURE'S BLUEPRINT IN SUPPORT OF RESTORATIVE JUSTICE

The United States has the largest penal system in the world. Our legal system fuels this massive penal presence, and following the precedent of British Law, it is rooted in principles of punishment and retribution. This is in stark contrast to other systems of law that have made more room for the possibility of caring for all its constituents by providing opportunities for restoring wholeness and wellbeing through rehabilitation and reconciliation.

We all need to care deeply about the impact of crime on everyone – including offenders and victims. We should care about the impact on their communities and see them, ultimately, as our communities too. We should all take responsibility for promoting, securing, and administering the principles and practice of Restorative Justice in order to transform the system into something better and more humane. Our country's abject failure to have a legal system that prioritizes and delivers on rehabilitation and reconciliation is a national disgrace.

Trauma is everywhere. Emotional distress is pervasive. Nearly everyone engaging in or exposed to crime and violence first survives it. In the absence of a Restorative Justice approach, our current legal system, as it stands, is a hellish instrument of racial and social control that is far reaching, characterized by systemic inequity and causing great harm to our individual and collective health and wellbeing.

NADA's style and technique can help in turning the tide. It has a proven track record of doing so. It takes strategic advantage of nature's blueprint in supporting the model paradigm of bio-psycho-social-cultural restoration and rehabilitation in the areas of mental health and substance misuse – areas that must be addressed effectively and efficiently if the Restorative Justice movement is to achieve the goals of rehabilitation and reconciliation as sustainable outcomes.

The one to five ear acupoints used in NADA and its nonverbal/nonjudgmental style and technique have much to offer in support of the practice and administration of Restorative Justice. NADA's style of engagement reliably results in better balancing of brain, mind, body, and behavior.

NADA builds upon both contemporary science and ageless wisdom healing traditions. It builds on traditions valuing healing over punishment and killing. It builds upon our inborn potential for personal and social redemptive restoration in this epoch of medico-legal injustice and mass incarceration. NADA is uniquely suited to supporting the establishment of an emerging new system of Restorative Justice.

DISCUSSION QUESTIONS:

How far have we come? Consider the murder of Brandon Bernard. Why do you think that even after such great opposition, the government moved forward with his execution? How could restorative justice principles have made a difference?

Think outside the box. Diagnostic categories often do not describe fully the person sitting in front of you. How might NADA help meet victims and offenders "where they are?"

Change takes time, but not all change requires a complete overhaul. How can incorporating NADA into existing practices and using existing personnel ease the process of change in "the real world?"

What are some of the ways that NADA can be used to help victims, offenders, and the greater community in which they live?

Psychotherapy is often done individually; however, NADA can be done in large group settings. What are the benefits of NADA with respect to cost and efficient use of personnel?

Consider the neuroscience. The mind and body are connected. Toxic emotions result in toxic behaviors. How does NADA work in helping to realign the mind and body for optimal decision-making and outcomes?

"The Year of Jubilee" Released Citizen Restoration and Re-Enfranchisement Act

ERICA FATIMA

"A just law is a man-made code that squares with the moral law or the law of God. An unjust law is a code that is out of harmony with the moral law. To put it in the terms of St. Thomas Aquinas: An unjust law is a human law that is not rooted in eternal law and natural law."[1]

-Dr. King

INTRODUCTION

This essay explores the ways in which mass incarceration has impacted American society and examines the collateral consequences for citizens post release. Further, it urges a new federal mandate to address some of the harms imposed by draconian, mandatory sentencing. First, the essay will explain "Jubilee" and discuss its goal. Finally, it concludes by providing solutions that set new maximum limits on the amount of time a person can serve. In so doing, it proposes the establishment of a reasonable timeline for mandatory release. The goal is to produce legislation that will usher in a new era of prison reform in America by highlighting the need for real reform and showing the necessity of providing restoration and re-enfranchisement rights for all citizens with felony convictions.

---

1   King, Martin Luther (July 24, 2014). *"Letter from a Birmingham Jail,* 1963 draft". The Martin Luther King, Jr. Research and Education Institute. Retrieved 30, June 2020.

I. A Policy Focused on Restoration, in Harmony with the Moral Law

The Year of Jubilee, Released Citizen Restoration and Re-Enfranchisement Act ("Jubilee RCRR Act") is a policy proposal to establish federal mandates for the immediate restoration and re-enfranchisement of *ALL* rights (emphasis added) to citizens released from state and federal prisons. It mandates federal sentencing limits: No person in the United States convicted of a felony or misdemeanor may serve more than *SEVEN* years for any crime, excluding violent offenses that contain some element of force or a threat of force against a person. Examples are the intentional violent crimes of murder, rape, kidnapping, and acts of violence against children. It also includes certain violent property crimes involving a strong likelihood of psychological trauma to the property owner; such as burglary[2] (the breaking and entering of a dwelling house at night with the intent to commit larceny, assault and battery, or any felony therein), and other State statutory crimes classified as violent felonies. The violent crimes enumerated are not intended as an exhaustive list of such felonies that fall outside the scope of this legislative Act. However, crimes not statutorily defined within the meaning of "violent," but viewed as a serious offense, for example, the illegal manufacture, distribution or possession of controlled substances that may be a felony, *ARE* covered under the Jubilee RCRR Act. The law is based on the Biblical principal that all slaves, (in this instance, prisoners) and indebted persons were to be set free and released from any outstanding debt owed, or indentured servitude, despite completing their terms. Members of the community were required to assist with food, clothing, shelter and with financial support so that the released person was fully restored back into the community. This principal also stands for the moral proposition that everyone needs mercy, grace and restoration. Each person belongs to a community, and the community is responsible for its member's wellbeing because at one point, past or present, everyone needs forgiveness and restoration. Accordingly, if a person used their land as collateral for a debt, during Jubilee, the property reverted back to the original owner and the original owner took possession free and clear of any liens or encumbrances.

Similarly, the Jubilee-RCRR Act restores all rights to persons released from prison, eliminates fines and mandatory fees upon release, eliminates probation requirements after time served, and uses public resources to provide housing, food allowances, employment, education, and other social services to ensure

---

2   Model Penal Code § 6.06 (American Law Institute. Proposed Final Draft (2017).

returning citizens are provided with necessary resources to begin successful reentry. In effect, Jubilee-RCRR Act is a paradigm shifting approach to mainstream concepts of sentencing policies and practices in order to produce more rational outcomes for both the individual and society. A key element of that change is a reconsideration of the scale of punishment in the United States, one of the driving forces that makes the American court system an outlier among democratic nations.[3]

To that end, the goal of this policy proposal explores the extent to which prevailing practices,[4] vis-a-vis length of sentencing, and permanent classification as a felon affects potential deterrent or rehabilitative objectives. It offers as an alternative, a solution to remedy outmoded felony sentencing practices in America by implementing federal statutes that immediately re-enfranchise U.S. citizens formally convicted of a felony and authorizes the permanent removal of felon, ex-felon or any other derivates that identify people by their past crimes from their records. Moreover, the Year of Jubilee, Released Citizen Restoration and Re-Enfranchisement Act ("Jubilee RCRR Act") joins with those collective voices in scholarship and policy, and other civic, faith-based, and community organizations[5] devoted to addressing the utility and efficiency of current federal sentencing practices,[6] the multi-faceted impacts imprisonment causes on entire communities,[7] and the collateral consequences of reentry after imprisonment. Starting from the premise that mass imprisonment[8] has had a profound and deleterious effect on society, both quantitatively and qualitatively, supported by data and decades of research, it is reasonable to conclude that the current state and federal penal systems do not work.[9] Innovative, problem-solving polices,

3   Justice Policy Institute. (2011). Finding Direction: Expanding Criminal Justice Options By Considering Policies of Other Countries.

4   *Long-Term-Sentences-Time-Reconsider-Scale-Punishment* www.sentencingproject.org/publications. Retrieved 30, June 2020.

5   See indexed list of organizations. *Who Pays: True Cost of Incarceration on Families*, www.ellabakercenter.org.

6   Western, B. (2006). Punishment and Inequality in America.

7   Travis, J. (2014). The Growth of Incarceration in the United States: Exploring Causes and Consequences. National Research Council.

8   Tonry, Michael. (2016). Sentencing Fragments: *Penal Reform in America.*

9   Hirsch, Adam J. (1992), The Rise of the Penitentiary: *Prisons and Punishment in Early America*, New Haven.

supported by people-centered approaches to reform and restoration, such as the Jubilee ACT, can provide policy and lawmakers with viable, scalable options.

The Jubilee RCRR Act posits: No person may serve more than seven years for a crime; (except for enumerated violent crimes) after which, any person having served or formally convicted of a felony is released, and completely liberated from any current or future debts pertaining to that crime. "[He] shall serve with you until the Year of the Jubilee; then he shall go out from you, he and his children with him, and go back to his own family, and return to the possession of his fathers; ... You shall not rule over him with harshness." *Leviticus* 25:39-43, KJV.

A. "We're #1!"—In Mass Incarceration. How Did We Get Here?

The United States is the world's leader in incarceration and has the longest sentencing anywhere around the globe.[10] Right now, there are more than 2.2 million people in the nation's prisons and jails—a 500% increase over the last 40 years.[11] And, seemingly, some states are earnestly competing in the "race to incarcerate"[12] to win a phantom prize for the most incarcerations in the nation. For example, in 2018, a total of twenty-two states had imprisonment rates that were higher than the nationwide average.[13] Louisiana had the highest rate (695 sentenced prisoners per 100,000 state residents), followed by Oklahoma (693 per 100,000), Mississippi (626 per 100,000), Arkansas (589 per 100,000), and Arizona (559 per 100,000). Conversely, Minnesota, Maine, Massachusetts, Rhode Island, and Vermont had the lowest imprisonment rates in the U.S., with each having fewer than 200 sentenced prisoners per 100,000 residents.[14]

This unprecedented rise of the prison population in the United States is inextricably linked to complex policy implementation by political leaders and criminal justice practitioners, many playing out false narratives, characterized by fear and scapegoating, despite increasing evidence that large-scale incarceration

---

10 Ye Hee Lee, M. (2015, July 7). Yes, U.S. Locks People Up at a Higher Rate Than Any Other Country. The Washington Post.

11 www.sentencingproject.org, The Sentencing Project compiles state-level criminal justice data from a variety of sources.

12 *Race to Incarcerate A Graphic Retelling* is an adapted work of inspired graphic storytelling by Sabrina Jones of Marc Mauer's landmark book on race, class, and the criminal justice system (2013).

13 https://www.sentencingproject.org/criminal-justice-facts/.

14 Most recent data compiled by the Bureau of Justice Statistics, U.S. Department of Justice.

is not an effective means of achieving public safety.[15] Moreover, the American penal system engages retributive[16] punishments akin to perpetual condemnation, including imposing draconian sentences, levying outlandish fines after release that may be converted into liens,[17] and, that if not paid, may allow states to reincarcerate[18] a released citizen. Additionally, a state may, after a person has completed their sentence, add years of probation under a "split sentencing"[19] mechanism. In so doing, convicted felons in America often live with life-long threats of imprisonment for previous crimes committed.

By contrast, other sovereign and industrialized nations, including indigenous tribes alike, do not adhere to the American penal system, but rather, implement more humane crime policies[20] in keeping with the ideals and moral justifications of sentencing guidelines that are restorative.[21] A call for serious reform is needed if America is ever to answer the moral question: for what offenses should we put people in prison? And for how long?[22] In so doing, perhaps, a more just and restorative system of punishments will arise while America grapples with the haunting question whether she has rehabilitated in fact many or most of the convicted defendants who have been sent to prison under the belief that a person convicted of a crime can be "cured" while incarcerated or under official supervision.[23]

15 U.S. Sentencing Commission. (2008). Alternative Sentencing: *Rehabilitative and Punitive Models and Evidence-Based Policy*. U.S. Sentencing Commission Symposium on Alternatives to Incarceration.

16 **Model Penal Code**. In 1962, the American Law Institute adopted a model Crimes Code called the Model Penal Code (MPC).

17 Frase, R.S. (2015 Mar 25). Why Have U.S. State and Federal Jurisdictions Enacted Sentencing Guidelines? University of Minnesota Sentencing Guidelines Resource Center. Retrieved 27, June 2020.

18 Courtney, L. (2017). A Matter of Time: The Causes and Consequences of Rising Time Served in America's Prisons. Urban Institute.

19 https://www.sentencingproject.org/criminal-justice-facts/.

20 Petteruti, A. (2011). Finding Direction: Expanding Criminal Justice Options By Considering Policies of Other Nations. Justice Policy Institute.

21 López-Lorca, B. (2016). Life Imprisonment in Latin America. Life Imprisonment and Human Rights.

22 *See, e.g., Tapia v. U.S.*, 131 S. Ct. 2382 (2011).

23 *How to End the Era of Mass Supervision*, by David Muhammad, executive director of the National Institute for Criminal Justice Reform.

B. Brief History of Mass Incarceration in America

Since time immemorial, human beings have committed anti-social acts. In response, governments enact laws that define crime and impose criminal punishments for violations. In the United States, every state, as well as the federal government, now has literally thousands of statutory provisions on the books that contain criminal penalties.[24] Primary rationales for enacting criminal laws start with a basic premise; to protect the public interest. This justification is often paired to outcome determinative purposes: deterrence, both general and specific; rehabilitation, including by isolation from society in prison,[25] and sometimes punitive retribution, aka "getting your just dessert."[26] However, it is rarely a one-size fits all approach.

Historically, governments use imprisonment as the main punishment to effectuate the intended results. The first prison in America, founded in 1790 by the Pennsylvanian Quakers, was designed to be less cruel and brutal than the dungeon prisons and jails.[27] So the Quakers created a place where prisoners could read scriptures and repent, the rationale—this would reform prisoners.[28] Later, in the Jacksonian Era, imprisonment and "rehabilitative labor"[29] became a popular form of criminal punishment. During the Progressive Era new concepts of the prison system, such as parole, indeterminate sentencing, and probation,[30] became mainstream practices in America. Overall, the goal of imprisonment, both nationally and abroad was deterrence, reformation, rehabilitation, and public safety.[31]

Most jurisdictions distinguish between crimes that are classified as "felonies" and "misdemeanors." The term felony originated from English common

---

24   "Mass Incarceration Costs $182 Billion Every Year". Equal Justice Initiative. February 6, 2017. Retrieved 11, July 2020.

25   Travis, J. (2014). The Growth of Incarceration in the United States: Exploring Causes and Consequences. National Research Council.

26   U.S. Sentencing Commission. (2008). Alternative Sentencing: Rehabilitative and Punitive Models and Evidence-Based Policy. U.S. Sentencing Commission Symposium on Alternatives to Incarceration.

27   https://valeriejenness.com/history-of-the-united-states-prison-system. Retrieved 8, July 2020.

28   Id.

29   https://en.wikipedia.org/wiki/History_of_United_States_prison_systems. Retrieved 8, July 2020.

30   National Probation and Parole Association, Standard Probation and Parole Act §§ 12 and 27 (1955).

31   http://www.pbs.org/moyers/journal/12282007/penalphilosophy.html. Retrieved 8, July 2020.

law, to describe an offense that, as Sir William Blackstone wrote, "comprises every species of crime, which occasioned at common law the forfeiture of lands or goods."[32] Felonies are the most serious offenses and often carry a harsher punishment, from two or more years imprisonment, to life in prison, or death in the case of the most serious felonies.[33] Misdemeanors are less serious offenses that are typically punished by a fine and/or a potential sentence of less than six months in jail. Blackstone also states that "[t]he idea of felony is indeed so generally connected with that of capital punishment, that we find it hard to separate them; and to this usage the interpretations of the law do now conform."[34]

C. Cruel and Unusual Punishment: "Still A Felon After I've Served My Time"[35]

When the United States rebranded its old polices of "law and order" to "The War on Crime,"[36] it added stricter mandatory sentencing laws that included longer terms of imprisonment: three-strikes laws,[37] and capital punishment.[38] The War on Crime has been credited with facilitating greater militarization of police and contributing to the startling increase in mass incarceration in the United States.[39] In 2018 in the U.S., there were 698 people incarcerated per

32 Blackstone, W. (1765). Commentaries on the Laws of England (Book IV chapter 7) Oxford: Clarendon Press.

33 Contempt for the poor in US drives cruel policies," says UN expert". OHCHR. Retrieved 25, June 2020.

34 Blackstone, W. (1765). Commentaries on the Laws of England (Book IV chapter 7) Oxford: Clarendon Press.

35 Nellis, (2017 May 3). Still Life: America's Increasing Use of Life and Long-Term Sentences. The Sentencing Project, Washington, D.C.

36 In modern politics, law and order, also known as Tough on Crime and the War on Crime, demands for a strict criminal justice system, especially in relation to violent and property crime, through stricter criminal penalties.

37 Schoener, N. (2018 Apr 30). Three Strikes Laws in Different States. LegalMatch.com.

38 U.S. Sentencing Commission. (2018). Recidivism Among Offenders Receiving Retroactive Sentence Reductions: The 2011 Fair Sentencing Act Guideline Amendment.

39 GENEVA (4 June 2018) – *The United States' principal strategy for dealing with extreme poverty is to criminalize and stigmatize those in need of assistance*, United Nations Human Rights, Office of the Commission, Human Rights Council Thirty-eighth session (18 June–6 July 2018). Agenda item 3. Retrieved 22, June 2020. https://www.ohchr.org/.

100,000;[40] giving America the dubious distinction of having the highest per-capita incarceration rate in the world. Incarceration became the go-to, over-utilized, primary form of punishment and rehabilitation for the commission of felony and other offenses.

Not surprisingly, the American penal system, steeped in traditions of systemic racism, especially following the demise of the Jim Crow era[41] as a means of social control over African Americans, continues to wield its power through draconian sentencing under mainstay monikers such as, "tough on crime," and "race to incarcerate."[42] As a result, imprisonment rates for sentenced black males is almost six times that of sentenced white males; at year-end 2017, (2,336 per 100,000 black male U.S. residents) compared to (397 per 100,000 white male U.S. residents).[43] There is a significant indication[44] that these uniquely American policies are products of recalcitrant racist ideologies and closely align with methods used to perpetuate racism in America.[45]

Subsequently, what has emerged, following widespread implementation of these political policy mandates, is a brutal form of cruel and unusual punishment that has been upheld by the United States Supreme Court. Any person, including U.S. citizens, convicted of a felony are irrevocably classified as a "felon,"[46] may be "permanently stripped of their rights,"[47] and face long-term legal consequences persisting after the end of paying "their debt to society."[48] In essence, felony convictions become punishments that are akin to life-long sentences because "ex-

---

40 Correctional Populations in the United States, 2013 (NCJ 248479). Published December 2014 by U.S. Bureau of Justice Statistics (BJS). By Lauren E. Glaze and Danielle Kaeble, BJS Statisticians.

41 Blackmon, Douglas A. (2008), Slavery by Another Name: The Re-Enslavement of Black Americans from the Civil War to World War II, New York.

42 *Race to Incarcerate A Graphic Retelling* is an adapted work of inspired graphic storytelling by Sabrina Jones of Marc Mauer's landmark book on race, class, and the criminal justice system (2013).

43 Most recent data compiled by the Bureau Of Justice Statistics, U.S. Department of Justice.

44 http://www.pbs.org/moyers/journal/12282007/penalphilosophy.html. Retrieved 8, July 2020.

45 Ella Baker Center for Human Rights, Forward Together, and Research Action Design (a collaborative participatory research project with 20 community-based organizations across the country to address this unjust legacy). Retrieved 3, July 2020.

46 The New Jim Crow: *Mass Incarceration in the Age of Colorblindness*, by Michelle Alexander (The New Press, 2010).

47 *See Richardson v. Ramirez*, 418 US 24, 94 S. Ct. 2655, 41 L. Ed. 2d 551 (1974).

48 *I Served My Prison Time. Why Do I Still Have to Pay?"* by, Courtney E. Martin, New York Times, (April 30, 2019). Ms. Martin is the author, most recently, of "*The New Better Off: Reinventing the American Dream.*" Retrieved 2, July 2020.

felons," remain felons, as it pertains to their criminal history and legal status.[49] In fact, felon status in the U.S. is not extinguished after sentence completion, even if parole, probation or early release is given.[50]

Some courts have held that federal courts have inherent ancillary authority to expunge criminal records where an arrest or conviction is found to be invalid or a clerical error is made.[51] Although, currently, there is no general federal expungement statute, and federal courts have no inherent authority to expunge records of a valid federal conviction,[52] notwithstanding, executive clemency[53] or a successful appeal. Thus, the vast majority of persons labeled "felon" retain that status indefinitely.[54] The rationale for such permanent punishment is incongruous with most justifications for criminal laws. In this way, punishment in the U.S. has become more retributive and punitive, rather than rehabilitative.[55] This has occurred despite judicial touting a standard of fairness that "does not offend traditional notions of fair play and substantial justice."[56]

Although all felonies remain serious crimes, concerns of proportionality (i.e., that the punishment fit the crime) have now prompted legislatures to require or permit the imposition of less serious punishments, ranging from lesser terms of imprisonment[57] to the substitution of a jail sentence or even the suspension of all incarceration contingent upon a defendant's successful completion of

---

49   Hirsch, Adam J. (1992), The Rise of the Penitentiary: Prisons and Punishment in Early America, New Haven.

50   Invisible Punishment: The Collateral Consequences of Mass Imprisonment. (Marc Mauer & Meda Chesney-Lind eds., 2002).

51   United States v. Sumner, 226 F.3d 1005, 1014 (9th Cir. 2000); see cases collected in Jane Doe v. United States, 110 F. Supp. 3d 448, 454, n. 16 (E.D.N.Y 2015); Hall v. Alabama, 2010 U.S. Dist. LEXIS 14082, at *22-30 (M.D. Ala. 2010).

52   See, e.g., United States v. Jane Doe, 833 F.3d 192 (2d Cir. 2016), vacating 110 F. Supp. 3d 448 (E.D.N.Y. 2015); United States v. Crowell, 374 F.3d 790, 792-93 (9th 2004), cert. denied, 543 U.S. 1070 (2005).

53   Felon Voting Rights." National Conference of State Legislatures, (September 2016). ("However, felons may qualify for restoration of some rights after a certain period of time has passed). Retrieved 30, June 2020.

54   Thinking About Prison and its Impact in the Twenty-First Century, by Marc Mauer, Walter Reckless Memorial Lecture, Ohio State Journal of Criminal Law. (April 14, 2004).

55   Devah Pager, The Mark of a Criminal Record, 108 AM. J. SOC. 937 (2003).

56   See generally, International Shoe Co. v. Washington, 326 U.S. 310 (1945).

57   Probation and Parole Systems Marked by High Stakes, Missed Opportunities, by Jake Horowitz Director Public Safety Performance Project (September 2018) www.pewtrusts.org.

probation.[58] In some jurisdictions, the term probation[59] applies only to community sentences (alternatives to incarceration), such as suspended sentences. In others, probation also includes supervision of those conditionally released from prison on parole.[60]

However, even where jurisdictions have moved away from the use of mandatory imprisonment, opting for probation, during the period of probation, a released citizen lives under duress and direct threat of being incarcerated for any violation of the restrictions as set forth by the court or probation officer; (however unreasonable,[61] sustainable, arbitrary, or interminably long). As recently as May 2020, an example of an unreasonable and cruel use of incarceration for probation violation made national news. A judge ordered a 15 year-old Black girl in Michigan locked up in juvenile detention for more than two months after she violated terms of her probation by not completing her online schoolwork,[62] despite the fact that the global pandemic (COVID-19) caused her school to migrate to a completely virtual format. Evidence presented by school officials—including the child's teacher, reported over 80% of all students had not completed their homework. This shameful example is just one of hundreds of thousands of cases in which the threat of a probation or parole violation is as bleak as a life sentence. As one judge stated, probation "has created a procedural vortex from which people on parole cannot escape and are at continual risk of being rearrested and reentered into the prison system."[63]

According to EXiT: Executives Transforming Probation and Parole, data shows that there are 4.5 million people, or one out of every 55 adults in the United States, under probation or parole supervision at any given time.[64] "Probation

---

58   U.S. Sentencing Commission. (2017). An Overview of Mandatory Minimum Penalties in the Federal Criminal Justice System.

59   Subramanian, R. & Delaney, R. (2014). Playbook for Change? States Reconsider Mandatory Sentences. Vera Institute of Justice.

60   Subramanian, R. & Delaney, R. (2014). Playbook for Change? States Reconsider Mandatory Sentences. Vera Institute of Justice.

61   Reingold, Paul (2017). "From Grace to Grids: Rethinking Due Process Protection for Parole." Journal of Criminal Law and Criminology. 107: 213–251.

62   A Teenager Didn't Do Her Online Schoolwork. So, a Judge Sent Her to Juvenile Detention, by Jodi S. Cohen https://www.propublica.org/.

63   Want-To-Shrink-The-Prison-Population-Look-At-Parole (2019) https://www.themarshallproject.org/.

64   How to End the Era of Mass Supervision, by David Muhammad, executive director of the National Institute for Criminal Justice Reform.

and parole have grown far too large because people are being supervised who should not be and are being kept on supervision for far too long . . . Far from being an aid to community reintegration as originally designed, community supervision too often serves as a tripwire to imprisonment, creating a vicious cycle of reincarceration for people under supervision for administrative rule violations that would rarely lead someone not under supervision into prison."[65] Today, prison, parole, and probation operations generate an $81 billion annual cost to U.S. taxpayers,[66] while police and court costs, bail bond fees, and prison phone fees generate another $100 billion in costs that are paid by individuals.[67]

If there is to be real change, so that our justice system aligns with the moral values espoused, and prominently displayed on the architrave of the United States Supreme Court, "Equal Justice Under Law,"[68] there must be a universal shift in American jurisprudence and its approach to punishment. That analysis should start at the beginning by addressing the following: what is the purpose of incarceration;[69] and, its immediate and collateral impact on society;[70] what are the responsibilities of the legislature, judges and prosecutors; and of federal and state agencies administering and supervising;[71] and are better methods available to meet changing relationships between imprisonment and public safety?

The Jubilee RCRR Act proposes that reform starts by ending obtuse, unenlightened, and often "anchored"[72] (the human tendency to rely too heavily on the first piece of information offered (the "anchor") when making decisions) sentencing. Moreover, despite vast scholarship, volumes of data analysis, and increasingly common-sense observance, that show the current sentencing

---

65   David Muhammad, executive director of the National Institute for Criminal Justice Reform. https://imprintnews.org.

66   Courtney, L. (2017). A Matter of Time: The Causes and Consequences of Rising Time Served in America's Prisons. Urban Institute.

67   NYTimes, Opinion: *I-Served-My-Prison-Time-Why-Do-I-Still-Have-To-Pay.* (April 30, 2019) www.nytimes.com.

68   https://www.supremecourt.gov.

69   Spelman, W. (2006). The Limited Importance of Prison Expansion. Retrieved 3, July 2020.

70   Marc Mauer, Invisible Punishment: The Collateral Consequences Of Mass Imprisonment (2002).

71   American Law Institute ("ALI") revised Model Penal Code, adopted 2017.

72   Bennett, M.W. (2014). Confronting Cognitive "Anchoring Effect" and "Blind Spot" Biases in Federal Sentencing: *A Modest Solution for Reforming a Fundamental Flaw.* Journal of Criminal Law & Criminology.

mechanisms employed today are not effective,[73] and in many ways have failed to keep the public safe, sentencing judges are influenced by anchors, even irrelevant anchors, to the same extent as lay people. The effects of the anchors are not reduced by the judges' actual experience.[74] Thus, drastic and oppressive incarceration sentences are meted out for even the most minor infractions across court systems today.

Consequently, a comprehensive reform agenda must include a repeal of all mandatory sentencing provisions across the board. In fairness, it is important to note that there are many legislative acts that are being introduced. This is a sign that reform may in fact be in the near future. For example, The First Step Act is lauded as a bipartisan, "once-in-a-generation" reform to America's prison and sentencing system to reduce recidivism, save tax dollars and promote safe communities. The Act uses evidence-based recidivism reduction programs to help inmates successfully return to society after serving their sentence. It also reduces some sentences for certain low-level, nonviolent offenders while preserving important law enforcement tools to tackle criminal enterprises. The United States Senate approved the Act by a vote of 87-12.

After the passage of the Act, Senator Cory Booker said, "Our country's criminal justice system is broken – and it has been broken for decades. You cannot deny justice to any American without it affecting all Americans. That's why the passage of the First Step Act tonight is so meaningful – it begins to right past wrongs that continue to deny justice to millions of Americans. This bill is a step forward for our criminal justice system. By no means can it be the only step – it must be the beginning of a long effort to restore justice to our justice system. But for the first time in a long time, with the passage of this Bill into law, our country will make a meaningful break from the decades of failed policies that led to mass incarceration, which has cost taxpayers billions of dollars, drained our economy, compromised public safety, hurt our children, and disproportionately harmed communities of color while devaluing the very idea of justice in America."[75]

73 First Step Act, a bipartisan "once-in-a-generation" reforms to America's prison and sentencing system to reduce recidivism, save tax dollars and promote safe communities. https://www.judiciary. senate.gov/press/rep/releases/senate-passes-landmark-criminal-justice-reform.

74 Bennett, M.W. (2014). Confronting Cognitive "Anchoring Effect" and "Blind Spot" Biases in Federal Sentencing: A Modest Solution for Reforming a Fundamental Flaw. Journal of Criminal Law & Criminology.

75 https://www.booker.senate.gov/.

Secondly, the Jubilee RCRR Act calls for a federal mandate ending the life-long penalization and stigma of "felon" and for the restoration and re-enfranchisement[76] of the legal and political status of returning citizens; and of current prisoners. The National Advisory Commission on Criminal Justice Standards and Goals, Corrections, Standard Report, 16.17, p. 592 (1973) observed: "Loss of citizenship rights — [including] the right to vote . . . — inhibits reformative efforts. If correction is to reintegrate an offender into free society, the offender must retain all attributes of citizenship. In addition, his respect for law and the legal system may well depend, in some measure, on his ability to participate in that system. Mandatory denials of that participation serve no legitimate public interest." Id., at 593.

To that end, the Jubilee RCRR Act recommends beginning with the basics—eradicating criminal records immediately upon release, and reclassifying "ex-felons"[77] simply to their rightful status as *Citizens*!

II. RESTORATION: The Issues of Collateral Consequences

Each year, the United States spends $80 billion[78] to lock away more than 2.4 million people in its jails and prisons—budgetary allocations that far outpace spending on housing, transportation, and higher education.[79] But costs run deeper than budget line items and extend far beyond the sentences served.[80] These costs are collateral consequences,"[81] and are rarely quantified or measured. They primarily impact incarcerated populations and the families and communities from whom they are separated. Collateral consequences are multiplicitous; impacting various segments of everyday life for those recovering

---

76 https://www.sentencingproject.org/news/8339/ Nicole D. Porter, The Sentencing Project's state and local advocacy efforts on sentencing reform, voting rights, and eliminating racial disparities in the criminal justice system. Her advocacy has supported criminal justice reforms in several states including Kentucky, Missouri, and California. Ms. Porter was named a "New Civil Rights Leader" by Essence Magazine for her work to eliminate mass incarceration.

77 "Federal Restoration of Rights, Pardon, Expungement & Sealing." Restoration of Rights Project. Collateral Consequences Resource Center. Retrieved 7, July 2020.

78 Marc Mauer Thinking-About-Prison-and-its-Impact-in-the-Twenty-First-Century.pdf.

79 Greenwood, P.W. & Turner, S. (2012) Probation and other Non-Institutional Treatment: *The Evidence Is In*. The Oxford Handbook of Juvenile Crime and Juvenile Justice.

80 U.S. Sentencing Commission. (2018). Recidivism Among Offenders Receiving Retroactive Sentence Reductions: The 2011 Fair Sentencing Act Guideline Amendment.

81 Marc Bauer, Invisible Punishment: The Collateral Consequences Of Mass Imprisonment (2002).

from the effects of imprisonment. Some broad categories in which felon and ex-felon status can have an ongoing, often grave impact: employment, housing, professional licenses (several types of professionals such as doctors, lawyers and nurses are required to self-report their criminal convictions to their respective licensing board). And, upon report or discovery of conviction, professionals often find themselves having to defend their future career prospects in administrative proceedings before licensure discipline panels, and may face sanctions that include probation with conditions, suspension or total revocation of the applicable professional license.[82] For those with immigration status – non-citizens who hold visas or green cards face the prospect of deportation if convicted of certain aggravated felonies or crimes of moral turpitude, including possible offenses listed by the federal government that can trigger deportation include crimes that can be considered misdemeanors.[83]

Other significant collateral consequences related to incarceration are residual fines and fees due after release. Both the returning citizen and, more often than not, their families are saddled with exorbitant fee-punishments[84] that, if not paid, can legally be converted into liens with a penalty of re-incarceration![85] Thus, the released citizen is swept into a vortex of perpetual punishment; and this, is certainly outside the moral laws of fair and just punishments. Finally, senior among collateral consequences is the legalized removal of voting rights for felons, and ex-felons. The U.S. Supreme Court made clear, "[A] criminal record was a factor that a state could lawfully take into consideration in determining the qualifications of voters. Because U.S. Const. amend. XIV, § 2, contained language suggesting that the practice of depriving felons of voting rights was acceptable, and because this practice was historically viewed as valid, respondents were not entitled to register as voters under the Equal Protection Clause of U.S. Const. amend. XIV." *Richardson v. Ramirez*, 418 U.S. 24, 26 (1974). In the end, families pay both the apparent and hidden costs while their loved ones serve out sentences

---

82 The Council of State Governments Justice Center. Frequently asked questions: Employment and education. National Reentry Resource Center. http://www.nationalreentryresourcecenter.org/faqs/employment-and-education#Q14.

83 Ditton, P.M. & Wilson, D.J. (1999) Truth in Sentencing in State Prisons. Bureau of Justice Statistics, U.S. Department of Justice.

84 "Some of the most common fees that handicap a parolee's successful re-entry are for body monitors." Reference: https://www.nytimes.com/2019/04/30.

85 Gottschalk, M. (2012). No Way Out? Life Sentences and the Politics of Penal Reform. Life Without Parole: America's New Death Penalty?

in our jails and prisons or are tethered to a never-ending cycle of probation or parole.[86] Moreover, these sentences produce diminishing returns for public safety, and are far out of line with practices of comparable nations and divert resources from more constructive interventions for public safety.

A. Eradicating the Felony Status After Time Served

Under the Jubilee RCRR Act, some of these collateral consequences will be mitigated and still others, eliminated for good. As noted previously, the reformation and restoration begins by eradicating the felony status. Many jurisdictions have examined the efficacy of expunging a felony record and have introduced varied iterations of legislation with this goal in mind. For example, in March 2020, Connecticut's State Joint Committee on Judiciary introduced Senate Bill CT S.B. 403[87] for the erasure of criminal records for certain misdemeanors and felony offenses. The bill passed both chambers with 95% of the vote.

Unfortunately, it did not become law because the executive allowed the deadline to pass. And, while Connecticut's Bill does not go as far as the Jubilee RCRR Act, it demonstrates that policy makers are working to reform the broken penal system by enacting laws that are in alignment with the moral law of "justice for all." Connecticut has become a leader in enacting laws to reform its penal system and sentencing laws. In 2008, Connecticut became the second state to authorize racial impact statements[88] for proposed criminal justice policies.[89] As a result, bills and amendments concerning pretrial or sentenced populations

---

86   Ayers, Edward L. (1984), Vengeance and Justice: Crime and Punishment in the 19th-Century American South, New York.

87   2020 Legislative Outlook CT S.B. 403.

88   Gottschalk, M. (2012). No Way Out? Life Sentences and the Politics of Penal Reform. Life Without Parole: America's New Death Penalty?

89   AN ACT CONCERNING THE BOARD OF PARDONS AND PAROLES, ERASURE OF CRIMINAL RECORDS FOR CERTAIN MISDEMEANOR AND FELONY OFFENSES AND PROHIBITING DISCRIMINATION BASED ON ERASED CRIMINAL HISTORY RECORDINFORMATION. Except as provided in subdivision (4) or (7) of this subsection, whenever any person has been convicted in any court of this state of a classified or unclassified misdemeanor, or a class c, d or e felony or an unclassified felony offense carrying a term of imprisonment of not more than ten years, all police and court records and records of the state's or prosecuting attorney or the prosecuting grand juror pertaining to such conviction shall be erased, or in the case of a felony conviction, provisionally erased under subparagraph (b) of subdivision (2) of this subsection or subparagraph (b) of subdivision (3) of this subsection: (a) at such time as provided in subdivision (2) of this subsection, or (b) following a petition by the convicted person, as provided in subdivision (3) of this subsection.

are now subject to racial impact analysis.[90] Racial impact statements are a tool for lawmakers to evaluate potential disparities of proposed legislation prior to adoption and implementation. Analogous to fiscal impact statements, they assist legislators in detecting unforeseen policy ramifications. Policymakers may then be able to modify legislation that would worsen existing racial disparities.[91]

B. The Black Family: Incarceration A Generational Massacre

The racial impact of mass incarceration imprisonment has always posed a set of burdens on the family members of people in prison, but none so much as to the African American Family.[92] The financial strains, psychological burdens, social stigma, and cycles of broken homes, especially, by the over-policing and snatching away of so many Black males, as young as 10 to 99 has caused untold collateral damage to generations Blacks in America.[93] Sentencing policies, implicit racial bias, and socioeconomic inequity contribute to racial disparities at every level of the criminal justice system.[94]

Today, people of color make up 37% of the U.S. population but 67% of the prison population. Overall, African Americans are more likely than White Americans to be arrested; once arrested, they are more likely to be convicted; and once convicted, they are more likely to face stiff sentences.[95] Black men are six times as likely to be incarcerated as White men, and Hispanic men are more than twice as likely to be incarcerated as non-Hispanic White men.[96]

Moreover, many collateral effects relate to the growing number of children who have a parent in prison. Current estimates place this figure at 1.5 million, but the racial dynamics of imprisonment produce a figure of about 1 in 14, for

90 Western, B. (2006). Punishment and Inequality in America.

91 Ghandnoosh, N. (2018, Mar 8). *Can We Wait 75 Years to Cut the Prison Population in Half?*. The Sentencing Project, Washington, D.C.

92 Spelman, W. (2006). The Limited Importance of Prison Expansion.

93 Gramlich, John. (2018, Jan 30). Five Facts About Crime in the U.S. Pew Research Center.

94 Mauer, M. & Ghandnoosh, N. (2014). *Fewer Prisoners, Less Crime: A Tale of Three States.* The Sentencing Project, Washington, D.C.

95 Glaze, L. & Maruschak, L. (2008). Parents in prison and their minor children. Washington, DC: Bureau of Justice Statistics.

96 U.S. Sentencing Commission. (2008). Alternative Sentencing: Rehabilitative and Punitive Models and Evidence-Based Policy. U.S. Sentencing Commission Symposium on Alternatives to Incarceration.

black children.[97] And, these figures only represent a one-day count, the proportion of black children who experience parental incarceration at some point in their childhood is considerably greater. In 2004, 52% of people in state prisons and 63% in federal prisons were parents of minor children. Most parents in prison are fathers (744,200 fathers compared to 65,600 mothers). The number of fathers in prison increased 76% and the number of mothers in prison increased 122% between 1991 and 2007.[98] But, how these children experience the imprisonment of their parents is largely a phenomenon of which we can only speculate, because America has never witnessed a time when prison affected such high numbers of families.[99]

Adding insult to injury, once parents are released from prison, they must be able to support their children. However, recently adopted federal policies continue to create extreme and sometimes insurmountable barriers to parents meeting their children's basic needs. For example, The Adoption and Safe Families Act of 1997 (AFSA) authorized the termination of parental rights when a child has been in foster care for 15 of the past 22 months. 1 in 30 (3%) of parents in state prisons have children in foster care. As of 2004, 58% of parents in state prison and 76% in federal prison were expected to still serve 12 months or more.[100] Shockingly, the Welfare Reform Act of 1996 imposed unduly harsh punishments on people convicted of felony drug crimes by *permanently* (emphasis added) denying them welfare benefits (TANF) and food stamps.[101]

Not surprisingly, the lifetime welfare ban has a disproportionate impact on African American and Latino families due to racially-biased drug policies[102] and the enforcement of those policies.[103] States now have the option of opting-out

---

97 https://www.sentencingproject.org/criminal-justice-facts/ Source Fact Sheet: Parents In Prison Sentencing project.org.

98 Glaze, L. & Maruschak, L. (2008). Parents in prison and their minor children. Washington, DC: Bureau of Justice Statistics.

99 Glaze, L. & Maruschak, L. (2008). Parents in prison and their minor children. Washington, DC: Bureau of Justice Statistics.

100 Mumola, C. (2000) Incarcerated parents and their children. Washington, DC: Bureau of Justice Statistics.

101 Federal Interagency Reentry Council. (2010). Reentry myth buster: On TANF benefits.

102 Lapidus, L., Luthra, N., Verma, A., Small, D., Allard, P., & Levingston, K. (2005). Caught in the net: The impact of drug policies on women and families. American Civil Liberties Union, Break the Chains: Communities of Color and the War on Drugs, the Brennan Center at NYU School of Law.

103 Legal Action Center. Opting out of federal ban on TANF and food stamps. http:www.lac.org/toolkit/TANF/TANF.htm.

of the felony conviction ban. As of 2011, fourteen states had completely opted out of the ban on TANF and eighteen had eliminated the ban for food stamps.[104] Twenty-six states have partially opted out of the TANF ban and twenty-two states have partially opted out of the food stamp ban. Some states, for example, apply the ban only to people convicted of distributing or manufacturing drugs, but not for possession, or they allow people to receive food stamps or TANF after completing their sentences and complying with other conditions such as participating in treatment or complying with conditions of probation.[105] Excessive incarceration brought about by lengthy prison terms that produce diminishing returns has negative consequences for public safety. At the federal level, the prison population expanded from (20,000 in 1980 to 189,000 by 2016).[106] The combined effect of the surge in drug prosecutions and the expansion of mandatory minimum sentences was a key factor in this growth. As of 2016, 55% of the federal prison population had been sentenced under a mandatory provision.[107] Because families support loved ones in the penal system, they often bear the burden to help those individuals re-acclimate to society after serving time. Four decades of unjust criminal justice policies have created a legacy[108] of collateral impacts that last for generations and are felt most deeply by women, low-income families, and communities of color.[109] For example, in 2007, 1.7 million children had a parent in prison on any given day. The number of children with parents in prison increased 80% between 1991 and 2007. One in 15 Black children, 1 in 42 Latino children, and 1 in 111 White children had a parent in prison in 2007. Black children are 7.5 times more likely and Hispanic children are 2.6 times more likely than are White children to have a parent in prison.[110]

These statics are abhorrent. The data expresses a seismic fault-line in the moral character of America. No matter the political view or partisan polarization,

---

104 Reference for this section: https://www.sentencingproject.org/publications/long-term-sentences-time-reconsider-scale-punishment.

105 Violent Crime Control and Law Enforcement Act of 1994, H.R.3355.ENR, 103d Cong. (1993).

106 Imprisoning America: The Social Effects of Mass Incarceration (Mary Pattillo et al. eds., 2004).

107 Prison Time Surges for Federal Inmates. (2015 Nov 18). Pew Charitable Trusts.

108 Blackmon, Douglas A. (2008), Slavery by Another Name: The Re-Enslavement of Black Americans from the Civil War to World War II, New York.

109 Imprisoning America: The Social Effects of Mass Incarceration (Mary Pattillo et al. eds., 2004).

110 Blackmon, Douglas A. (2008), Slavery by Another Name: The Re-Enslavement of Black Americans from the Civil War to World War II, New York.

it is universally understood that a nation is only as strong as its children who literally are the future. Accordingly, this is our clarion call; we must stop the mass incarceration of our citizens and enact legislation that invests in social interventions to reform, rehabilitate and re-enfranchise our citizen. Research indicates more effective ways to reduce crime is by examining the effects of incarceration parallel to other forms of intervention and their relative costs. In fact, by investing in these alternative mechanisms it will likely produce greater public safety benefits than expanding incarceration.[111]

While the Jubilee RCRR Act is not a panacea for the massive reforms needed to redress the ills of mandatory sentencing and lifetime punishments, it can be a useful federal policy in reform if enacted.

C. Employment Crisis: No Want to Hire An "Ex-Felon"

A report by the Ella Baker Center estimates that more than 600,000 people returned home from prison— and the previous year, and the year before that.[112] A vast majority of people leaving jail or prison had no jobs. Those who did earned a median annual income of $2,500 per year. Who will hire citizens with a felony record? Getting a job with a prison record has always been challenging, but the new dynamics of imprisonment extend this problem to non-offenders as well in African American communities.

Employment discrimination is defined as limiting, segregating, or classifying a job applicant or employee in a way that adversely affects the opportunities or status of such applicant or employee because of the disability of such applicant or employee.[113] However, if one is a convicted felon, the reality is employers discriminate.[114] Although, disguised as policy to protect the public, these laws also yield the same racially biased, disastrous effects as those aforementioned.[115]

---

111 Women's Prison Association. (2003). WPA Focus on Women & Justice: Barriers to Reentry.

112 Ella Baker Center for Human Rights, Forward Together, and Research Action Design launched a collaborative participatory research project with 20 community-based organizations across the country to address this unjust legacy.

113 Hilliard v. BellSouth Medical Assistance Plan, 918 F. Supp. 1016,

114 42 U.S.C.S. § 2000e (LexisNexis, Lexis Advance through Public Law 116-155, approved August 8, 2020).

115 Harry J. Holzer et al., Will Employers Hire Former Offenders? Employer Preferences, Background Checks, and Their Determinants, in IMPRISONING AMERICA: THE SOCIAL EFFECTS OF MASS INCARCERATION 205 (Mary Pattillo et al. eds., 2004).

However, all hope is not lost. For example, the Illinois General Assembly found that it is in the public interest to do more to give Illinois employers access to the broadest pool of qualified applicants possible, protect the civil rights of those seeking employment, and ensure that all qualified applicants are properly considered for employment opportunities and are not pre-screened or denied an employment opportunity unnecessarily or unjustly.[116] Thus, the State legislature implemented legislation called, "Ban the Box."[117] In effect, it prohibits employers from inquiring about criminal records until after making a conditional offer. The Act does not prohibit an employer from notifying applicants in writing of the specific offenses that will disqualify an applicant from employment in a particular position due to federal or State law or the employer's policy.

Connecticut has one of the nation's most comprehensive employment protections for its returning citizens. Employer inquiries about erased criminal record are prohibited, as well as discrimination on basis of erased criminal record, provisional pardon or certificate of rehabilitation.[118]

There are a myriad of other collateral consequences attached to a felony record. Convicted felons are not a protected class under the Fair Housing Act and many landlords require criminal background checks. The Department of Housing and Urban Development (HUD) General Counsel has issued guidance on when such restrictions may violate the Fair Housing Act because of their disparate impact on persons of color or with disabilities.[119] Nevertheless, finding suitable housing continues to be a challenge if one has a criminal record.[120]

In closing, America needs substantially downsized, less punitive, and more hopeful, equitable and restorative prison policies. The biblical example of the Jubilee Year provides a strong model to remove the barriers that make it harder for individuals with criminal records to turn their lives around.[121]

---

116 820 ILCS 75/5.

117 820 ILCS 75/15 (LexisNexis, Lexis Advance through P.A. 101-650 of the 2020 Session of the 101st Legislature).

118 Conn. Gen. Stat. § 31-51i.

119 https://www.hud.gov/sites/documents/HUD_OGCGUIDAPPFHASTANDCR.PDF.

120 https://www.monroecountylawyers.com/blog/2018/02/lifelong-debt-to-society-7-collateral-effects-of-felony-convictions-in-michigan.

121 Reference: https://imprintnews.org/justice/how-to-end-the-era-of-mass-supervision.

Does the distinction between just and unjust laws have any reality in practice? How do we reach a consensus in our divided society on whether a law violates the moral law or "the law of God?"

What effect did the change from "law and order" to the "war on crime" have on the rights of those accused and convicted of crimes?

Is the Jubilee Year Forgiveness Program workable in modern society? Why did it work in ancient Jewish society?

Why should crimes related to violence be restricted under the Jubilee Act? What if this is a crime of violence that has a low recidivism rate?

Is the statute overbroad in its clemency approach? Would you recommend any other limitations to the Act beyond or instead of the violence restriction?

Does grounding the Jubilee Act in biblical text make it more or less palatable to legislators and the public? Is it proper to ground laws on biblical or other religious texts in a pluralistic society? Arguments for and against the death penalty often cite biblical texts. How has that effected the death penalty abolition movement?

Traditional attributes of restorative justice are that offenders accept responsibility for their anti-social acts and that they take some steps to repair the harm to their victims. Does the Jubilee Act meet those requirements?

Kathleen M. Bankhead, J.D., Independent Juvenile Ombudsman, Illinois Department of Juvenile Justice; Ass't States Attorney, Cook County, Illinois (Ret.)

Terezie Bukova, JD, Faculty of Law, Masaryk University (Czech Republic).

Dr. Kenneth Carter, Lead Psychiatric Physician in Primary Care-Mental Health Integration in the Veterans Administration Health Care System; President of the National Acupuncture Detoxification Association (NADA) – a not-for-profit healthcare organization with national and international reach.

Alison Chan, J.D., University of San Francisco Law School.

Elizabeth Clarke, JD, Founder and President, Juvenile Justice Initiative of Illinois.

Fania Davis, Ph.D., J.D., Founding Director, Restorative Justice for Oakland Youth; lecturer and author, "The Little Book of Race and Restorative Justice (2019).

Erica Fatima, Second Year Law Student, UIC Law School; BA in Mass Media Communications from DePaul University.

Wilma Friesema, Licensed Marriage and Family Therapist (MFT), EPIC 'Ohana Engagement Specialist (Honolulu, Hawaii).

Stephanie Glassberg, J.D., UIC Law School.

Lenka Krickova, JD, Faculty of Law, Masaryk University (Czech Republic).

Joy Lindberg Lee, Certified Substance Abuse Counselor; Former Markham Court Administrator and Community Attache.

Gina Marotta, JD, DePaul Law School; Career Coach and Spiritual Advisor.

Judge Sheila M. Murphy (Ret.), Retired Judge Circuit Court of Cook County, Illinois; Adjunct Professor, UIC Law School; Co-Director of the UIC Law School Restorative Justice Project.

Thomas R. Murray, J.D., UIC Law School.

Charles Pyle, United States Magistrate Judge, Southern District Arizona.

Patrick Murphy-Racey, Photo journalist, Roman Catholic Dean in the Diocese of Knoxville, Tennessee, and Chaplain to the Knoxville Police Department. He is the son of Judge Sheila Murphy (ret.).

Ashley Schoenborn, J.D., UIC Law School.

Michael P. Seng, Professor, UIC Law School; Director of the UIC Law School Fair Housing Legal Support Center; Co-Director, of the UIC Law School Restorative Justice Project.

Allison Trendle, J.D., UIC Law School.

Dr. Diana Uchiyama, Attorney and Psychologist, Director, Attorney Assistance Program for the State of Illinois

Daniela Velez-Clucas, JD, UIC Law School; Immigrant Children's Protection Project, National Immigration Justice Center, Heartland Alliance.

Ian Wolff, Ph.D. Candidate and the grandson of Judge Sheila Murphy (Ret.)

The editors would like to thank UIC Law School students **Alison Chan, Thomas Hudson Cross, Dana Devlin, Julia Donaldson, Courtney Krznarich, Deija Swanson, and Allison Trendle** for their assistance in editing selected chapters in this book.

CPSIA information can be obtained
at www.ICGtesting.com
Printed in the USA
BVHW041120081021
618415BV00002B/6

9 781600 425387